Teacher Resource Book

VISIONS

Basic Language and Literacy

Caroline Linse

Jane Yedlin

THOMSON

HEINLE

Australia • Canada • Mexico • Singapore • United Kingdom • United States

THOMSON

™

HEINLE

VISIONS TEACHER RESOURCE BOOK

Caroline Linse and Jane Yedlin

Publisher: *Phyllis Dobbins*

Director of Development: *Anita Raducanu*

Senior Developmental Editor and Contributor : *Jill Korey O'Sullivan*

Developmental Editor: *Tania Maundrell-Brown*

Associate Developmental Editor: *Yeny Kim*

Associate Developmental Editor: *Kasia Zagorski*

Editorial Assistant: *Audra Longert*

Production Supervisor: *Mike Burggren*

Marketing Manager: *Jim McDonough*

Manufacturing Manager: *Marcia Locke*

Director, ELL Training and Development: *Evelyn Nelson*

Photography Manager: *Sheri Blaney*

Production Editor: *Samantha Ross*

Development: *Sheita Pfeiffer, Jennifer Bixby*

Design and Production: *Publicom, Inc.*

Cover Designer: *Studio Montage*

Printer: *Globus Printing Company*

Printed in the United States of America
1 2 3 4 5 6 7 8 9 10   08 07 06 05 04 03

For more information contact Heinle, 25 Thomson Place, Boston, Massachusetts 02210 USA,
or you can visit our Internet site at http://www.heinle.com

For permission to use material from this text or product contact us:

Tel   1-800-730-2214

Fax   1-800-730-2215

Web www.thomsonrights.com

ISBN: 0-8384-0386-7

Contents

Visions Program Components iv

Visions Basic Scope & Sequence vii

Scientifically Based Research in the *Visions Basic* Program x

Lesson Plans 1

CHAPTER A 1   CHAPTER 4 65
CHAPTER B 11   CHAPTER 5 73
CHAPTER C 21   CHAPTER 6 81
CHAPTER D 31   CHAPTER 7 87
CHAPTER 1 39   CHAPTER 8 95
CHAPTER 2 49   CHAPTER 9 103
CHAPTER 3 57   CHAPTER 10 111

Answer Key to Activity Book 115

Reading Fluency Teacher Notes for Activity Book 125

READING FLUENCY CHART ... 125
CHAPTER 1 126   CHAPTER 6 131
CHAPTER 2 127   CHAPTER 7 132
CHAPTER 3 128   CHAPTER 8 133
CHAPTER 4 129   CHAPTER 9 134
CHAPTER 5 130   CHAPTER 10 135

Resources 136

PERSONAL DICTIONARY 136   PRINT ALPHABET (S-Z) 151
STUDENT INFORMATION FORM 137   CURSIVE ALPHABET (A-I) 152
WEB 138   CURSIVE ALPHABET (J-R) 153
VENN DIAGRAM 139   CURSIVE ALPHABET (S-Z) 154
CLUSTER MAP 140   LETTER TILES: CAPITAL LETTERS A-M 155
SUNSHINE ORGANIZER 141   LETTER TILES: CAPITAL LETTERS N-Z 156
TIMELINES 142   LETTER TILES: LOWERCASE LETTERS a-m ... 157
SENSE CHART 143   LETTER TILES: LOWERCASE LETTERS n-z ... 158
PARAGRAPH 144   WORD TILES: SHORT AND LONG VOWELS 159
INTERVIEW 145   WORD TILES: DIGRAPHS AND BLENDS 160
STEP-BY-STEP INSTRUCTIONS .. 146   NUMERALS 1-10 161
FRIENDLY LETTER 147   NUMERALS 11-20 162
WRITING LINES 148   CALENDAR 163
PRINT ALPHABET (A-I) 149   GAME INSTRUCTIONS 164
PRINT ALPHABET (J-R) 150

Program Overview

Visions is Heinle's newest language development program that supports students at four levels, from pre-literacy to transition into the mainstream classroom.

Visions: Basic Language and Literacy provides support for students with little or no knowledge of written English. Students progress from letter recognition and formation, phonics/phonemic awareness, vocabulary building, and reading and writing. In **Visions: Language, Literature, Content,** Levels A, B, and C, students learn and practice skills and strategies to meet grade-level standards and achieve academic success.

For Students		Basic Level	Level A	Level B	Level C
Student Book	offers accessible, authentic literature with a balance of fiction and non-fiction, including excerpts from novels, short stories, plays, poetry, narratives, biographies, and informational and content-based readings. The Basic Level systematically presents letter formation, sound-symbol relationships, phonics, and phonemic awareness for newcomer students with little or no literacy skills. Vocabulary building as well as reading and writing at the sentence and paragraph level are emphasized.	●	●	●	●
Activity Book	emphasizes reinforcement and practice of standards-based knowledge and highlights state test-taking skills. Basic Level extends opportunity for student practice of basic reading and writing skills, and includes beginning level content readings.	●	●	●	●
Student Handbook	provides helpful summaries of strategies and review material for student reference.	●	●	●	●
Heinle Reading Library	offers 18 soft cover classics tied to the themes of *Visions*: Language, Literature, Content, and designed for student independent reading.		●	●	●
Basic Mini-Readers	are lively, contemporary stories carefully designed so that students practice the sounds, letters, grammar, and vocabulary presented in the text and in new contexts. The mini-readers are contained in each student's Basic Activity Book.	●			
Student CD-ROM	provides an opportunity for interactive practicing, reteaching, and reinforcing of listening/speaking skills, reading skills, and phonics/phonemic awareness.	●	●	●	●
Audio CDs*	feature all reading selections recorded for auditory learning and building listening/speaking skills and reading fluency.	●	●	●	●
Newbury House Dictionary with CD-ROM	helps students develop essential dictionary and vocabulary building skills. Features a pronunciation CD-ROM.		●	●	●
Basic Newbury House Dictionary	is designed for beginning-level students to transition from bilingual and picture dictionaries, and provides clear sample sentences, abundant graphics, and activities.	●			
More Grammar Practice Workbook	helps students learn and review essential grammar skills.		●	●	●
Website http://visions.heinle.com	features additional skill-building activities for students.	●	●	●	●

*Also featured on Audio Tape.

Components-At-A-Glance

For Teachers		Basic Level	Level A	Level B	Level C
Teacher Edition	contains point-of-use lesson suggestions and multi-level activities developed specifically to meet state standard requirements.		●	●	●
Teacher's Resource Book	provides easy-to-use and implement lesson plans aligned with state standards. Additional support includes graphic organizers to support lesson activities, CNN® video transcripts, Video Worksheets for students, and a summary of each reading in English and translated into Cambodian, Haitian Creole, Hmong, Cantonese, Spanish, and Vietnamese. School-to-Home Newsletters, in English and the six languages, encourage family involvement. Basic Level includes scripts, extensive teaching notes and step-by-step teacher instructions. **Also available on CD-ROM for teacher customization.**	●	●	●	●
Assessment Program	features diagnostic tests and standards-based quizzes, tests, and exams to ensure accountability, with checklists and tracking systems to monitor individual student progress. **Also available on CD-ROM with ExamView® test-generating software, which allows teachers to create customized tests in minutes from a test bank for each chapter.**	●	●	●	●
Transparencies	offer graphic organizers, reading summaries, and grammar charts for interactive teaching. Basic Level transparencies focus on key concepts for literacy-level students.	●	●	●	●
Staff Development Handbook and Video	provide step-by-step training for all teachers.	●	●	●	●
CNN® Video	features thematic news segments from today's headlines to help build content comprehension through meaningful and realistic viewing activities.		●	●	●
Website http://visions.heinle.com	features additional teaching resources and an opportunity for teachers to share classroom management techniques with an online community.	●	●	●	●

VISIONS BASIC Teacher Resource Book • Copyright © Heinle

Visions: Basic Language and Literacy

Visions: Basic Language and Literacy provides students with the language development and school survival skills needed to succeed while introducing them to the basic reading and writing elements they'll need to progress.

STUDENT BOOK

- Chapters A–D feature the most basic literacy skills, essential vocabulary development, and phonics and phonemic awareness instruction.

- Chapters 1–10 provide continued vocabulary and language development and phonics instruction as well as step-by-step reading and writing skill-building activities that align with state standards.

ACTIVITY BOOK

The Activity Book provides scaffolding and practice activities as well as reading fluency practice. A content area reading is included in each chapter. In addition, mini-readers accompany Chapters 1-10. These readers provide practice in reading, and comprehension skills, and word study.

STUDENT CD-ROM

The Student CD-ROM provides an opportunity for teaching, practicing, and reinforcing spelling skills, listening and speaking skills, phonics and phonemic awareness, and reading skills.

AUDIO CD (OR CASSETTE)

The Audio CD (also available on cassette) includes listening and speaking activities from the student book and recordings of the readings. In addition, the content area readings from the Activity Book are included.

SCOPE AND SEQUENCE

	Letters and Sounds	Language and Vocabulary	Reading And Writing
CHAPTER A **At School** page 2	Consonants: *b, g, m, s, t* Vowel: *a*	Greetings Introductions Mr./Mrs./Miss/Ms.	Introductions
CHAPTER B **In the Classroom** page 14	Consonants: *c, d, f, n, p* Vowel: *o*	*Where are you from?* Countries/Nationalities Colors Numbers 1–10	The American Flag
CHAPTER C **Classmates** page 28	Consonants: *h, j, l, v, x* Vowels: *i, u*	Clothes *How old are you?* Numbers 11–20 Parts of the Body	Sentences and Questions
CHAPTER D **Around the School** page 40	Consonants: *k, q, r, w, y, z* Vowel: *e*	School Places, Objects, and People Prepositions Asking For and Giving Directions	School Workers

	Vocabulary	Listening and Speaking	Build Vocabulary	Grammar	Word Study	Use Prior Knowledge	Build Background	Text Structure	Reading	Beyond Reading	From Reading to Writing	Projects
CHAPTER 1 In the School Office page 52	In the School Office	Making Requests	The Calendar: Days of the Week Months of the Year Ordinal Numbers	Subject Pronouns Possessive Adjectives	Short Vowels	Information About You	Parents and Guardians	A Form	Student Information Form	Scan for Information	Filling Out a Form Writing Dates Writing Phone Numbers Writing Addresses	Project 1: Make a Class Birthday Book Project 2: Make a Class Calendar
CHAPTER 2 About My Family page 66	Family Members Pets	Describing People	Adjectives for Describing People	Present Tense of be Present Tense of be: Negative Contractions with be	Long Vowels: a, i, o, u	Describe a Baby	Dimples	Rhyming Poem	"My Baby Brother" by Mary Ann Hoberman	Find Words That Rhyme Shared Reading	Description of a Family Member	Project 1: Family Member Presentation Project 2: Make and Organize Rhyme Cards
CHAPTER 3 After School page 80	Activities	Talking About Activities	Sports and Arts Activities	Simple Present	Long e Sound: ee, ea	Trying Something New	Roller Skating	Free Verse Poem	"74th Street" by Myra Cohn Livingston	Organize Pictures Retell the Story Act Out the Poem	Paragraph About a Favorite Activity	Project 1: Activities Collage Project 2: Favorite Activity Presentation
CHAPTER 4 Home page 94	Homes Rooms of a Home	Talking About Activities in Different Rooms	Furniture and Objects in Different Rooms of a Home	there is / there are	Compound Words	Feelings About Home	Petunias	Vignette	"A House of My Own" by Sandra Cisneros	Think About the Picture Compare with Words	Paragraph About a Future Home	Project 1: Create Your Dream Home Project 2: Find Compound Nouns
CHAPTER 5 The Community page 108	Community Places and Transportation	Talking About Community Places and Transportation	Time and Schedules	Present Continuous -ing Spelling Rules	Digraphs: ch, sh, th, wh, ng	Newspapers	Community Service	Newspaper Article	Newspaper Articles Who / What / When / Where / Why	Scan for Information	Informational Paragraph	Project 1: Make a Transportation Graph Project 2: Create a School Newspaper

VISIONS BASIC Teacher Resource Book • Copyright © Heinle

VISIONS BASIC Teacher Resource Book • Copyright © Heinle

	Vocabulary	Listening and Speaking	Build Vocabulary	Grammar	Word Study	Use Prior Knowledge	Build Background	Text Structure	Reading	Beyond Reading	From Reading to Writing	Projects
CHAPTER 6 Food page 122	Breakfast, Lunch, and Dinner Foods	Talking About Foods and Meals	Table Settings	Count and Noncount Nouns	Plural Count Nouns: Spelling and Pronunciation	What Foods Are Healthy?	Pyramids	Informational Text	"The Food Guide Pyramid"	Analyze Your Diet Compare Your Diet to the Food Guide Pyramid	Paragraph About Diet Topic Sentence and Details	Project 1: Make a Food Pyramid Poster Project 2: Make a Class Recipe Book
CHAPTER 7 Money page 136	Coins and Bills	Talking About Money and Prices	Ways to Pay	Comparative Adjectives	The Prefix re-	What Do You Wish For?	Gold	Myth	"King Midas and the Golden Touch"	Make a Story Timeline Retell the Story	Opinion Paragraph Phrases for Expressing Options	Project 1: Make a Menu Project 2: Create a Store
CHAPTER 8 Jobs page 150	Jobs	Talking About Jobs	Job Tools and Objects	Object Pronouns	The Suffix -er	How Do You Order Fast Food?	Cash Registers	"How-To" Narration	"How to Take a FastFood Order"	Illustrate the Order of Events Retell the Sequence of Events Act Out the Sequence of Events	"How-To" Paragraph Sequence Words	Project 1: Invite a Guest Speaker to Class Project 2: Give a "How-To" Presentation
CHAPTER 9 Holidays page 164	Holidays	Talking About Holidays	Holidays Throughout the Year	Past Tense: be and Regular Verbs	Consonant Clusters: s Blends	Leaders	Peaceful Protest	Biography	"Martin Luther King Jr.: American Leader"	Fill In a Timeline Draw a Picture	Autobiography	Project 1: American Holiday Presentation Project 2: Timeline of a Famous American's Life
CHAPTER 10 Feelings page 178	Feelings	Talking About Feelings	Verbs Related to Feelings	Future Tense with will Future Tense with will: Negative Contractions with will	Long and Short Vowel Review	Feelings About the First Day of School	Monsters	Poem	"Patti Bennett" by Mel Glenn	Compare and Contrast	Personal Letter Greeting and Closing	Project 1: Keep a Diary Project 2: Act It Out

The 100 Most Frequently Used English Words............ 192
Learning Strategies 193
Grammar Reference................................. 195
Glossary 200
Skills Index... 203
Credits 210

Learning to read involves a number of different skills. Students must combine knowledge about sounds, letter names, letter shapes, vocabulary, and sentence structure with world knowledge. Learning to read a language with an alphabet, such as English, is different than learning how to read a language written with characters, such as Chinese.

Phonemic Awareness

Learning to read and write an alphabetic language like English is dependent upon the learner's understanding that spoken words are composed of smaller sound units, or phonemes. It is obvious to those of us who already know how to read and write that a word like *book* has three sounds or phonemes, /b/, /oo/, and /k/. Research reveals that many learners do not perceive words as segment-able into separate sound units. This can be particularly true of English language learners (ELLs) who have limited experience listening to standard English speech. However, awareness of the separate phonemes that make up a word is critical for matching those sounds with letters to "sound out" or "decode" a word.

The ability to hear the individual phonemes that compose a word may be developed and enhanced through oral activities that call attention to rhythm, rhyme, alliteration and other sound qualities of words. English language learners who are from environments that are not rich in literacy are among those most likely to benefit greatly from such activities. (Adams, 1998) (Blachman, 2000) (Snow, Burns & Griffin, 1998) (Verhoeven, 1999)

Knowledge of Letter Shapes and Names

Learning to read and write depends upon the ability to visually discriminate one letter from another. Learners must be aware of the features of shape that differentiate written letters (graphemes) such as *o,* and *u;* or *m* and *n.* They must also learn to recognize directional orientations that differentiate letters with similar graphic features such as *d, b, p;* and *q;* or *w* and *m.* As if that were not enough, literacy learners must also learn the one-to-one correspondence between distinctly shaped pairs of upper case and lower case letters such as *A* and *a* and *G* and *g.* Learners who have not been immersed since early childhood in a rich print environment featuring the Roman alphabet may require extensive practice in recognizing and discriminating the 26 letters in their upper and lower case forms.

Moreover, research indicates that the ability to identify letters by name is a strong predictor of learning to read. Letter names provide a system of labels for talking about and classifying graphemes, the symbols that make up words. Letter names provide a bridge from students' recognition of letter shapes to their mapping of sounds onto these shapes. (Adams, 1995) (New Standards Primary Literacy Committee, 1999) (Snow, Burns & Griffin, 1998)

Explicit Phonics Instruction

Explicit phonic instruction teaches the relationships between sounds (phonemes) and the printed letters (graphemes). Students are first taught the sounds made by consonants at the beginnings of words. Then students are taught the sounds of consonants at the ends of words, vowel sounds, and blends. (Pinnel & Fountas, 1998) (Snow, Burns & Griffin, 1998)

Word Identification Skills

Students need to know how to pronounce and to understand the printed words that they encounter. Students learn to decode, or sound out words, applying their knowledge of grapheme (letter)/phoneme (sound) correspondence. Other types of knowledge needed for word identification include: knowledge of word parts such as roots and affixes, knowledge of the visual configurations of high frequency words that cannot easily be sounded out (*the, he, were*), and knowledge of how to use context clues. (Adams, 1995) (New Standards Primary Literacy Committee, 1999)

Fluency

Reading fluency refers to the ability to read aloud smoothly without frequent or lengthy pauses for word identification. Fluent reading has prosody (phrasing,

VISIONS BASIC Teacher Resource Book • Copyright © Heinle

rhythm, and intonation) appropriate to the meaning. Research supports repeated guided oral reading of texts as the most effective instruction for achieving fluency. Texts that recycle or spiral vocabulary across lessons help students develop fluency and comprehension. (Fountas & Pinnel, 1996) (Hiebert, 1999) (Stahl, Heuback, & Cramond, 1997)

Spelling Instruction

Spelling instruction supports both writing and reading skills, teaching students the various patterns in which letters clustered together to form sounds and words. Spelling instruction supports students as they go from being emergent to proficient readers. (Ehri, 1997) (Pinnel, & Fountas, 1998) (Templeton, & Morris, 2000)

Vocabulary Instruction

To support reading comprehension, vocabulary instruction should increase the number of words known and the depth of such knowledge, including multiple meanings for words used in school. New words are best learned in context and in relation to other words. Vocabulary instruction should also teach students word analysis strategies involving prefixes, suffixes and root words. Vocabulary knowledge involves understanding words in both spoken and written form. Word learning requires multiple encounters with a word in its various contexts. Research identifies limited vocabulary knowledge as the greatest impediment to reading comprehension among English language learners. Research demonstrates that vocabulary instruction to ELLs can promote gains in word knowledge and in reading comprehension. (Anderson, 1999) (Garcia, 2000) (Blachowitz & Fisher, 2000) (Beck & McKeown, 1991) (Nation, 1990)

Comprehension Strategies

Simply sounding out individual words is not reading. Reading involves making meaning from print. Students can be helped to build reading comprehension in a variety of ways. These include pre-reading activities to elicit, assess, and build on students'

prior knowledge of the topic and vocabulary. Guiding questions give students goals for their reading, and a preview of chapter headings and sections provide a helpful map of what to expect. Teachers can engage students in monitoring comprehension as they read by helping them to paraphrase and summarize chunks of text as they read. Helping students to figure out what is going to happen next or what type of information may be provided next is an example of a simple but effective reading comprehension strategy. (Anderson, 1999) (Carrell, Devine, & Eskey, 1988) (Pressley, 2000) (Pritchard, 1990)

Integration of Listening, Speaking, Reading, and Writing

Language use consists of four distinct skills or modalities: listening, speaking, reading, and writing, practiced in combination with one another. For example, when there is a speaker, there is usually a listener as well. Writers have readers to interpret and enjoy their work. Listening and reading are considered receptive skills, and speaking and writing are considered productive skills. Progress in the four skills may be uneven but is inter-related. Good instruction should integrate all four modalities. For example, students could listen to a story, talk about it, read the story or a related story for themselves and then respond in writing. (Echevarria, Vogt, & Short, 2000) (Ediger, 2001) (Peregoy & Boyle, 1997) (Goldenberg, 1993) (Goldenberg & Pathey-Chavez, 1995)

Learning Strategies

Learning strategies refer to the way that learners successfully tackle different learning tasks such as memorizing a word list, writing a report, or studying for a test. Students who are effective at learning use a variety of strategies to complete their assignments. These strategies include different ways of getting ready to perform a task, actually performing the task, and working with others to complete the task.

References

Adams, M.J. *Beginning to Read: Thinking and Learning about Print.* Cambridge, MA: MIT Press, 1995.

Adams, M.J. "The Elusive Phoneme." *American Educator:* Spring/Summer 1998.

Anderson, N. *Exploring Second Language Reading.* Boston: Heinle and Heinle Publishers, 1999.

Beck, I. and McKeown, M. "Conditions of Vocabulary Learning." Kamil, Mosenthal. Pearson, and Barr (Eds.) *Handbook of Reading Research.* Mahwah, NJ: Lawrence Erlbaum, 2000.

Blachman, B.A. "Phonological Awareness." Kamil, Mosenthal. Pearson, and Barr (Eds.) *Handbook of Reading Research.* Mahwah, NJ: Lawrence Erlbaum, 2000.

Blachowitz, C.L.Z. and Fisher, P. "Vocabulary Instruction" in Kamil, Mosenthal. Pearson, and Barr (Eds.) *Handbook of Reading Research.* Mahwah, NJ: Lawrence Erlbaum, 2000.

Carrell, P., Devine, J.; & Eskey, D. (Eds.) *Interactive approaches to Second Language Reading.* Cambridge, UK: Cambridge University Press, 1998.

Chamot, A.U., Dale, M., O'Malley, J.M., & Spanos, G. "Learning and problem-solving strategies of ESL students." *Bilingual Research Journal* 16 (1992): 133.

Chamot, A.U., & O'Malley, J. *The Calla Handbook.* Reading, MA: Addison-Wesley, 1995.

Echevarria, J.; Vogt, M., Short, D. *Making Content Comprehensible for English Language Learners.* Needham Heights: Allyn & Bacon, 2000.

Ediger, A. "Teaching Children Literacy Skills in a Second Language." Celce-Murcia (Ed.) *Teaching English as a second or foreign language.* Boston, MA: Heinle & Heinle, 2001.

Ehri, L. "Learning to spell and learning to read are one in the same, almost." Perfetti, & Fayol (Eds.) *Learning to spell: research, theory, and practice across languages.* Mahwah, NJ: Lawrence Erlbaum, 2000.

Fountas, I.C. & Pinnel, G.S. *Guided Reading.* Portsmouth, NH: Heinnemann, 1996.

Garcia, G.E. "Bilingual Children's Reading." Kamil, Mosenthal. Pearson, and Barr (Eds.) *Handbook of Reading Research.* Mahwah, NJ: Lawrence Erlbaum, 2000.

Goldenberg, C. "Instructional conversations: Promoting comprehension through discussion." *The Reading Teacher,* 46 (1993): 316–326.

Goldenberg, C. & Pathey-Chavez, G. "Discourse Processes in Instructional Conversations: Interactions Between Teacher and Transition Readers." *Discourse Processes* 19 (1995): 57–74.

Hiebert, E. "Text Matters in Learning to Read." *Reading Teacher* (1999): 552–568.

Nation, P. *Teaching and Learning Vocabulary.* Boston, MA: Heinle & Heinle, 1990.

New Standards Primary Literacy Committee. *Reading and Writing Grade by Grade: Primary Literacy Standards for Kindergarten Through Third Grade.* Pittsburgh, PA: National Center on Education and the Economy, 1999.

Oxford, R. "Language Learning Strategies." *The Cambridge Guide to Teaching English to Speakers of Other Languages.* Cambridge, UK: Cambridge University Press, 2001.

Peregoy, S. & Boyle, O. *Reading, Writing, and Learning in ESL.* White Plains, NY: Longman, 1997.

Pinnel, G.S. and Fountas, I.C., "Word Matters: Teaching Phonics and Spelling." *The Reading/Writing Classroom,* 1998.

Pressley, M. "What should comprehension instruction be the instruction of?" Kamil, Mosenthal. Pearson, and Barr (Eds.) *Handbook of Reading Research.* Mahwah, NJ: Lawrence Erlbaum, 2000.

Pritchard, R. "The effects of cultural schemata in text processing." *Reading Research Quarterly:* 25 (1990): 273–295.

Snow, C.E., Burns, M.S., & Griffin, S. (Eds). *Preventing reading failure in young children.* Washington, DC: National Academy Press, 1998.

Stahl, S.A., Heuback, K., & Cramond, B. *Fluency-oriented Reading Instruction.* National Reading Research Center, 1997.

Templeton, S. and Morris, D. "Spelling. . ." Kamil, Mosenthal. Pearson, and Barr (Eds.) *Handbook of Reading Research.* Mahwah, NJ: Lawrence Erlbaum, 2000.

Verhoeven, L. (1999). "Second language reading." In Wagner, Vanes, & Street (Eds.), *Literacy: An international handbook.* Boulder: West view Press.

VISIONS BASIC Teacher Resource Book • Copyright © Heinle

Chapter A At School

Materials

Student Book: pp. 2–13
Activity Book: pp. 1–8
Audio: Chapter A
Student CD-ROM: Chapter A
Teacher Resource Book: Lesson Plan, pp. 1–10, Teacher Resources, pp. 148–162
Transparencies

Themes

School   Greetings
People   Introductions
The Alphabet

Learning Strategies

Look for patterns in language
Use prior knowledge to understand meaning
Monitor oral and written language production
Use contrastive analysis to acquire new vocabulary
Use imagery memorization to help learn the alphabet

Listening

Use active listening comprehension to follow directions
Understand expressions and vocabulary: school, greetings
Recognize and distinguish phonological elements: *a, b, g, s, m,* and *t*
Listen to and extract meaning from audio recording
Analyze and evaluate spoken discourse for appropriate audience (casual/formal)
Infer meaning from actions and visual context

Speaking

Identify people
Ask for and give information, such as name
Exchange greetings
Produce phonological elements of newly acquired vocabulary

Reading

Learn sound/symbol relationships in the English phonological system
Recognize directionality of words in English
Develop basic sight vocabulary

Writing

Distinguish between uppercase and lowercase letters
Use capitalization with reference to proper names and titles

Viewing and Representing

Interpret a visual image
Use visual cues to derive meaning

Introductory Activities

a. **Use prior knowledge** Chapters A–D are intended for students who have had no formal literacy background or for those who are not familiar with the English alphabet. However, most students have been exposed to some degree of print through various everyday objects.

b. **Use print from the environment to derive meaning** Bring to class familiar objects with labels on them, such as food packages or newspaper ads. Have students identify letters or words. The lesson introduces the sounds and letters *a, b, g, m, s,* and *t.* The items you bring may reinforce these letters, but should more importantly heighten awareness of environmental print. Students should gain confidence and curiosity to want to explore the printed world.

c. **Recognize letters of the alphabet** Point out letters displayed in the classroom or ask students to find examples in the room.

Chapter Opener (Student Book, pp. 2–3)

a. **Listening skills: Infer meaning** Introduce the word pair *boy/girl* to the class. Use hand gestures to prompt a boy to stand up as you say the word *boy.* Then have a girl stand up when you say *girl.* Do this several times. Then introduce the word pair *teacher/student.* Point to yourself as you say the word *teacher.* Point to a few students (boys and girls) and say *student* each time.

b. **Use visual cues** Play a game similar to *Simon Says* by gesturing the class to stand, sit, bow, smile, turn, etc., as you call out the words *boy, girl, student,* or *teacher.* For example, say: *Boys stand up. Girls stand up. Boys turn around. Girls sit down. Teachers sit down.*

c. **View illustrations: Identify people** Refer to the picture on pages 2–3. Point out the individuals in the picture and say the words: *boy, girl, student,* and *teacher.* Ask students to repeat the words. Introduce *school* by pointing to the building in the picture. Next, explain the words *man* and *woman.*

1 Listen and point. (Student Book, p. 2)

a. **Learn graphic cues** Help students locate Activity *1. Listen and point* on page 2. Call attention to the corresponding icons for the

activity. Demonstrate the listening icon for the class by pointing to your ear as you say the word *listen.* Then say the first word *boy.* Point to the picture of the boy and the corresponding word as you say *boy.* Show the class your index finger and repeat the gesture as you say the word *point,* showing your finger placement on the page. Now prompt the class and say: *Point to the word boy.* Then point to the word *boy.*

b. **Use nonverbal cues** Play the audio or read the script. Give students visual cues throughout the activity by pointing to your ear when it is time for students to listen, and then by pointing to the book when it is time for them to point.

c. **Associate sounds with printed words** Encourage students to follow your example of first listening to the words and then pointing to them.

d. **Ask for assistance.** Stop and repeat the activity several times if necessary. Encourage students to ask for assistance as needed.

Audioscript 🎧

1. Listen and point.

Point to the picture of the boy. Point to the word *boy.*
Point to the picture of the girl. Point to the word *girl.*
Point to the picture of the man. Point to the word *man.*
Point to the picture of the woman. Point to the word *woman.*
Point to the picture of the student. Point to the word *student.*
Point to the picture of the teacher. Point to the word *teacher.*
Point to the picture of the school. Point to the word *school.*

Pronunciation Pointer

Demonstrate the pronunciation shift between the words *man* and *woman.* Note that the stress on the first syllable in the word *woman* changes the vowel sound in the second syllable.

2 Listen and repeat. (Student Book, p. 2)

a. **Learn graphic cues** Help students locate *Activity 2. Listen and repeat.* Call attention to the corresponding icons.

b. **Use active listening to follow directions** Point to your ear and say the word *listen.* Then say: *Listen to the word boy.* Now prompt the class with a hand gesture and say the word *repeat*. Then say: *Repeat the word boy*. Gesture for the class to say *boy - boy*. Point to your ear once more and say again: *Listen to the word boy*. Now prompt the class with a hand gesture and say: *Repeat the word: boy - boy*. Gesture for the class to say *boy*.

c. **Associate sounds with printed words** Play the audio or read the script. Encourage students to follow your example of first listening to the words and then repeating them.

d. **Monitor oral production** Students may need extra practice giving a choral response the first few times. Encourage everyone to speak. Stop and repeat the activity several times if necessary, but refrain from making corrections in pronunciation at this point.

Activity Book, p. 1: Left to Right Directionality
Activity Book, p. 2: Top to Bottom Directionality
Activity Book, p. 3: Shape Recognition

Letters and Sounds

Consonants: *b, g, m, s, t*

Vowel: *a*

③ **Listen and repeat.** (Student Book, p. 4)

a. **Use graphic cues** Have students look at page 4. Help them locate *Activity 3. Listen and repeat*. Call attention to the corresponding icons.

b. **Use active listening to follow directions** Point to your ear and say the word *listen*. Then say the first line: *Listen to the letter sound m*. Now prompt the class with a hand gesture and say the word *repeat*. Then say: *Repeat the letter sound* /m/: /m/. Gesture for the class to say /m/. Then say: *Listen to the word man*. Now prompt the class with a hand gesture and say the word *repeat*. Then say: *Repeat the word: man - man*. Gesture for the class to say *man*.

c. **Recognize phonological elements** Play the audio or read the script. Give students visual cues throughout the activity by pointing to your ear when it is time for students to listen, and then by pointing to the class when it is time for them to repeat.

d. **Monitor oral production** Students may need extra practice giving a choral response the first few times. Encourage everyone to speak. Repeat the activity several times if necessary, but refrain from making corrections in pronunciation at this point.

Pronunciation Pointer

Some students may notice the difference in pronunciation between *ch* in *teacher* and *ch* in *school*. Without bringing too much attention to this difference, simply acknowledge that the *ch* in school is irregular.

④ **Listen and repeat.** (Student Book, p. 4)

a. **Use graphic cues** Help students locate *Activity 4. Listen and repeat* on page 4. Call attention to the corresponding icons.

b. **Use active listening to follow directions** Point to your ear and say the word *listen*. Then say the first line: *Listen to the letter sound and the word*: /m/ - *man*. Now prompt the class with a hand gesture and say the word *repeat*. Then say: *Repeat the sound of the letter and the word*: /m/ - *man*. Gesture for the class to say: /m/ - *man*.

c. **Recognize phonological elements** Play the audio or read the script. Give students visual cues throughout the activity by pointing to your ear when it is time for students to listen, and then by pointing to the class when it is time for them to repeat.

d. Produce phonological elements Encourage everyone to speak. Practice both choral response and prompted individual responses.

e. Monitor oral production Students may need extra practice giving responses the first few times. Stop and repeat the activity several times if necessary, but refrain from making corrections in pronunciation at this point.

Audioscript 🎧

4. Listen and repeat.
Listen to the letter sound and the words. Repeat the letter sound and the words.
/m/ man; /m/ map; /m/ mop; /s/ school; /s/ student; /s/ sun; /t/ teacher; /t/ tack; /t/ table

Pronunciation Pointer

The initial consonant clusters in the words *school* and *student* will be challenging to Spanish speakers. In Spanish there are no voiceless consonant blends beginning with *s*. Consequently, Spanish speakers will insert the /e/ sound prior to these blends. Point out to students the Spanish words *escuela* (school) and *estudiante* (student). Have students practice omitting the initial vowel sound in these two words, saying 'scuela and 'studiante. Transition the pronunciation from *escuela* to *school* and from *estudiante* to *student*.

Language Transfer and Interference

Haitian-Creole: The English consonant *s* has an approximate sound in Haitian-Creole.

Spanish: The vowel sound /a/ has an approximate sound in Spanish. The letter *g* in Spanish carries the *h* sound before the vowels *e* or *i*.

Vietnamese: The short vowel sound /a/ has an approximate match in Vietnamese. The consonants *b* and *t* have approximate sounds in Vietnamese.

Culture Note
Contrastive Analysis

English and Spanish have many words in common that have Latin roots. Have students look for and keep track of such similar words. Some examples to share with the class are: *año/annual; asistente/assitant; auditorio/auditorium; diferente/different; difícil/ difficult; dirección/direction*

⑤ **Trace.** (Student Book, p. 4)

a. Learn graphic cues Have students locate *Activity 5. Trace.*

b. Use active listening to follow directions Point your index finger and trace the capital letter *M* and the lowercase letter *m* on the board. Say the letter as you trace it on the board. Repeat this motion with both your left and right hand to indicate to students that they may write with whichever hand is more comfortable. Turn to the class and trace in the air as you say the word *trace*.

c. Write letters of the alphabet Draw students' attention to the tracing arrows in the book. Then trace the letters again as you say the word *trace*.

d. Distinguish between uppercase and lowercase Gesture to the class and show the size difference between the capital and lowercase letters. Say the word *capital* as you point to *M* and indicate that it is larger than *m*. Write on the board: *capital letter = uppercase letter*. Explain that both terms mean the same thing.

e. Monitor written production Have students trace over the letters with their index finger. Make sure that all students are tracing correctly. Demonstrate the general top to bottom, left to right directionality conventions for writing, or guide students to follow the direction of the arrows on the page. Encourage students to ask for assistance as needed.

Literacy Note
Directionality of Words in English

Some languages, such as Hebrew and Arabic, are written from right to left. Students of these native languages may need to be reminded of the left to right directionality of English.

Activity Book, p. 4: Consonants: m, s, t

6 **Listen and repeat.** (Student Book, p. 5)

Use graphic cues Help students locate *Activity 6. Listen and repeat* on page 5. Call attention to the corresponding icons. Refer to the general guidelines for *Listen and repeat* in *Activity 3* in this chapter.

Audioscript 🎧

6. Listen and repeat.

Listen to the letter sound: /a/
Repeat the letter sound: /a/
Listen to the word: *apple apple apple*
Repeat the word: *apple apple apple*

Listen to the letter sound: /b/
Repeat the letter sound: /b/
Listen to the word: *boy boy boy*
Repeat the word: *boy boy boy*

Listen to the letter sound: /g/
Repeat the letter sound: /g/
Listen to the word: *girl girl girl*
Repeat the word: *girl girl girl*

7 **Listen and repeat.** (Student Book, p. 5)

a. Use graphic cues Help students locate *Activity 7. Listen and repeat* on page 5. Call attention to the corresponding icons. Refer to the general guidelines for *Listen and repeat* in *Activity 3* in this chapter.

b. Interpret a visual image Review the nine vocabulary words by pointing to the corresponding pictures to convey meaning as you say the words.

Audioscript 🎧

7. Listen and repeat.

Listen to the letter sound and the words.
Repeat the letter sound and the words.
/a/ apple; /a/ ant; /a/ animals; /b/ boy; /b/ bag; /b/ bat; /g/ girl; /g/ gas; /g/ gate

Literacy Note

You may want to point out that the final *s* in *animals* indicates the plural form of the word.

8 **Trace.** (Student Book, p. 5)

Learn graphic cues Have students locate *Activity 8. Trace.* Refer to the general guidelines for *Trace* in *Activity 5*.

Activity Book, p. 5: Consonants: b, g; Vowel: a

Language and Vocabulary

9 **Listen and point.** (Student Book, p. 6)

Learn graphic cues Help students locate *Activity 9. Listen and point* on page 6. Call attention to the corresponding icons for the activity. Refer to general guidelines for *Listen and point* in *Activity 1* of this chapter.

Audioscript 🎧

9. Listen and point.

Listen to the boy. Point to the words.
Hi. My name is Tran. What's your name?

Listen to the girl. Point to the words.
Hi. My name is Ana.

Listen to the girl. Point to the words.
Hi. My name is Lisa. What's your name?

Listen to the boy. Point to the words.
Hi. My name is Emilio.

Punctuation Note

Point out the punctuation marks /./ and /?/. Make note for Spanish students that in English a question mark appears only at the end of a sentence in contrast to the Spanish convention of an inverted question mark /¿/ at the beginning of a question followed by an upright question mark /?/ at the end of a question.

¿Cuál es su nombre? / What's your name?

10 Listen and repeat. (Student Book, p. 6)

a. Use graphic cues Help students locate *Activity 10. Listen and repeat* on page 6. Refer to general guidelines for *Listen and repeat* in *Activity 3*.

b. Extract meaning from audio recording Play the audio or read the script. Give students visual cues throughout the activity by pointing to your ear when it is time for students to listen, and then by pointing to the class when it is time for them to repeat. Use animated gestures to enhance comprehension of the dialogue.

Audioscript 🎧
10. **Listen and repeat.**

Listen to the words. Repeat the words.
Hi. My name is Tran. What's your name?
Hi. My name is Ana.

Listen to the words. Repeat the words.
Hi. My name is Lisa. What's your name?
Hi. My name is Emilio.

Pronunciation Pointer
Demonstrate to the class that the inflection of a speaker's voice must rise at the end of a question, but drops at the end of a statement. Motion with your hand the rising and falling intonation as you say the dialogue.

11 **Introduce yourself.** (Student Book, p. 6)

a. **Learn graphic cues** Help students locate *Activity 11. Introduce yourself* on page 6. Call attention to the corresponding icons for the activity. Demonstrate the dialogue and use explicit voice modulations to differentiate between the different speakers in the dialogue.

b. **Ask for and give information** Ask for a volunteer to practice the dialogue with you in front of the class. Use greeting gestures to enhance meaning. Then line the class up in two rows (A and B) facing each other. Prompt students to practice introducing themselves to their partners. After each introduction, have the last person in row A move to the front of the row. Repeat the activity until everyone in row A has met everyone in row B.

c. **Self-monitor oral production** Encourage students to monitor themselves by comparing their speech to the text and to that of others as they practice the dialogue several times with different partners.

Activity Book, p. 6: Write the Alphabet

12 **Listen and point.** (Student Book, p. 7)

Learn graphic cues Help students locate *Activity 12. Listen and point* on page 7. Call attention to the corresponding icons for the activity. Refer to general guidelines for *Listen and point* in *Activity 1* of this chapter.

Audioscript 🎧
12. **Listen and point.**

Listen to the words. Point to the words.
Good morning. My name is Mrs. Garcia. I'm your teacher.
Hello, Mrs. Garcia. My name is Ana.

Culture Note
Explain to students that *Hello* is a more formal form of greeting than *Hi*. It is preferable to use this form with adults. If someone initiates the use of the informal *Hi* you may then use *Hi* as well.

13 **Listen and repeat.** (Student Book, p. 7)

Use graphic cues Help students locate *Activity 13. Listen and repeat* on page 7. Refer to general guidelines for *Listen and repeat* in *Activity 3*.

Audioscript 🎧
13. **Listen and repeat.**

Hello. My name is Mrs. Garcia. I'm your teacher.
Hello, Mrs. Garcia. My name is Ana.

14 **Listen and repeat.** (Student Book, p. 7)

a. **Learn graphic cues** Help students locate *Activity 14. Listen and repeat* on page 7. Call attention to the corresponding icons for the activity. Refer to general guidelines for *Listen and repeat* in *Activity 3* of this chapter.

b. **Evaluate spoken discourse for appropriate audience** Play the audio or read the script. Give students visual cues throughout the activity to help enhance the context.

Audioscript 🎧
14. **Listen and repeat.**

Listen to the words. Point to the words.
Hello. I'm Mrs. Green.
Hello. I'm Miss Rana.
Hi. I'm Mr. Smith.
Hi. I'm Ms. Allen.

Culture Note

Explain that *Mr., Mrs., Ms.,* and *Miss* are courtesy titles used before a person's last name as a formality and sign of respect. These are similar to *Sr., Sra.,* and *Srta.* (*Señor, Señora,* and *Señorita*) in Spanish. Explain that *Mr.* is used for men; *Mrs.* is used for married women; *Ms.* may be used for women regardless of marital status; and *Miss* is used for unmarried women or girls. Point out that these titles must begin with an uppercase letter, and the abbreviated forms must end with a period. Ask students what the courtesy titles are in their languages. Explain that in American schools, students address teachers by their title and last name, not as *Teacher*.

Letters and Sounds

Consonants: *b, g, m, s, t*

Vowel: *a*

⓯ **Blend letter sounds.** (Student Book, p. 8)

a. Use graphic cues Have students open their books to page 8. Help them locate *Activity 15. Blend the letter sounds.*

b. Learn sound/symbol relationship Make three large flash cards with the letters *b, a, t* on each respectively. Call out the individual letter sounds /b/, /a/, and /t/ several times while holding up the card for each corresponding sound. Hold up the card for *b* as you tell students that this is the letter for the sound /b/. Then blend together the initial consonant and medial vowel "*ba*" as you hold up the two corresponding cards. Next sound out the final consonant *t* several times. Finally sound out all three-letter sounds and blend them together to pronounce the word *bat.*

c. Look for patterns in language Use large flash cards with the letters: *b, a, t.* Call on individual students to say the word *bat* while you hold up the corresponding letter cards. Have the class repeat the word.

d. Understand new vocabulary Be sure students know the meaning of the word *bat* by showing a picture or using appropriate props for the word. Emphasize that the letters they are learning represent sounds in words that correspond to items.

e. Blend phonological elements into words Go through the activity chorally with the class or ask for volunteers to blend the letter sounds into words. Emphasize that the *a* sound in all these words is a short /a/.

Audioscript 🎧

15. Blend the letter sounds.

Listen to the letter sounds. Point to the letters. Listen to the words.

b a t	*bat, bat, bat*
b a g	*bag, bag, bag*
g a s	*gas, gas, gas*
m a n	*man, man, man*
s a t	*sat, sat, sat*
t a g	*tag, tag, tag*

Pronunciation Pointer

Indicate to students that although they can hear the final consonant clearly in the activity, in the conversation of native speakers the final consonant is often muted in words such as *bat, bag, tag, tack,* and *sat.* Put your hand in front of your mouth when saying the words to demonstrate the varying degree of aspiration with these final consonants. Have students do the same.

⓰ **Write the letters.** (Student Book, p. 8)

a. Use graphic cues Help students locate *Activity 16. Write the letters* on page 8. Demonstrate how to write the letters *a, b, g, m, s,* and *t.* Ask student volunteers to come to the board. Guide them to write the letters on the board.

b. Write letters of the alphabet Have students complete the activity by copying the letters as shown in the text. Indicate to students that they must write each letter several times on a line as shown from left to right. Point out that the letter *g* has a tail that must dip below the center guide line. All the other letters must be written above the center guide.

c. Monitor written production Monitor students' writing. Some non-literate students may need assistance holding the pencil correctly or properly positioning the paper. Encourage students to write letters in the same size, and to space letters equally apart on a line.

⓱ **Write the words.** (Student Book, p. 9)

a. Use graphic cues Help students locate *Activity 17. Write the words* on page 9. Review the six words in the activity by pointing to each picture and asking the class for the correct vocabulary word. Draw three dashes next to each other on the board and model the activity by writing the example <u>b</u> <u>a</u> <u>t</u> above the corresponding dashes on the board. Show students that there are six items in the activity and that each should be written on a separate line.

b. Write letters of the alphabet Have students complete the activity by copying the words in their notebook. Indicate that they must write one letter per dash.

c. Monitor written production Check to see that students are correctly copying words in the appropriate space. Encourage them to write letters of the same size.

18 **What's the missing letter?** (Student Book, p. 9)

a. Use graphic cues Have students open their books to page 9. Help them locate *Activity 18. What's the missing letter?* Review the six words in the activity by pointing to each picture on the left and asking the class for the correct vocabulary word. Next, copy the example *b a g* on the board. Show a picture of a bag to the class and ask the class what the item is. If the class doesn't offer an answer, say the word *bag*.

b. Write letters of the alphabet Have students complete the activity in their notebook and fill in the missing letter for each word in the appropriate space. Indicate that they must write one letter per dash.

c. Monitor written production Check to see that students are filling in the correct letter for each word in the appropriate space on their page. Look for inversion errors particularly with the letters *b, m, n,* and *s*.

19 **Listen and point.** (Student Book, p. 10)

Use graphic cues Have students open their books to page 10. Help them locate *Activity 19. Listen and point.* Refer to general guidelines for *Listen and point* in *Activity 1* of this chapter.

Audioscript 🎧
19. Listen and point.
Look at the alphabet letters. Listen to the letter names in the song. Point to the letters: *A B C D E F G H I J K L M N O P Q R S T U V W X Y and Z. Now I know my ABC's from the letter A to Z.*

20 **Listen and repeat.** (Student Book, p. 10)

Use graphic cues Have students open their books to page 10. Help them locate *Activity 20. Listen and repeat.* Refer to general guidelines for *Listen and repeat* in *Activity 3* of this chapter. **Note:** If students are uncomfortable singing the alphabet song, have them chant the letters.

Audioscript 🎧
20. Listen and repeat.
Look at the alphabet letters. Listen to the letter names in the song. Sing the song: *A B C D E F G H I J K L M N O P Q R S T U V W X Y and Z. Now I know my ABC's from the letter A to Z.*

21 **Write the letters.** (Student Book, p. 10)

a. Use graphic cues Have students open their books to page 10. Help them locate *Activity 21. Copy the letters.*

b. Write letters of the alphabet Have students complete the activity by writing the 52 uppercase and lowercase letters of the alphabet in their notebooks. First, have them write all the uppercase letters in one column. Then, have them write all the lowercase letters next to the uppercase ones.

c. Distinguish between uppercase and lowercase Encourage students to compare and contrast between the uppercase and lowercase letters for each letter. Point out similarities for the following letters: *c, f, i, j, k, m, o, p, s, t, u, v, w, x, y, z* and differences in: *a, b, d, e, g, h, l, n, q, r.*

d. Use imagery memorization Have students draw pictures in their notebooks to help them remember the uppercase and lowercase for the 10 less similar letters: *a, b, d, e, g, h, l, n, q, r.* For example, indicate that capital *B* loses its upper loop, or that capital *R* drops its leg.

22 Point and match. (Student Book, p. 11)

a. Use graphic cues Have students open their books to page 11. Help them locate *Activity 22. Point and match.*

b. Develop basic sight vocabulary Point to the picture for item one and solicit the correct vocabulary word. Then ask a volunteer to point out the word that corresponds to the image. Have all students point to the correct word and repeat it after you. Do the activity with the class as a group.

Answer key
22. Point and match.

1. boy	3. girl	5. man	7. gate
2. bat	4. bag	6. map	8. sun

23 Point and match. (Student Book, p. 11)

a. Use graphic cues Have students open their books to page 11. Help them locate *Activity 23. Point and match.*

b. Develop basic sight vocabulary Point to the word *bag* on the left and ask a volunteer to read it out loud. Then have the class chorally read the four words to the right as you point to each word. Point to the target word *bag* once more and have a volunteer locate the same word in the list on the right. Trace a circle with your finger around the correct answer. Do the activity with the class.

Reading and Writing

24 Read and speak. (Student Book, p. 12)

a. Use graphic cues Have students open their books to page 12. Help them locate *Activity 24. Read and speak.* Ask for volunteers to help you demonstrate the activity.

b. Give information about yourself Have students work in pairs and practice the dialogue several times.

c. Monitor oral production Check to make sure that the students are correctly reading the dialogue script and correctly inserting their own personal information. Have students practice both roles in the dialogue.

Punctuation Note
Explain that *I'm* is a contraction for *I am* and *what's* is a contraction for *what is*. Write *I am* and *what is* on the board and underneath write *I'm* and *what's*. Then cross out the *a* in *am* and circle the apostrophe in *I'm* and cross out the *i* in *is* and circle the apostrophe in *what's*.

25 Write the words. (Student Book, p. 12)

a. Use graphic cues Have students open their books to page 12. Help them locate *Activity 25. Write the words.* Draw students' attention to the example box to the right of the first number. Point to the letters *m* and *y*.

b. Write vocabulary words Have students copy the activity in their notebooks and rewrite the words on the left in corresponding boxes to the right. Make sure students know that they must write one letter per box.

Answer key
25. Write the words.

1. my   2. name   3. is   4. what's   5. your

26 Write the sentences. (Student Book, p. 12)

a. Use graphic cues Have students open their books to page 12. Help them locate *Activity 26. Write the sentences.* Read: *What's your name?* Point to each word as you read.

b. Write sentences Write: *What's your name?* on the board. Have students write the sentence in their notebook. Remind them to begin from the left and move across as they write the sentence.

c. Proofread writing Encourage students to compare their writing to the original sentence in the text. Have them draw a line under any mistakes they notice.

d. Correct writing Have students correct the mistakes they may have made by rewriting the sentence carefully with the correction.

Literacy Note
Capitalization of Proper Nouns
Point out that in English all personal names must begin with the uppercase form of the letter.

Activity Book, p. 7: Write Sentences
Activity Book, p. 8: Reading

Review

Words (Student Book, p. 13)

Develop basic sight vocabulary Have students make a set of personal bilingual flash cards for themselves. Help them locate the list of words on page 13. Have them write the English word on one side and the word in their home language on the back, or draw or paste a picture as a visual cue as appropriate.

Expressions (Student Book, p. 13)

Recognize directionality of words in English Have each group member create a name card that says *Hello. My name is* _____.

The alphabet (Student Book, p. 13)

Identify letters in environmental text Have students search through magazines, newspapers, and flyers to identify letters of the alphabet. Help students recognize letters in various fonts as well as cursive variations. Divide the class into groups of four or five and have them cut out several examples of each letter to be used in a collage.

Chapter B In the Classroom

Materials

Student Book: pp. 14–27
Activity Book: pp. 9–16
Audio: Chapter B
Student CD-ROM: Chapter B
Teacher Resource Book: Lesson Plan, pp. 11–20, Teacher Resources, pp. 148–162
Transparencies

Themes

School Items
The Alphabet
Introductions
Nationality

The Flag
Colors
Numbers

Learning Strategies

Look for patterns in language
Monitor oral and written language production
Use contrastive analysis to acquire new vocabulary
Use semantic mapping to acquire new vocabulary
Make connections across content areas

Listening

Use active listening comprehension to follow directions
Understand expressions and vocabulary: introductions, school items, colors, and numbers,
Recognize and distinguish phonological elements: *c, d, f, n, o,* and *p.*
Listen to and extract meaning from audio recording
Infer meaning from actions and visual context

Speaking

Identify nationalities, colors, and numbers 1–10
Ask for and give information, such as name and nationality
Initiate authentic discourse with peers
Produce phonological elements of newly acquired vocabulary

Reading

Learn sound/symbol relationships in the English phonological system
Recognize directionality of words in English
Develop basic sight vocabulary
Participate in shared reading

Writing

Distinguish between uppercase and lowercase letters
Use capitalization rules with reference to proper names and nationalities
Construct correct sentences

Viewing and Representing

Interpret a visual image
Use visual cues to derive meaning

Introductory Activity

Use print from the environment to derive meaning Make large flash cards of the words on pages 14-15. Use the cards to label objects in your classroom for the following words: *board, chair, clock, computer, desk, door, flag,* and *window*. This can provide students with continual reinforcement.

Chapter Opener (Student Book, pp. 14-15)

a. View illustrations: Classroom items
Have students look at the picture on pages 14-15. Point out the various personal items a student might have and say the words: *backpack, book, notebook, pen,* and *pencil.* Now introduce items found in a classroom such as: *board, computer, eraser,* and *flag.*

b. Use semantic mapping to acquire new vocabulary Draw a T-chart on the board and label it *Student / Classroom.* Now have students help you classify the new vocabulary words into these two categories. Come up with other possible categories, such as *Items to Write With / Furniture.*

1 Listen and point. (Student Book, p. 14)

a. Learn graphic cues Help students locate *Activity 1. Listen and point* on page 14. Call attention to the corresponding icons for the activity. Point to your ear and say the word *listen.* Then say *backpack,* pointing to the picture of the backpack. Show the class your index finger and repeat the gesture as you say the word *point,* showing your finger placement on the page. Now prompt the class and say the word *point.* Then point to the word *backpack.*

b. Use nonverbal cues Play the audio or read the script. Give visual cues by pointing to your ear when it is time for students to listen, and by pointing to the book when it is time to point.

Audioscript 🎧

1. Listen and point.
Point to the picture of the backpack. Point to the word *backpack.*
Point to the picture of the board. Point to the word *board.*
Point to the picture of the book. Point to the word *book.*
Point to the picture of the chair. Point to the word *chair.*
Point to the picture of the classroom. Point to the word *classroom.*
Point to the picture of the clock. Point to the word *clock.*
Point to the picture of the computer. Point to the word *computer.*
Point to the picture of the desk. Point to the word *desk.*
Point to the picture of the door. Point to the word *door.*
Point to the picture of the eraser. Point to the word *eraser.*
Point to the picture of the flag. Point to the word *flag.*
Point to the picture of the marker. Point to the word *marker.*
Point to the picture of the notebook. Point to the word *notebook.*
Point to the picture of the pen. Point to the word *pen.*
Point to the picture of the pencil. Point to the word *pencil.*
Point to the picture of the window. Point to the word *window.*

2 Listen and repeat. (Student Book, p. 14)

a. Use graphic cues Have students look at page 14. Help them locate *Activity 2. Listen and repeat.* Call attention to the corresponding icons.

b. Use active listening to follow directions Point to your ear and say the word *listen.* Then say: *Listen to the word backpack.* Prompt the class with a hand gesture and say the word *repeat.* Say: *Repeat the word backpack, backpack.* Gesture for the class to say *backpack.*

c. Associate sounds with printed words Play the audio or read the script. Give visual cues by pointing to your ear when it is time for students to listen, and by pointing to the class when it is time for them to repeat.

VISIONS BASIC Teacher Resource Book   •   Copyright © Heinle

d. **Monitor oral production** Students may need extra practice giving a choral response the first few times. Encourage everyone to speak. Stop and repeat the activity if necessary, but refrain from making corrections at this point.

e. **Identify classroom objects** For additional practice, point to objects that are in your classroom and have students identify them. Encourage students to ask: *What's this?* Answer, writing any new words on the board.

Audioscript

2. Listen and repeat.

backpack, backpack / board, board / book, book / chair, chair / chalk, chalk / classroom, classroom / clock, clock / computer, computer / desk, desk / door, door / eraser, eraser / flag, flag / marker, marker / notebook, notebook / pen, pen / pencil, pencil / window, window

Activity Book, p. 9: In the Classroom

Letter and Sounds

Consonants: *c, d, f, n, p*

Vowel: *o*

③ Listen and repeat. (Student Book, p. 16)

a. **Use graphic cues** Help students locate *Activity 3. Listen and repeat* on page 16. Call attention to the corresponding icons.

b. **Use active listening to follow directions** Point to your ear and say the word *listen*. Then say the first line: *Listen to the letter sound: c.* Prompt the class with a hand gesture and say the word *repeat*. Say: *Repeat the sound /k/: /k/.* Gesture for the class to say */k/*. Then say: *Listen to the word computer.* Now prompt the class with a hand gesture and say the word *repeat*. Say: *Repeat the word: computer - computer.* Gesture the class to say *computer*.

c. **Recognize phonological elements** Play the audio or read the script. Give visual cues by pointing to your ear when it is time for students to listen, and by pointing to the class when it is time for them to repeat.

d. **Produce phonological elements** Encourage everyone to speak. Practice choral responses.

e. **Monitor oral production** Students may need extra practice giving a choral response the first few times.

Audioscript

3. Listen and repeat.

Listen to the letter sound: *c:* /k/
Repeat the letter sound: /k/
Listen to the word: *computer, computer, computer*
Repeat the word: *computer, computer, computer*

Listen to the letter sound: /d/
Repeat the letter sound: /d/
Listen to the word: *desk, desk, desk*
Repeat the word: *desk, desk, desk*

Listen to the letter sound: /f/
Repeat the letter sound: /f/
Listen to the word: *flag, flag, flag*
Repeat the word: *flag, flag, flag*

Language Transfer and Interference

Spanish: The English vowel sound /o/ has an approximate sound in Spanish, but is not represented by the letter *o*.

Vietnamese: The short vowel sound /o/ has an approximate match in Vietnamese.

The letter *d* is confusing for Vietnamese speakers. It may be replaced by *j, y,* or *z*.

④ Listen and repeat. (Student Book, p. 16)

Use graphic cues Help students locate *Activity 4. Listen and repeat* on page 16. Refer to the general guidelines for *Listen and repeat* in Activity 3 of this chapter.

Audioscript

4. Listen and repeat.

Listen to the sound of the letter and the word.
Repeat the sound of the letter and the word.
/K/ *computer*, /K/ *cap*, /K/ *cat*, /d/ *desk*, /d/ *door*, /d/ *dog*, / f/ *flag*, /f/ *foot*, /f/ *fan*

Pronunciation Pointer

Some students may notice the difference in pronunciation between *door* and *foot*. You may indicate that most commonly the double o sound in English is pronounced as in *moon*. Both *door* and *foot* are somewhat less common variant vowel sounds.

5 **Point to the beginning letter.** (Student Book, p. 16)

a. **Learn graphic cues** Have students locate *Activity 5. Point to the beginning letter* on page 16. Call attention to the corresponding icon.

b. **Use active listening to follow directions** Point your index finger to the picture of a cap and say *cap, cap.* Call out the following letter sounds: /d/, /k/, and /s/ as you point to their corresponding letters. Repeat the word *cap* and the sound /k/ and point to the letter *c* as you repeat the sound /k/.

c. **Identify new vocabulary** Make flash cards with the following images: *cap, dog, fan, computer, door,* and *cat.* (You may wish to ask students to draw the images on the flash cards.) Write the word on the other side for later use. Point to the picture on a flash card and ask: *What's this?*

d. **Learn sound/symbol relationships** Call on three volunteers to say the three letter sounds that follow each image. Ask students to identify the letter sound that matches the beginning sound of the word for the item on the flash card. Do the activity with the class as a group or call on volunteers.

6 **Listen and repeat.** (Student Book, p. 17)

Use graphic cues Have students open their books to page 17. Help them locate *Activity 6. Listen and repeat.* Refer to the general guidelines for *Listen and repeat* in *Activity 3.*

Audioscript 🎧

6. **Listen and repeat.**
Listen to the letter sound: /n/
Repeat the letter sound: /n/
Listen to the word: *notebook, notebook, notebook*
Repeat the word: *notebook, notebook, notebook*

Listen to the letter sound: /o/
Repeat the letter sound: /o/
Listen to the word: *office, office, office*
Repeat the word: *office, office, office*

Listen to the letter sound: /p/
Repeat the letter sound: /p/
Listen to the word: *pencil, pencil, pencil*
Repeat the word: *pencil, pencil, pencil*

7 **Listen and repeat.** (Student Book, p. 17)

a. **Use graphic cues** Have students open their books to page 17. Help them locate *Activity 7. Listen and repeat.* Refer to the general guidelines for *Listen and repeat* in *Activity 3.*

b. **Interpret a visual image** Review the nine vocabulary words by pointing to the corresponding pictures to convey meaning.

c. **Reinforce new vocabulary** Point to various items in the class from the list of new words and ask: *What is this?* Prompt students for an answer. Alternatively, ask students to identify the correct item as you ask: *Show me a pen.*

Audioscript 🎧

7. **Listen and repeat.**
Listen to the letter sounds and the words.
Repeat the letter sounds and the words.
/n/ *notebook,* /n/ *nose,* /n/ *newspaper,*
/o/ *office,* /o/ *on,* /o/ *orange,*
/p/ *pencil,* /p/ *pen,* /p/ *pizza*

8 **Point to the beginning letter.** (Student Book, p. 17)

a. **Learn graphic cues** Have students locate *Activity 8. Point to the beginning letter* on page 17. Call attention to the corresponding icon.

b. **Develop basic sight vocabulary** Point to the picture of the nose on the left and say *nose* several times, stressing the initial consonant /n/. Point to the first letter and ask: *Nose?* Nod your head to indicate that it is the correct match. Then point to the second letter and say /m/. Shake your head to show it is not the correct sound. Do the same with the last letter, saying the sound /o/. Do the activity orally with the class, having students point to the beginning letters.

c. **Recognize phonological elements** Hold up your book and call on volunteers to come up and point to the correct letter.

Answer key
8. Point to the beginning letter.
1. **n** m o; nose
2. a **o** f; orange
3. **p** b g; pen
4. a c **o**; office
5. m **n** c; notebook
6. **p** g b; pizza

Activity Book, p. 10: Consonants: c, d, f, n, p: Vowel: o

Language and Vocabulary

9 **Listen and point.** (Student Book, p. 18)

Learn graphic cues Help students locate *Activity 9. Listen and point* on page 18. Refer to general guidelines for *Listen and point* in *Activity 1* of this chapter.

Audioscript 🎧

9. **Listen and point.**

Listen to the boy. Point to the words.
I'm Tran. I'm from Vietnam.

Listen to the boy. Point to the words.
My name is Pablo. I'm Colombian. Where are you from?

Listen to the girl. Point to the words.
I'm Irina. I'm from Russia.

10 **Listen and repeat.** (Student Book, p. 18)

Use graphic cues Have students open their books to page 18. Help them locate *Activity 10. Listen and repeat.* Refer to general guidelines for *Listen and repeat* in *Activity 3.*

Audioscript 🎧

10. **Listen and repeat.**

Listen to the words. Repeat the words.
A: I'm Tran. I'm from Vietnam.
B: My name is Pablo. I'm Colombian. Where are you from?
C: I'm Irina. I'm from Russia.

11 **Listen and repeat.** (Student Book, p. 19)

a. **Use graphic cues** Have students open their books to page 19. Help them locate *Activity 11. Listen and repeat.* Refer to general guidelines for *Listen and repeat* in *Activity 3.*

b. **Make connections across content areas** Use a world map or globe to locate all of the countries listed in the activity and to identify the home countries and nationalities of all the students in the class.

Audioscript 🎧

11. **Listen and repeat.**

Listen to the countries. Repeat the countries. Listen to the nationalities. Repeat the nationalities.
Brazil: Brazilian / China: Chinese / Colombia: Colombian / Cuba: Cuban / Guatemala: Guatemalan / Haiti : Haitian / Mexico : Mexican / Russia: Russian / United States: American /Vietnam: Vietnamese

Punctuation Note

Point out that names of countries, nationalities, and languages are always capitalized. Have students point to the capital letters.

12 **Work with a partner.** (Student Book, p. 19)

a. **Learn graphic cues** Help students locate *Activity 12. Work with a partner* on page 19. Call attention to the corresponding icons.

b. **Ask for and give information** Pair students with partners and have them ask each other the questions modeled in the book.

c. **Monitor oral production** Remind students to distinguish between the name of a country and the adjectival form used for the nationality.

Activity Book, p. 11: Greetings
Activity Book, p. 12: Conversations

Letter and Sounds

Consonants: *c, d, f, n, p*

Vowel: *o*

13 **Blend the letter sounds.** (Student Book, p. 20)

a. **Use graphic cues** Have students open their books to page 20. Help them locate *Activity 13. Blend letter sounds.* Call attention to the corresponding icons.

b. **Learn sound/symbol relationship** Make three large flash cards with the letters *c, a,* and *t* on each respectively. Call out the individual letter sounds /k/, /a/, and /t/ several times while holding up the corresponding card.

Then hold up the *c* and *a* cards and blend the initial consonant and medial vowel: /ka/. Next, sound out the final consonant /t/ several times. Finally sound out all three sounds and blend them together to pronounce the word *cat*.

c. Look for patterns in language Call on individual students to say the word *cat* while you hold up the corresponding word card. Have the class repeat the word several times. Then change the first letter card from a *c* to a *b* and have the students sound out the new word: *bat*. Change the final consonant *t* to an *n* to create the next word on the list: *fan*.

d. Use visual cues to derive meaning Be sure students know the meaning of the word *cat* by showing a picture of a cat to emphasize that the letter combinations represent sounds in words that correspond to objects.

e. Participate in shared reading Go through the activity chorally with the class or ask for volunteers to blend the letter sounds into words. Emphasize that the *a* sound in all these words is a short /a/.

Audioscript 🎧

13. Blend the letter sounds.

Listen to the letter sounds. Point to the letters. Listen to the words.

c a t:		*cat, cat, cat*
f a n:		*fan, fan, fan*
n a p:		*nap, nap, nap*
d o t:		*dot, dot, dot*
p o t:		*pot, pot, pot*
d o g:		*dog, dog, dog*

Listen to the letter sounds. Say the letter sounds. Listen to the word. Say the words.

c a t:		*cat, cat, cat*
f a n:		*fan, fan, fan*
n a p:		*ap, nap, nap*
d o t:		*dot, dot, dot*
p o t:		*pot, pot, pot*
d o g:		*dog, dog, dog*

⑭ What's the missing letter? (Student Book, p. 20)

a. Learn graphic cues Help students locate *Activity 14. What's the missing letter?* on page 20. Call attention to the corresponding icon.

b. Write letters of the alphabet Have students write the missing letter for each word in their notebook. Indicate that they must write one letter per dash.

Answer key
14. What's the missing letter?
1. dog   2. fan   3. pot   4. cat   5. nap

---

⑮ Say the words. (Student Book, p. 20)

a. Use graphic cues Have students open their books to page 20. Help them locate *Activity 15. Say the words.* Call attention to the corresponding icon.

b. Recognize phonological elements Point to the letters of each word and have students sound them out and then blend them to say the word.

c. Self-monitor oral production Some students may need extra practice distinguishing between the vowel sounds /o/ and /a/. Demonstrate these vowel sounds with exaggerated articulation. Use a mirror to help students observe themselves as they produce these vowel sounds.

⑯ Write the words. (Student Book, p. 21)

a. Use graphic cues Have students open their books to page 21. Help them locate *Activity 16. Write the words.*

b. Use active listening to follow directions Review the words by pointing to each picture on the left and asking for the correct word. Demonstrate the example by drawing three blank boxes on the board. Show a picture of a fan and ask: *What's this?* If the class doesn't offer an answer, say the word *fan*. Ask students to repeat the word *fan* and sound out the first two letters as you write them on the board. Then solicit the final consonant sound and write *n* in the appropriate blank box.

c. Learn sound/symbol relationships Have students fill in the missing letters in their notebook. Indicate that they must write one letter per box.

d. Monitor written production Check to see that students are filling in the correct letters for each word in the appropriate space. Look for inversion errors and substitutions.

VISIONS BASIC Teacher Resource Book • Copyright © Heinle

Answer key

16. Write the words.

1. fan   2. cat   3. dog   4. pot

17 Spell the words. (Student Book, p. 21)

a. Use graphic cues Have students open their books to page 21. Help them locate *Activity 17. Spell the words.* Call attention to the corresponding icons.

b. Produce phonological elements Have students copy the activity. Play the audio or read the script. Have students spell the words by writing the correct letters in the corresponding boxes.

c. Monitor written production Check to see that students are filling in the correct letters for each word in the appropriate space on their papers. Repeat the audio as necessary.

Audioscript 🎧

17. Spell the words.

Listen to the words. Write the words.

1. *nap, nap, nap*
2. *cat, cat, cat*
3. *dog, dog, dog*
4. *fan, fan, fan*

18 Find the words. (Student Book, p. 21)

a. Use graphic cues Have students open their books to page 21. Help them locate *Activity 18. Find the words.*

b. Recognize directionality of words Make flash cards with the letters *n, a,* and *f* on each respectively. Put the cards on the board in the sequence *n a f* and ask the class: *Is this a word?* Then move the n to the end and ask if *a f n* is a word. Rearrange the cards as *f a n* and ask the class if this is a word. Once the class has identified the correct sequence, demonstrate to the class that in English word are always read from left to right. Do the rest of this activity with the class since student vocabulary is not strong enough to do this word jumble activity independently.

Answer key

18. Find the word.

1. n a f	**fan**	4. t a c	**cat**	
2. a g b	**bag**	5. g a t	**tag**	
3. n a m	**man**			

Activity Book, p. 13: Blending Sounds

Reading and Writing

19 View and match. (Student Book, p. 22)

a. Use graphic cues Have students open their books to page 22. Help them locate *Activity 19. View and match.*

b. Develop basic sight vocabulary Point to the picture for the example and solicit the correct vocabulary word. Ask a volunteer to point to the word that corresponds to the image. Trace a circle around the correct answer to demonstrate. Do the activity with the entire class.

Answer key

19. View and match.

1. **door** desk
2. bag **flag**
3. **desk** book
4. flag **foot**

20 Listen and read. (Student Book, p. 22)

a. Use graphic cues Have students open their books to page 22. Help them locate *Activity 20. Listen and read.*

b. Interpret a visual image Show the class the pictures on page 22 and point out the various people. Point to the teacher and say: *Mrs. Garcia is a teacher.* Point to the American girl and say: *Lisa. Lisa is American.* Point to the Mexican girl and say *Ana. Ana is Mexican.*

c. Infer meaning Point to your book on your desk and say: *This is my book.* Then point to a student's book and say: *That is your book.* Repeat the words *this* and *that,* emphasizing the locality of the objects with your gestures.

d. Extract meaning from audio recording Play the audio or read the script. Replay or reread the script a second time, this time reading it chorally with the class.

e. Participate in shared reading Ask two volunteers to read and act out the script with you in front of the class. Then divide the class into groups of three to practice reading the dialogue several times. Have students change roles each time.

Audioscript 🎧
20. Listen and read.

*A: My name is Mrs. Garcia. I'm a teacher.
This is my classroom. This is my desk.
B: Hi. My name is Lisa. I'm a student. I'm
American.
C: Hi. I'm Ana. I'm from Mexico. I'm a
student. That is my school.*

㉑ Write about yourself. (Student Book, p. 22)

a. Use graphic cues Have students open
their books to page 22. Help them locate
Activity 21. Write about yourself.

b. Construct correct sentences Have
students copy the activity and fill in the
appropriate answers. Students may need to
refer to *Activity 11* on page 19 for help.

c. Use basic capitalization rules Remind
students to use capital letters with both
their name and the name of their country.

㉒ Listen and read. (Student Book, p. 23)

a. Use graphic cues Have students open
their books to page 23. Help them locate
Activity 22. Listen and read.

b. Interpret a visual image Show the
picture of the American flag and say
American flag. Point to the stars and say
stars. Point to the stripes and say *stripes.*
Point to the each color of the flag and say
red, white, and *blue* respectively.

c. Extract meaning from audio recording
Play the audio or read the script. Point out
the various details of the flag as described
in the script. Reread the script, this time
reading it chorally with the class.

Audioscript 🎧
22. Listen and read.
The American Flag

*This is the American flag.
It is red, white, and blue.
It has thirteen stripes and fifty stars.
The stripes are red and white.
The stars are white on a square of blue.
What does this flag mean to you?*

㉓ What are the missing words? (Student
Book, p. 23)

a. Use graphic cues Have students open
their books to page 23. Help them locate
Activity 23. What are the missing words?

b. Construct correct sentences Have
students copy the activity and fill in the
appropriate answers. Students may need to
refer to *Activity 22* for help.

Answer key
23. What are the missing words?
1. flag   2. blue   3. stars   4. red

Culture Note
Students may be interested to know that the 50
stars represent the 50 states, and the 13 stripes
represent the 13 original colonies.

Language and Vocabulary

㉔ Listen and repeat. (Student Book, p. 24)

Use graphic cues Help students locate
Activity 24. Listen and repeat on page 24.
Refer to general guidelines for *Listen and
repeat* in *Activity 3.*

Audioscript 🎧
24. Listen and repeat.

1	one	one computer
2	two	two desks
3	three	three backpacks
4	four	four students
5	five	five chairs
6	six	six dogs
7	seven	seven books
8	eight	eight caps
9	nine	nine pens
10	ten	ten pencils

㉕ Trace the numbers. (Student Book, p. 25)

a. Use graphic cues Have students open
their books to page 25. Help them locate
Activity 25. Trace the numbers.

b. Use active listening to follow directions
Point your index finger and trace the
numeral *1* on the board. Say the word *one*
as you trace. Repeat this motion with both
your left and right hands to indicate that
students may write with whichever hand is
more comfortable. Turn to the class and
trace in the air and say *trace.*

c. Write numbers Draw students' attention
to the tracing arrows in the book. Then
trace the numerals again as you say the
word *trace.*

d. Monitor written production Have students trace over the numerals with their index finger. Make sure that all students are tracing correctly. Demonstrate the general top to bottom, left to right directionality for writing, or guide students to follow the direction of the arrows on the page. Encourage students to ask for assistance as needed.

Culture Note

Some students may cross the numeral *7* and the numeral *0* or write *9* with a tail similar to the letter *g*. At this point, do not discourage students from writing numbers in this manner, but make sure they recognize the American form. Suggest that *9* with a tail may be confused for the letter *g*.

26 What are the missing numbers? (Student Book, p. 25)

a. Use graphic cues Have students open their books to page 25. Help them locate *Activity 26. What are the missing numbers?*

b. Recite number sequence Do a choral chant with your class of the number sequence 1–10. Have students hold up their fingers as they say the numbers. For an extra challenge, have students count backwards from 1 to 10.

c. Write the numbers Have students copy the activity and fill in the missing numbers. Remind them to begin from the left and move across to the right.

Answer key

26. What are the missing numbers?

1 **2** 3 4 **5** 6 7 **8** 9 10

27 What are the missing letters? (Student Book, p. 25)

a. Use graphic cues Have students open their books to page 25. Help them locate *Activity 27. What are the missing letters?*

b. Develop basic sight vocabulary Make five flash cards. On one side of the cards spell out the numbers one to five respectively and on the opposite side write the corresponding numerals. Review the numbers with the class by holding out the cards randomly. Ask: *How do you spell the*

number one? Then turn the cards over and hold the numeral side up and ask volunteers to say the number and spell it.

c. Use active listening to follow directions Copy the example *one* on the board as shown in the student book but with blank boxes for the letters *o* and *a*. Point to the numeral 1 in the book and hold up one finger as you say the word *one*. Repeat the word *one*, putting stress on the sound /n/ as you point to the letter *n* on the board. Say the word *one* again and write in the first letter. Then solicit the final *e* from the class.

d. Write the numbers Copy the activity on the board. Call on volunteers to fill in the missing letters. Indicate to students that they must write one letter per box. Have students copy the correct answers onto a piece of paper.

e. Monitor written production Check that students are filling in correct letters for each word in appropriate spaces.

Answer key

27. What are the missing letters?

1. **o** n **e**
2. **t** w **o** o i
3. **t** h r **e** e
4. f **o** u **r**
5. f **i** v **e**

Activity Book, p. 14: Numbers

Language and Vocabulary

28 Listen and repeat. (Student Book, p. 26)

a. Use graphic cues Have students open their books to page 26. Help them locate *Activity 28. Listen and repeat.* Refer to general guidelines for *Listen and repeat* in *Activity 2.*

b. Reinforce understanding Repeat the activity and act out modified versions. For example, place a red pen on your desk and ask: *Where is my red pen?* Solicit an answer from the class by pointing to the correct response in the book.

c. Initiate authentic discourse with peers Pair students with partners and have them ask original questions using the model in the book.

Audioscript 🎧

28. Listen and repeat.

red, red, red
blue, blue, blue
purple, purple, purple,
black, black, black
brown, brown, brown
green, green, green
yellow, yellow, yellow
orange, orange, orange
pink, pink, pink
white, white, white

Listen and repeat.

1. *A: Where is my blue pen?*
   B: Its on your desk.
2. *A: Where is your green backpack?*
   B: Its under my chair.
3. *A: Is this your black pen?*
   B: Yes, it is..
4. *A. Where is your red notebook?*
   B: Its in my backpack.
5. *A: Where is the pink marker?*
   B: Its on the desk.
6. *A: Is that my yellow pencil?*
   B: No, it isn't.

Activity Book, p. 15: Colors
Activity Book, p. 16: Math

Review

Words (Student Book, p. 27)

a. Develop basic sight vocabulary Make large flash cards with the new vocabulary words. Pass out the cards among students. Point to students randomly and have them call out the word they are holding.

b. Initiate authentic discourse with peers Line several students up in front of the class and have them try to make a question or sentence, such as: *Where are the stripes?* or *The window isn't under the clock* or *It's in the backpack.* Encourage students to experiment. Don't worry about strict grammatical structure at this point, as long as other students understand the message.

Colors (Student Book, p. 27)

Make connections across content areas Create Color by Number illustrations of the various flags representative of your student population. Make a coloring key to correspond to the colors on the flags. Display the key on the board for the entire class to follow. Demonstrate to the class by coloring one flag. Hand out blank flags and coloring pencils. Ask students to color in the flags according to the key. You can later laminate the flags and use them to decorate the class.

Numbers (Student Book, p. 27)

Ask for and give information Make three sets of flash cards, one set with the numbers 1–10 spelled out, the second set with the numerals 1–10, and the third set with 1–10 familiar objects on each card respectively. Hand out the cards and have students circulate around the room to find the two other matching partners. Encourage students to talk by saying: *I'm number 2* or *I have two pens.*

Expressions (Student Book, p. 27)

Ask for and give information To reinforce oral use of the expressions, have students ask and answer the question, going in a chain around the room. Start by asking: *Where are you from?* Prompt students to answer: *I'm from __. I'm __.* Make sure that students include *from* in their answer. Some students may be from a different country, but be American citizens. Be sure students show respect for others.

Chapter C Classmates

Use with student text page 28–39

Materials

Student Book: pp. 28–39
Activity Book: 17–24
Audio: Chapter C
Student CD-ROM: Chapter B
Teacher Resource Book: Lesson Plan, pp. 21–30; Teacher Resources, pp. 148–162
Transparencies

Themes

The Alphabet
Clothing
Numbers
Parts of the Body

Learning Strategies

Look for patterns in language
Monitor oral and written language production

Listening

Use active listening comprehension to follow directions
Understand expressions and vocabulary: introductions, school items, colors, and numbers
Recognize and distinguish phonological elements: *h, j, l, v, x, i,* and *u*
Listen to and extract meaning from audio recording
Infer meaning from actions and visual context

Speaking

Identify clothing, parts of the body, and numbers 11–20
Ask for and give information, such as age, descriptions, and locations
Initiate authentic discourse with peers
Produce phonological elements of newly acquired vocabulary

Reading

Learn sound/symbol relationships in the English phonological system
Develop basic sight vocabulary
Participate in shared reading

Writing

Distinguish between uppercase and lowercase letters
Use capitalization and punctuation rules with reference to sentences and questions
Construct correct sentences

Viewing and Representing

Interpret a visual image
Use visual cues to derive meaning
Describe how illustrations support text

Introductory Activity

Infer meaning Bring to class various articles of clothing as props. Include several types of each of the following items, if possible: hat, jacket, jeans, shirt, shoes, skirt, sneakers, and sweater. Hold out each item and say the corresponding word. You may even want to put on some of the articles of clothing as you repeat the words. The clothing will be used later in a game.

Chapter Opener (Student Book, pp. 28–29)

a. View illustrations: Supporting text Refer to the picture on pages 28–29. Point out the group of students and say the word *classmates*. Then show two students standing near one another and say the word *friend*. You may want to use the Spanish word *amigo* to clarify understanding for some of your students or act out the meaning of the word. Point to pairs of students and say: *classmates*. Then gesture for two of them to shake hands as you say: *friends*.

b. Recognize new vocabulary Create two sets of flash cards with the words for each article of clothing you brought into class. Hold up the flash cards and have students repeat the words to reinforce the new vocabulary.

c. Play a game based on teamwork This game is a good ice-breaker, and students enjoy it. Pile the clothing props on a table in front of the room. Divide the class into two teams and have them stand on opposite sides of the room. Have one student from each team stand by the pile of clothing and have another student ready to "dress" him/her. Teams work simultaneously, but the flash cards are shuffled. Give each team a set of flash cards. In this game, the team reads out one of the flash cards to the student who will be dressing his/her teammate. This student must run to the pile, find the correct article of clothing, and hand it to the other student who has been standing by the clothes. This student must put on the article of clothing. The teams must work quickly and correctly. The winning team is the one that reads through the entire set of flash cards, dressing the teammate with the most clothing items.

① **Listen and point.** (Student Book, p. 28)

a. Learn graphic cues Help students locate *Activity 1. Listen and point* on page 28. Call attention to the corresponding icons for the activity. Demonstrate by pointing to your ear and saying the word *listen*. Then say the word *classmates*. Point to the picture of the classmates and the corresponding word as you say *classmates*. Show your index finger and repeat the gesture as you say the word *point*, showing your finger placement on the page. Now prompt the class and say the word *point*. Then point to the word *classmates*.

b. Use nonverbal cues Play the audio or read the script. Give visual cues by pointing to your ear when it is time to listen, and by pointing to the book when it is time to point.

c. Monitor oral production Students may need extra practice giving a choral response the first few times. Encourage everyone to speak. Stop and repeat the activity if necessary, but refrain from making corrections at this point.

Audioscript 🎧

1. Listen and point.

Point to the pictures of the classmates. Point to the word *classmates*.
Point to the picture of the friend. Point to the word *friend*.
Point to the picture of the hat. Point to the word *hat*.
Point to the picture of the jacket. Point to the word *jacket*.
Point to the picture of the jeans. Point to the word *jeans*.
Point to the picture of the shirt. Point to the word *shirt*.
Point to the picture of the shoes. Point to the word *shoes*.
Point to the picture of the skirt. Point to the word *skirt*.
Point to the picture of the sneakers. Point to the word *sneakers*.
Point to the picture of the sweater. Point to the word *sweater*.

② **Listen and repeat.** (Student Book, p. 28)

a. Use graphic cues Have students look at page 28. Help them locate *Activity 2. Listen and repeat*. Demonstrate by pointing to your ear and saying the word *listen*. Then say the word *classmates*. Now prompt the class and say *Repeat*.

VISIONS BASIC Teacher Resource Book • Copyright © Heinle

Repeat the word *classmates*. Gesture for the class to repeat.

b. Recognize phonological elements Play the audio or read the script. Give students visual cues by pointing to your ear when it is time for students to listen, and by pointing to the class when it is time for them to repeat.

c. Monitor oral production Encourage everyone to speak. Stop and repeat the activity several times if necessary, but refrain from making corrections at this point.

Audioscript 🎧

2. Listen and repeat.

classmates, classmates / friend, friend / hat, hat / jacket, jacket / jeans, jeans / shirt, shirt / shoes, shoes / skirt, skirt / sneakers, sneakers/ sweater, sweater

Activity Book, p. 17: Classmates and Clothing

Letters and Sounds

Consonants: *h, j, l, v, x*

Vowels: *i, u*

3 Listen and repeat. (Student Book, p. 30)

a. Use graphic cues Help students locate *Activity 3. Listen and repeat* on page 30. Demonstrate for the class by pointing to your ear and saying the word *listen*. Then say the first two lines of the audioscript: *Listen to the letter sound h. Repeat the letter sound: h.* Now prompt the class with a hand gesture to repeat. Say: *Repeat the letter sound: h.* Gesture for the class to repeat.

b. Recognize phonological elements Play the audio or read the script. Give students visual cues by pointing to your ear when it is time for students to listen, and then by pointing to the class when it is time for them to repeat.

c. Monitor oral production Students may need extra practice giving a choral response the first few times. Encourage everyone to speak. Stop and repeat the activity if necessary. Refrain from making corrections at this point.

Audioscript 🎧

3. Listen and repeat.

Listen to the letter sound: /h/
Repeat the letter sound: /h/
Listen to the word: *hat, hat, hat.*
Repeat the word: *hat, hat, hat.*

Listen to the letter sound: /j/
Repeat the letter sound: /j/
Listen to the word: *jacket, jacket, jacket.*
Repeat the word: *jacket, jacket, jacket.*

Listen to the letter sound: /l/
Repeat the letter sound: /l/
Listen to the word: *leg, leg, leg.*
Repeat the word: *leg, leg, leg.*

Listen to the letter sound: /u/
Repeat the letter sound: /u/
Listen to the word: *up, up, up.*
Repeat the word: *up, up, up.*

4 Listen and repeat. (Student Book, p. 30)

Use graphic cues Help students locate *Activity 4. Listen and repeat* on page 30. Refer to the general guidelines for *Listen and repeat* in *Activity 3* of this chapter.

Audioscript 🎧

4. Listen and repeat.

Listen to the letter sounds and the words. Repeat the letter sounds and the words. /h/ hair; /h/ hand; /j/ jeans; /j/ jog; /l/ library; /l/ leaf; /u/ up; /u/ under

5 Point to the beginning letter. (Student Book, p. 30)

a. Learn graphic cues Have students locate *Activity 5. Point to the beginning letter* on page 30. Call attention to the corresponding icon.

b. Use active listening to follow directions Demonstrate by reading the first word *leg* three times. Then call out the following letter sounds: /h/ /j/ /l/ as you point to their corresponding letters. Repeat the word *leg* and the sound /l/. Circle the letter *l* with your finger as you repeat the sound /l/.

c. Learn sound/symbol relationships Monitor students to make sure they are pointing to the correct letter as you say the words. As an alternative, you can write the numbers and letters on the board, and have students come to the board and point as you say the words.

Answer key

5. Point to the beginning letter.

1. leg	h	j	**l**	4. jog	l h **j**	
2. hand	j	**h**	l	5. hat	j l **h**	
3. library	**l**	j	h	6. jeans	h l **j**	

6 **Listen and repeat.** (Student Book, p. 31)

Use graphic cues Have students open their books to page 31. Help them locate *Activity 6. Listen and repeat.* Refer to the general guidelines for *Listen and repeat* in *Activity 3.*

Audioscript 🎧

6. Listen and repeat.

Listen to the letter sound: /v/
Repeat the letter sound: /v/
Listen to the word: *van, van, van.*
Repeat the word: *van, van, van.*

Listen to the letter sound: /ks/
Repeat the letter sound: /ks/
Listen to the word: *x-ray, x-ray, x-ray.*
Repeat the word: *x-ray, x-ray, x-ray.*

Listen to the letter sound of the letter: /i/
Repeat the letter sound: /i/
Listen to the word: *in, in, in.*
Repeat the word: *in, in, in.*

Language Transfer and Interference

Spanish: The vowel sounds /i/ and /u/ have approximate sounds in Spanish.

Haitian-Creole: The short vowel sound /u/ does not occur in Haitian-Creole as it does in English.

Vietnamese: The short vowel sound /i/ does not occur in Vietnamese as it does in English.

7 **Listen and repeat.** (Student Book, p. 31)

Use graphic cues Have students open their books to page 31. Help them locate *Activity 7. Listen and repeat.* Refer to the general guidelines for *Listen and repeat* in *Activity 3.*

Audioscript 🎧

7. Listen and repeat.

Listen to the letter sounds and the words.
Repeat the letter sounds and the words.
/v/ van; /v/ video; /x/ x-ray; /i/ in; /i/ insect

8 **Point to the beginning letter.** (Student Book, p. 31)

Learn graphic cues Have students locate *Activity 8. Point to the beginning letter* on page 31. Refer to the general guidelines for *Point to the beginning letter* in *Activity 5.*

Answer key

8. Point to the beginning letter.

1. jeans	**j**	h	l	4. video	l f **v**	
2. van	h	f	**v**	5. in	**i** h f	
3. insect	d	**i**	u	6. up	**i** o u	

Activity Book, p. 18: Consonants: h, j, l, v, x; Vowels: i, u

Language and Vocabulary

9 **Listen and repeat.** (Student Book, p. 32)

Learn graphic cues Help students locate *Activity 9. Listen and repeat* on page 32. Call attention to the corresponding icons. Refer to the general guidelines for *Listen and repeat* in *Activity 3.*

Audioscript 🎧

9. Listen and repeat.

Listen to the words. Repeat the words.

A: *Hi. My name is Linda.*
B: *How old are you?*
A: *I'm 15 years old.*

A: *These are my friends. Irina is Russian.*
B: *How old is Irina?*
A: *She's 14 years old.*

A: *Emilio is my friend, too. He's from Mexico.*
B: *How old is Emilio?*
A: *He's 14 years old.*

10 **Listen and repeat.** (Student Book, p. 32)

a. Use graphic cues Have students open their books to page 32. Help them locate *Activity 10. Listen and repeat.* Refer to the general guidelines for *Listen and repeat* in *Activity 3.*

b. Infer meaning from visual content Ask: *What are these? These are dots. What color are they?* Have students count the first group of dots with you, counting aloud from one to eleven.

VISIONS BASIC Teacher Resource Book • Copyright © Heinle

Audioscript 🎧
10. Listen and repeat.

11	eleven
12	twelve
13	thirteen
14	fourteen
15	fifteen
16	sixteen
17	seventeen
18	eighteen
19	nineteen
20	twenty

Pronunciation Pointer

In pronouncing the teen numbers, place emphasis on the "teen" syllable in preparation for contrast with the numbers *30, 40,* etc.

Activity Book, p. 19: Classmates
Activity Book, p. 20: Numbers

⑪ **Listen and repeat.** (Student Book, p. 33)

Use graphic cues Have students open their books to page 33. Help them locate *Activity 11. Listen and repeat.* Refer to the general guidelines for *Listen and repeat* in *Activity 3.*

Audioscript
11. Listen and repeat. 🎧

Look at the boy. Look at the words. These are the parts of the body. Listen and repeat.
body, body; head, head; arm, arm; leg, leg; neck, neck; stomach, stomach; elbow, elbow; hand, hand; fingers, fingers; knee, knee; foot, foot

Look at the girl. Look at the words. These are the parts of the head and face. Listen and repeat.
head, head; face, face; ear, ear; hair, hair; eye, eye; nose, nose; cheek, cheek; lips, lips; chin, chin; mouth, mouth; teeth, teeth

⑫ **Work with a partner.** (Student Book, p. 33)

a. **Learn graphic cues** Help students locate *Activity 12. Work with a partner* on page 33. Call attention to the corresponding icons for the activity.

b. **Ask for and give information** Pair students with partners and have them ask each other the questions modeled in the activity. Model working with a volunteer. Say: *We are partners. I am working with a partner.*

c. **Initiate authentic discourse with peers** Encourage students to extend the activity by substituting other parts of the body.

d. **Monitor oral production** Remind students to distinguish between possessive pronouns *my/your* and demonstrative pronouns *this/that.*

Letters and Sounds

Consonants: *h, j, l, v, x*

Vowels: *i, u*

⑬ **Blend the letter sounds.** (Student Book, p. 34)

a. **Use graphic cues** Have students open their books to page 34. Help them locate *Activity 13. Blend the letter sounds.* Call attention to the corresponding icons.

b. **Learn sound/symbol relationship** Create three large flash cards with the letters *v, a,* and *n* on each respectively. Call out the individual letter sounds /v/, /a/, and /n/ several times while holding up the corresponding card. Then hold up the *v* and *a* cards and blend the initial consonant and medial vowel: /va/. Next, sound out the final consonant /n/ several times. Finally sound out all three sounds. Blend them together to pronounce *van.*

c. **Use visual cues to derive meaning** Be sure students know the meaning of the word *van.* Show a picture to emphasize that letters represent sounds in words that correspond to objects.

Audioscript 🎧

13. Blend the letter sounds.

Listen to the letter sounds. Point to the letter sounds. Listen to the words.

v a n	*van, van, van*
j o g	*jog, jog, jog*
l i p	*lip, lip, lip*
s i x	*six, six, six*
h u g	*hug, hug, hug*
c u p	*cup, cup, cup*

Listen to the letter sounds. Say the letter sounds. Listen to the words. Say the words.

v a n	*van, van, van*
j o g	*jog, jog, jog*
l i p	*lip, lip, lip*
s i x	*six, six, six*
h u g	*hug, hug, hug*
c u p	*cup, cup, cup*

⑭ What's the missing letter? (Student Book, p. 34)

a. Learn graphic cues Help students locate *Activity 14. What's the missing letter?* on page 34. Call attention to the corresponding icon for the activity.

b. Write letters of the alphabet Have students copy the activity in their notebooks and fill in the missing letter for each word. Indicate that they must write one letter per box. Some students may need to refer to *Activity 13* for review.

Answer key

14. What's the missing letter?

1. hug	h **u** g
2. six	s i **x**
3. cup	c **u** p
4. van	**v** a n
5. jog	j o **g**

⑮ Say the words. (Student Book, p. 34)

a. Use graphic cues Have students open their books to page 34. Help them locate *Activity 15. Say the words.* Call attention to the corresponding icon.

b. Recognize phonological elements Point to the letters of each word and have students sound them out and then blend them to say the words in the activity.

c. Self-Monitor oral production Some students may need extra practice distinguishing between the vowel sounds /o/ and /u/. Demonstrate these vowel

sounds with exaggerated articulation. Use a mirror to help students observe themselves as they produce these vowel sounds.

Activity Book, p. 21: Vowels: i, u

⑯ Write the words. (Student Book, p. 35)

a. Use graphic cues Have students open their books to page 35. Help them locate *Activity 16. Write the words.*

b. Use visual cues to derive meaning Review the words by pointing to each picture on page 34 and asking: *What's this?* Demonstrate the example in *Activity 16* by drawing three blank boxes on the board. Show the picture of *jog* and ask a volunteer to act it out. Ask students to repeat the word *jog* and sound out the first two letters as you write them on the board. Then solicit the final consonant sound and write *g* in the appropriate blank box.

c. Monitor written production Have students copy the activity on a piece of paper. Check to see that students are filling in the correct letters for each word in the appropriate space. Look for errors and substitutions such as *o* for *u* or *v* for *u*.

⑰ Spell the words (Student Book, p. 35)

a. Use graphic cues Have students open their books to page 35. Help them locate *Activity 17. Spell the words.* Call attention to the corresponding icons.

b. Produce phonological elements Have students copy the activity. Play the audio or read the script. Have students spell the words by writing the correct letters in the corresponding boxes.

c. Monitor written production Check to see that students are filling in the correct letters for each word in the appropriate space. Repeat the audio as necessary.

d. Ask for and give information To check students' work, ask: *How do you spell van?* Help students spell it aloud. Ask this question about each of the words. Then have volunteers ask classmates the same questions. This is a useful question for students to learn and use in class.

Audioscript 🎧

17. Spell the words.

Listen to the words. Write the words.

1. *van, van, van*
2. *cup, cup, cup*
3. *hug, hug, hug*
4. *jog, jog, jog*

18 **Is the beginning sound the same?** (Student Book, p. 35)

a. Use graphic cues Have students open their books to page 35. Help them locate *Activity 18. Is the beginning sound the same?* Call attention to the corresponding icon.

b. Use active listening to follow directions Point to the picture on the left of item 1: *hug*. Ask a volunteer to identify the word. Repeat the word *hug*. Ask the class what the initial sound is in the word. Then ask a volunteer to identify the picture on the right: *hand*. Repeat the word *hand*. Ask the class what the initial sound is in this word. Now say *hug* and *hand* several times. Ask if the beginning sound is the same or different. Confirm that they are the same. Point to the word *same* in the book and trace a circle with your finger.

c. Distinguish between phonemic elements Show students how to number their piece of paper from 1–5. Have students work with a partner from a different language background. Have them first identify what the words are, and then determine if the initial sound they hear is the same or different. Have students write out the word *same* or *different* next to the appropriate number on their paper.

Answer key

18. Is the beginning sound the same?

1. hug / hand	same
2. van / fan	different
3. x-ray / six	different
4. jog / jeans	same
5. lip / library	same

Language Transfer and Interference

Spanish: The letter *h* has no corresponding sound in Spanish. The sound /h/ is represented by the letters *j* and by the letter *g* before the vowels *e* or *i*. In many cases the letter *v* will sound like a soft *b*, as in the Spanish word for green: *verde /berde/.*

Vietnamese: The letter *l* can have the sound of *r*: *load > road*

Activity Book, p. 22: Parts of the Body

Reading and Writing

19 **Read and match.** (Student Book, p. 36)

a. Use graphic cues Have students open their books to page 36. Help them locate *Activity 19. Read and match.*

b. Use active listening to follow directions Point to the word on the left in the item 1 example and say *hug*. Ask a volunteer to point to the word on the right that matches the example on the left. Trace a circle around the correct answer to demonstrate the activity.

c. Develop basic sight vocabulary Have students copy the activity in their notebooks. Students should work independently to find the correct answers.

20 **Listen and read.** (Student Book, p. 36)

a. Use graphic cues Have students open their books to page 36. Help them locate *Activity 20. Listen and read.*

b. Interpret a visual image Show the class the picture on page 36 and point to Martha. Say: *This is Martha. Martha has brown hair. She has blue eyes.*

c. Extract meaning from audio recording Play the audio or read the script. Replay or reread the script a second time. Then read it chorally with the class.

VISIONS BASIC Teacher Resource Book • Copyright © Heinle

Audioscript 🎧
20. Listen and read.

This is Martha. She is a student. She is 14 years old. Her hair is brown. Her eyes are blue. She is my friend. Is she your friend, too?

21 **What are the missing words?** (Student Book, p. 37)

a. Use graphic cues Have students open their books to page 37. Help them locate *Activity 21. What are the missing words?*

b. Describe how illustrations support text Have students to look at the picture of Emilio on page 37. Ask the class: *What color is Emilio's hair?* Point to your own hair to provide a cue. Then ask: *What color are his eyes?* Point to your own eyes.

c. Construct correct sentences Have students copy the activity in their notebooks and fill in the appropriate answers.

Answer key
21. What are the missing words?
This **is** Emilio. He is **a** student.
He **is** 14 years old.
His **hair** is black. His eyes **are** brown.
He is **my** friend.

22 **Listen and read.** (Student Book, p. 37)

a. Use graphic cues Have students open their books to page 37. Help them locate *Activity 22. Listen and read.*

b. Understand the use of punctuation marks Show the class the chart on page 37. Explain that the examples on the left are sentences and they end with a period. The examples on the right are questions and they end with a question mark. Explain that these are different forms of sentences and that all sentences in English must begin with a capital letter.

c. Extract meaning from audio recording Play the audio or read the script. Replay or reread the script. Point out the significant punctuation examples from activity 20 on page 36. Read it chorally with the class. Provide more punctuation examples for the class.

Audioscript 🎧
22. Listen and read.

Look at the sentences. Listen to the sentences.
I'm a student.
His hair is brown.

A sentence begins with a capital letter. A sentence ends with a period.

Look at the questions. Listen to the questions.
Is this your pen?
How old are you?

A question begins with a capital letter. A question ends with a question mark.

23 **Add the punctuation.** (Student Book, p. 37)

a. Use graphic cues Have students open their books to page 37. Help them locate *Activity 23. Add the punctuation.*

b. Use correct punctuation and capitalization Have students copy the activity in their notebooks and fill in the appropriate answers. Students may need to refer to *Activity 22* for help.

Answer key
23. Add the punctuation.
1. What's your name**?**
2. My name is Ana**.**
3. Where are you from**?**
4. I'm from Mexico**.**
5. How old is Irina**?**
6. She is 16**.**

Activity Book, p. 23: Friends

Language and Vocabulary

24 **Listen and repeat.** (Student Book, p. 38)

Use graphic cues Have students open their books to page 38. Help them locate *Activity 24. Listen and repeat.* Refer to the general guidelines for *Listen and repeat* in *Activity 3.*

Audioscript 🎧
24. Listen and repeat.

A: How many girls are there in this class?
B: There are 14 girls in this class. How many girls are there in your class?
A: There are 11 girls in my class. There are 13 boys.
B: How many teachers are there?
A: There is one teacher.

㉕ **Talk about the picture.** (Student Book, p. 38)

a. Use graphic cues Have students open their books to page 38. Help them locate *Activity 25. Talk about the picture.*

b. Describe illustrations Look at the picture on page 38. Describe several details in the picture using sentences such as: *There is a blue backpack. There are two windows.* Point to other objects in the picture to prompt students to make sentences. *Ask the class: Where is the backpack?* Point to the backpack under a desk to provide a cue. Then say: *The backpack is under a desk.* Ask other similar questions. Then ask: *What color is the backpack?* If the class does not offer an answer say: *The backpack is blue.*

c. Construct correct sentences Have students work with a partner and ask each other questions based on the picture. Write a few examples on the board to help students generate new questions such as *What do you see? How many ___ are there? Where is/are the ___? What color is the ___?*

Activity Book, p. 24: A Catalogue Page

Review

Clothing (Student Book, p. 39)

Clothing I Spy To reinforce and practice clothing and color vocabulary, play this game with students. Say: *I spy blue sneakers.* Prompt students to say *here* when they find the blue sneakers. Continue in the same way, saying different clothing and colors. As an alternative, the student who says *here* first becomes the next person to say *I spy.*

Parts of the Body (Student Book, p. 39)

Simon says Practice parts of the body by playing Simon Says. Model the game first, touching what you name. For example: *Simon says touch your arm. Simon says touch your cheek. Touch your hair.* Practice together until students understand that if they follow the command when you don't say *Simon says,* they are out. You can have everyone stand, and then students sit down when they are out.

Expressions (Student Book, p. 39)

Scrambled sentences To practice the expressions listed on the review page, write the words for each sentence or question on separate index cards. Keep the cards for each sentence together with a paper clip. Change sentences to fit the ability of your students. For example, you could write: *There are three books on the desk.* Hand out the cards to small groups of students, and have students exchange cards as they finish each sentence.

Chapter D Around the School

Materials

Student Book: pp. 40–51
Activity Book: pp. 25–32
Audio: Chapter D
Student CD-ROM: Chapter D
Teacher Resource Book: Lesson Plan, pp. 31–38, Teacher Resources, pp. 148–162
Assessment Program: pp. 9–18
Overhead Transparencies

Themes

School Building
The Alphabet
Directions
Possession

Learning Strategies

Use inductive reasoning
Use prior knowledge
Look for patterns in language
Monitor oral and written language production
Understand learning strategies, such as circumlocution
Use accessible language and learn new and essential language

Listening

Use active listening comprehension to follow directions
Understand expressions and vocabulary regarding directions and school building
Recognize and distinguish phonological elements: *k, q, r, w, y, z,* and short *e*
Listen to and extract meaning from audio recording
Infer meaning from actions and visual context

Speaking

Ask for and give information, such as directions
Initiate authentic discourse with peers
Produce phonological elements of newly acquired vocabulary

Reading

Learn sound/symbol relationships in the English phonological system
Develop basic sight vocabulary
Participate in shared reading

Writing

Distinguish between uppercase and lowercase letters
Introduce orthographic rules, such as writing *qu* together
Use capitalization and punctuation rules with reference to sentences and questions
Construct correct sentences

Viewing and Representing

Interpret a visual image
Use visual cues to derive meaning

Introductory Activity

Use prior knowledge Make or bring magazine pictures of some common signs students might see around the school or in town. These might include signs for men's/women's bathrooms, handicap facilities, public telephone, bus stop, pedestrian or bike zones, stop, yield, etc. Have students guess the meaning of these signs.

Chapter Opener (Student Book, pp. 40–41)

a. View illustrations: Supporting text Refer to the picture on pages 40–41. Point out the various parts of the school in the picture and say the words: *hall, bulletin board, locker,* and *stairs.* Ask students to repeat these words. Now introduce the words *library, bookcase, bookshelf,* and *librarian* by pointing out these images in the picture. Explain the words *cafeteria* and *gym.* Note that the word *gym* is short for *gymnasium.*

b. Listening skills: Infer meaning Take a tour of the school with your class. Point out the following: *hall, bulletin board, locker, stairs, library, bookcase, bookshelf, librarian, cafeteria,* and *gym.* If possible, arrange for the class to briefly meet the librarian, nurse, secretary, and principal. Also make sure to point out the school bathrooms and to teach your students the words that appear on the bathroom doors at your particular school. You may want to mention that bathrooms are sometimes called restrooms, and signs on restrooms can say *Ladies/Gentlemen* or *Women/Men.* If your school has two or more floors, explain to students that in English the ground floor is called the first floor, the next is called the second, etc.

c. Use visual cues Have students help you create a map of your school. Have students label places with graphic icons they come up with themselves. For example, they might use a fork and knife to label the cafeteria; a book to label the library; a basketball to label the gym, and so forth.

❶ Listen and point. (Student Book, p. 40)

a. Learn graphic cues Help students locate *Activity 1. Listen and point* on page 40. Call attention to the corresponding icons for the activity.

b. Use active listening to follow directions Demonstrate by pointing to your ear and

saying the word *listen.* Then say the word *bookcase.* Point to the picture of the hall and the corresponding word as you say *bookcase.* Show your index finger and repeat the gesture as you say the word *point,* showing your finger placement on the page. Now prompt the class and say the word *point.* Then point to the word *bookcase.*

c. Use nonverbal cues Play the audio or read the script. Give visual cues by pointing to your ear when it is time to listen, and by pointing to the book when it is time to point.

Audioscript 🎧

1. Listen and point.

Point to the picture of the bookcase. Point to the word *bookcase.*
Point to the picture of the bookshelf. Point to the word *bookshelf.*
Point to the picture of the *bulletin board.* Point to the word *bulletin board.*
Point to the picture of the cafeteria. Point to the word *cafeteria.*
Point to the picture of the gym. Point to the word *gym.*
Point to the picture of the hall. Point to the word *hall.*
Point to the picture of the librarian. Point to the word *librarian.*
Point to the picture of library. Point to the word *library.*
Point to the picture of the locker. Point to the word *locker.*
Point to the picture of the stairs. Point to the word *stairs.*

❷ Listen and repeat. (Student Book, p. 40)

a. Use graphic cues Help students locate *Activity 2. Listen and repeat* on page 40. Demonstrate by pointing to your ear and saying the word *listen.* Then say the word: *bookcase.* Now prompt the class and say *repeat.* Say: *Repeat the word bookcase.* Gesture for the class to repeat.

b. Recognize phonological elements Play the audio or read the script. Give students visual cues by pointing to your ear when it is time for students to listen, and by pointing to the class when it is time for them to repeat.

c. Monitor oral production Encourage everyone to speak. Stop and repeat the activity several times if necessary, but refrain from making corrections at this point.

Audioscript 🎧

Audioscript 🎧

2. Listen and repeat.

bookcase, bookcase; bookshelf, bookshelf; bulletin board, bulletin board; cafeteria, cafeteria; gym, gym; hall, hall; librarian, librarian; library, library; locker, locker; stairs, stairs

Activity Book, p. 25: Around the School

Letters and Sounds

Consonants: *k, q, r, w, y, z*

Vowel: *e*

③ Listen and repeat. (Student Book, p. 42)

a. Use graphic cues Help students locate *Activity 3. Listen and repeat* on page 42. Demonstrate for the class by pointing to your ear and saying the word *listen*. Then say the first line: *Listen to the letter sound /k/*. Now prompt the class with a hand gesture and say: *Repeat. Repeat the letter sound /k/*. Gesture for the class to say: */k/*.

b. Recognize phonological elements Play the audio or read the script. Give students visual cues by pointing to your ear when it is time for students to listen, and then by pointing to the class when it is time for them to repeat.

c. Monitor oral production Students may need extra practice giving a choral response the first few times. Encourage everyone to speak.

Audioscript 🎧

3. Listen and repeat.

Listen to the letter sound: */k/*
Repeat the letter sound: */k/*
Listen to the word: *key, key, key*
Repeat the word: *key, key, key*

Listen to the letter sound: */r/*
Repeat the letter sound: */r/*
Listen to the word: *ring, ring, ring*
Repeat the word: *ring, ring, ring*

Listen to the letter sound: */w/*
Repeat the letter sound: */w/*
Listen to the word: *window, window, window*
Repeat the word: *window, window, window*

④ Listen and repeat. (Student Book, p. 42)

Use graphic cues Help students locate *Activity 4. Listen and repeat* on page 42.

Refer to the general guidelines for *Listen and repeat* in *Activity 3* of this chapter.

Audioscript 🎧

4. Listen and repeat.

Listen to the letter sounds and the words.
Repeat the letter sounds and the words.
/k/ key; /k/ king; /k/ kite; /r/ ring; /r/ rose; /r/ rain; /w/ window; /w/ water; /w/ woman

⑤ Point to the beginning letter. (Student Book, p. 42)

a. Learn graphic cues Have students locate *Activity 5. Point to the beginning letter* on page 42. Call attention to the corresponding icon.

b. Use active listening to follow directions Demonstrate with item 1 by saying the word *woman* three times. Then call out the following letter sounds: */k/, /w/,* and */r/* as you point to their corresponding letters. Repeat the word *woman* and the sound */w/*. Point to the letter *w* with your finger as you repeat the sound */w/*.

c. Learn sound/symbol relationships Follow the same procedure for each of the items. Have students point to the letter that matches the beginning sound they hear.

Answer Key

5. Point to the beginning letter.

1. woman	k	**w**	r
2. window	r	**w**	k
3. king	r	**k**	w
4. water	k	r	**w**
5. ring	w	k	**r**
6. rain	w	**r**	k

⑥ Listen and repeat. (Student Book, p. 43)

a. Use graphic cues Help students locate *Activity 6. Listen and repeat* on page 43. Refer to the general guidelines for *Listen and repeat* in *Activity 3*.

b. Introduce an orthographic rule Explain to the class that the letter *q* must always be followed by the letter *u* in English. Tell the students that this is a special spelling rule. Write the following examples on the board, underlining *qu: quarter, quiet, queen*.

Audioscript 🎧

6. **Listen and repeat.**
Listen to the letter sound: /y/
Repeat the letter sound: /y/
Listen to the word: *yellow, yellow, yellow*
Repeat the word: *yellow, yellow, yellow*

Listen to the letter sound: /z/
Repeat the letter sound: /z/
Listen to the word: *zipper, zipper, zipper*
Repeat the word: *zipper, zipper, zipper*

Listen to the letter sound: /kw/
Repeat the letter sound: /kw/
Listen to the word: *quarter, quarter, quarter*
Repeat the word: *quarter, quarter, quarter*

Listen to the letter sound: /e/
Repeat the sound: /e/
Listen to the word: *egg, egg, egg*
Repeat the word: *egg, egg, egg*

Language Transfer and Interference

Spanish: The /kw/ sound does occur in Spanish, but it does not correspond with the letter *q*. In Spanish the /kw/ sound is represented by the letters *cu* as in *cuatro /kwatro/: four.* The letter *q* in Spanish has the sound *k* as in *queso /keso/: cheese.* Spanish speakers will often pronounce *y* as *j*, saying: *jes* instead of *yes.* There is no exact sound transfer in Spanish for the letter *z*.

Haitian-Creole: The short vowel sound /e/ does not occur in Haitian-Creole as it does in English.

Vietnamese: The short vowel sound /e/ has an approximate sound in Vietnamese. There is no exact sound transfer in Vietnamese for the letters *w, y,* and *z.*

7 **Listen and repeat.** (Student Book, p. 43)

Use graphic cues Help students locate *Activity 7. Listen and repeat* on page 43. Refer to the general guidelines for *Listen and repeat* in *Activity3*

Audioscript 🎧

7. **Listen and repeat.**
Listen to the letter sounds and the words.
Repeat the letter sounds and the words.
/y/ yellow; /y/ yes; /z/ zipper; /z/ zebra; /kw/ quarter; /kw/ queen; /e/ egg; /e/ elbow

8 **Point to the beginning letter.** (Student Book, p. 43)

Learn graphic cues Have students locate *Activity 8. Point to the beginning letter* on page 43. Refer to the general guidelines for Point to the beginning letter in *Activity 5.*

Answer key

8. Point to the beginning letter.

1. egg	**e**	o	u	4. rose	**r** l n
2. yellow	g j	**y**		5. key	l **k** t
3. zipper	s	**z**	x	6. queen	j g **q**

Activity Book, p. 26: Consonants: k, q, r, w, y, z; Vowel: e

Language and Vocabulary

9 **Listen and point.** (Student Book, p. 44)

Learn graphic cues Help students locate *Activity 9. Listen and point* on page 44. Call attention to the corresponding icons. Refer to the general guidelines for *Listen and point* in *Activity 1.*

Audioscript 🎧

9. **Listen and point.**
This is a map of a school. Look at the first floor of the school. Point to the first floor. Find the main office. The main office is next to the entrance. Point to the main office. Find the elevator. The elevator is next to the stairs. Point to the elevator. Find the cafeteria. The cafeteria is across from the bathrooms. Point to the cafeteria. Find the bathrooms. The girls' bathroom is on the left. The boys' bathroom is on the right. Point to the girls' bathroom. Point to the boys' bathroom. Now look at the second floor. Find the library. The library is next to the stairs. Point to the library. Find the nurse's office. The nurse's office is across from the library. Point to the nurse's office.

10 **Listen and repeat.** (Student Book, p. 45)

Use graphic cues Help students locate *Activity 10. Listen and repeat* on page 45. Refer to the general guidelines for *Listen and repeat* in *Activity 3.*

Audioscript 🎧

10. Listen and repeat.

Listen to the girls.
A: Excuse me. Where's the gym?
B: It's on the left. It's next to Room 102.
A: Thanks.

Now repeat.
A: Excuse me. Where's the gym?
B: It's on the left. It's next to Room 102.
A: Thanks.

Listen to the boys.
A: Excuse me. Where's the nurse's office?
B: It's on the second floor. Go up the stairs. It's on the left. It's next to the bathrooms.
A: Thanks.

Now repeat.
A: Excuse me. Where's the nurse's office?
B: It's on the second floor. Go up the stairs. It's on the left. It's next to the bathrooms.
A: Thanks.

Culture Note

Call attention to the use of polite language, particularly the expression *Excuse me* as a way of getting someone's attention. Mention that *thanks* is less formal than *thank you*. Discuss where to use these expressions. Ask: *Where can we say Excuse me?* Prompt answers like *in the classroom, in the cafeteria, in the school office.* Ask: *What do we say to the principal-thanks or thank you?* Continue with similar questions about speaking to the school librarian, a teacher, a friend, and a classmate.

Literacy Note

Write on the board: *contraction: it is—it's, I am—I'm* to introduce the term *contraction*. Ask students to find other contractions in the Activity 10 conversation. Explain that contractions are an informal form.

Also note that the possessive form is introduced for the first time here with the word *nurse's*. Write on the board *nurse's office* and point out the *'s* but do not expand on it. Simply state that this apostrophe shows possession and is not the same as the apostrophe in a contraction Say: *This means that it is the office of the nurse. It is the nurse's office.* Also point out that this *s* does not indicate plural form.

⑪ **Answer the questions about your school.** (Student Book, p. 45)

a. Learn graphic cues Help students locate *Activity 11. Answer the questions about your school* on page 45. Call attention to the corresponding icon for the activity.

b. Respond to oral commands Give commands for students to act out to reinforce new vocabulary. For example, say: *Look right. Look left. Look at the classmate next to you. Look at the classmate across from you.*

c. Ask and give information Practice this activity orally with the class. Emphasize the different types of question forms such as information, yes/no, and choice. Indicate the corresponding answer types. Reinforce the contrasting intonation patterns of questions and statements. Bring attention to the *wh-* questions words *where* and *what* used here. Have students describe their classroom.

Answer key

11. Answer the questions about your school.

1. Is the nurse's office on the first floor?
   Yes, it is. *or* No, it isn't.
2. Is the cafeteria next to the gym?
   Yes, it is. *or* No, it isn't.
3. Is the gym on the first floor or the second floor?
   It's on the ___ floor.
4. Where is the library?
   It's ___.
5. Where is the main office?
   It's ___.
6. What is across from the main office?
   The ___ is across from the main office.

Activity Book, p. 27: In the School
Activity Book, p. 28: Where is it?

Letters and Sounds

Consonants: *k, q, r, w, y, z*

Vowel: *e*

⑫ **Blend the letter sounds.** (Student Book, p. 46)

a. Use graphic cues Help students locate *Activity 12. Blend the letter sounds* on page 46. Call attention to the corresponding icons.

b. Learn sound/symbol relationship Create three large flash cards with the letters *t, e,* and *n* on each respectively. Call out the individual letter sounds /t/, /e/, and /n/ several times while holding up the corresponding card. Then hold up the *t* and *e* cards and blend the initial consonant and medial vowel /te/. Next, sound out the final consonant /n/ several times. Finally sound out all three sounds. Blend them together to pronounce *ten*.

c. Use visual cues to derive meaning Be sure students know the meaning of the word *ten*. Show a picture to emphasize that the letters *t e n* represent the sounds in the word *ten* that corresponds to the number of objects.

Audioscript 🎧

12. Blend the letter sounds.

Listen to the letter sounds.
Point to the letter sounds. Listen to the words.

t e n	ten, ten, ten
b e d	bed, bed, bed
j e t	jet, jet, jet
w e t	wet, wet, wet
y e s	yes, yes, yes
r e d	red, red, red

Listen to the letter sounds. Say the letter sounds. Listen to the words. Say the words.

t e n	ten, ten, ten
b e d	bed, bed, bed
j e t	jet, jet, jet
w e t	wet, wet, wet
y e s	yes, yes, yes
r e d	red, red, red

13 What's the missing letter? (Student Book, p. 46)

a. Learn graphic cues Help students locate *Activity 13. What's the missing letter?* on page 46. Call attention to the icon.

b. Write letters of the alphabet Have students fill in the missing letter for each word in their notebook. Indicate that they must write one letter per box. Some students may need to refer to *Activity 12.*

Answer key

13. What's the missing letter?

1. r e **d**
2. w e **t**
3. t e **n**
4. **j** e t
5. b **e** d

14 Say the words. (Student Book, p. 47)

a. Use graphic cues Help students locate *Activity 14. Say the words* on page 47. Call attention to the corresponding icon.

b. Recognize phonological elements Point to the letters of each word and have students sound them out and then blend them to say the word in the lesson.

c. Self-monitor oral production Some students may need extra practice pronouncing *w, j,* or *r.* Demonstrate these sounds with exaggerated articulation. Use a mirror to help students observe themselves as they pronounce these letter sounds.

15 Write the words. (Student Book, p. 47)

a. Use graphic cues Help students locate *Activity 15. Write the words* on page 47.

b. Use active listening to follow directions Review the words by pointing to each picture and asking for the correct word. Demonstrate the example by drawing three blank boxes on the board. Point to the picture *jet* and ask what the word is. If the class doesn't offer an answer, say the word *jet.* Ask students to repeat the word *jet* and sound out the first two letters as you write them on the board. Then solicit the final consonant sound and write *t* in the appropriate blank box.

c. Learn sound/symbol relationships Have students copy the activity in their notebooks. Then have them fill in the missing letters in the appropriate boxes in their notebook. Indicate that they must write one letter per box.

d. Monitor written production Check to see that students are filling in the correct letters for each word in the appropriate spaces. Look for errors and substitutions.

16 Spell the words. (Student Book, p. 47)

a. Use graphic cues Help students locate *Activity 16. Spell the words* on page 47. Call attention to the corresponding icons.

b. Produce phonological elements Have students copy the activity in their notebooks. Play the audio or read the script. Have students spell the words by writing the correct letters in the corresponding boxes.

c. Monitor written production Check to see that students are filling in the correct letters for each word in the appropriate space in their notebooks. Repeat the audio as necessary.

Audioscript

16. Spell the words.
Listen to the words. Write the words.1.
1. *jet, jet, jet*
2. *bed, bed, bed*
3. *yes, yes, yes*
4. *red, red, red*

Activity Book, p. 29: Vowel: e

Reading and Writing

17 Read and match (Student Book, p. 48)

a. Use graphic cues Help students locate *Activity 18. Read and match* on page 48.

b. Look for patterns in language Point to the letter *y* on the left side of item 1. Ask a volunteer to point to the letters that exactly match it from the choices on the right. Trace a circle with your finger around the correct answers to demonstrate.

c. Look for patterns in language Write the letters *b, d, p, q,* and *h* on the board and point out that the loop in *b, d, p,* and *q* is connected whereas the loop in *h* is not. Have students note the position of the loop in *b, d, p,* and *q.* Next write the letters *l, i, I, t, r, f,* and *j.* Indicate that although all these letters are made with a single vertical stroke, the lowercase *i* has a dot on top, the uppercase *I* is crossed on the top and bottom, the letter *t* is crossed in the middle and may have a hook in the bottom right, the letter *f* is crossed and has a hook on the top right, the letter *r* has a shorter stem than *f* and is not crossed, and the letter *j* is dotted with a hook on the bottom left. Then write *h, n, m, u, v,* and *w.* Distinguish the difference in the length of the stem for *h* and *n,* the number of hoops between n and *m,* the rotation of *n* and *u, m* and *w,* as well as the pinch at the base of *v* as opposed to the rounded base of *u.* Lastly compare the letters *s* and *z* contrasting the curves in *s* to the sharp corners of *z,* as well as their being inverted.

d. Distinguish between phonemic elements Copy the activity on the board. Work with the class to find the matching letters.

18 Read and match. (Student Book, p. 48)

a. Use graphic cues Help students locate *Activity 18. Read and match* on page 48.

b. Use active listening to follow directions Point to the word on the left in item 1 and say *office.* Ask a volunteer to point to the word on the right that matches the example on the left. Trace a circle around the correct answer to demonstrate the activity.

c. Develop basic sight vocabulary Have students copy the activity in their notebooks. Students should work independently to find the correct answers.

19 Listen and read. (Student Book, p. 49)

a. Use graphic cues Have students open their books to page 49. Help students locate *Activity 19. Listen and read.*

b. Interpret a visual image Show the class the pictures on page 49 and point to Ms. Fernandez in the first picture and say: *This is Ms. Fernandez. She is the school principal. This is her office.*

c. Extract meaning from audio recording Play the audio or read the script. Replay or reread the script. Read it chorally with the class.

Audioscript

19. Listen and read.
I'm Ms. Fernandez. I'm the principal. This is my office. It's on the first floor. My office is inside the main office. The main office is next to the entrance.

I'm Mr. Soto. I'm the gym teacher. This is the gym. It's on the first floor. The gym is on the left of the main entrance. It's next to Room 102.

My name is Mrs. Walsh. I'm the school nurse. My office is on the second floor. It's across from the library. It's a nice office. There's a desk for me and a bed for sick students.

20 **Answer the questions.** (Student Book, p. 49)

a. **Use graphic cues** Help students locate *Activity 20. Answer the questions* on page 49.

b. **Construct correct sentences** Have students copy the activity in their notebooks and fill the appropriate answers. Some students may need to refer to *Activity 19* for help.

Answer key

20. Answer the questions.
1. Mrs. Walsh is the **nurse.**
2. Mr. Soto is the **gym teacher.**
3. **Ms. Fernandez** is the principal.
4. The gym is next to **room** 102.
5. The nurse's office is across from the **library.**

Activity Book, p. 30: People and Rooms

Language and Vocabulary

21 **Listen and repeat.** (Student Book, p. 50)

Use graphic cues Help students locate *Activity 21. Listen and repeat* on page 50. Refer to the general guidelines for *Listen and repeat* in *Activity 3*.

Audioscript 🎧
21. Listen and repeat.

Listen.
A: Excuse me. Is this the Lost and Found?
B: Yes, it is.
A: I lost my backpack. Maybe it's here.
B: Is this your backpack?
A: No, it isn't. Mine is green.
B: Is this yours?
A: Yes, that's mine. Thank you.

Now repeat.
A: Excuse me. Is this the Lost and Found?
B: Yes, it is.
A: I lost my backpack. Maybe it's here.
B: Is this your backpack?
A: No, it isn't. Mine is green.
B: Is this yours?
A: Yes, that's mine. Thank you.

22 **What are the missing words?** (Student Book, p. 50)

a. **Use graphic cues** Have students open their books to page 50. Help students locate *Activity 22. What are the missing words?*

b. **Construct correct sentences** Have students copy the activity in their notebooks. Remind them to use a capital letter for the first word of a sentence.

c. **Practice dialogue with peers** Pair students to work as partners and ask each other questions based on the activity. Encourage them to use the activity as a model to generate new questions. Be sure they foster respect for others.

Answer key

22. What are the missing words?
1. A: Is this **your** backpack?
   B: No, **it** isn't. Mine **is** red.
2. A: Is this **your** jacket?
   B: **No,** it isn't. **Mine** is black.
3. A: Is this **your** baseball cap?
   B: Yes, it **is.** Thank **you.**

Activity Book, p. 31: Mine and Yours
Activity Book, p. 32: Social Studies: Reading a Map

Review
Words (Student Book, p. 51)

Understand circumlocution Review vocabulary for places and things in the school by giving students cues, and having students tell the name of the place or thing. Model the first cue. Here are some sample cues you can use.

1. It has many books, but it has no door. [bookcase]
2. Go here if you are hungry. [cafeteria]
3. This is a place to wash your hands. [bathroom]

Expressions (Student Book, p. 51)

Use inductive reasoning skills Create a series of clues for a Scavenger Hunt for places around the school. For each group, write five clues. For example: *It is next to the nurse's office. The door is green.* The first group who returns to class with the list of places "wins."

VISIONS BASIC Teacher Resource Book • Copyright © Heinle

Chapter 1 In the School Office

Materials

Student Book: pp. 52–65
Activity Book: pp. 33–40, Mini-Reader 1
Audio: Chapter 1
Student CD-ROM: Chapter 1
Teacher Resource Book
    Lesson Plan: pp. 41–48
    Reading Fluency: p. 126
    Resource Masters: Personal Dictionary, p. 136; Student Information Form, p. 137; Web, p. 138;
        Venn Diagram, p. 139; Numerals 1–20, pp. 161–162; Calendar, p. 163
Assessment Program: pp. 19–22
Transparencies

Themes

School Office   Forms
Calendar   Ordinal Numbers

Learning Strategies

Look for patterns in language
Monitor oral language production
Make connections across content areas: mathematics

Listening

Use active listening comprehension to follow directions
Understand expressions and vocabulary: days of the week, months of the year, ordinal numbers,
    subject pronouns, and possessive adjectives
Recognize and distinguish phonological elements: short vowels
Listen to and extract meaning from audio recording
Infer meaning from actions and visual context

Speaking

Identify ordinal numbers, days of the week, months of the year
Ask for and give information

Reading

Read authentic documents such as a Student Information Form
Learn sound/symbol relationships in the English phonological system: short vowels
Develop basic sight vocabulary
Participate in shared reading

Writing

Complete a form
Use capitalization and punctuation rules with reference to days of the week, months of the year, and
    abbreviations
Employ complex grammatical structures such as: nominative and possessive cases

Viewing and Representing

Use visual cues to derive meaning
Produce visuals to support text
Interpret and evaluate visual images

Chapter Opener (Student Book, pp. 52–53)

a. View illustrations: Supporting text Refer to the picture on p. 52. Point out the following office supplies and equipment: *calendar, copy machine, keyboard, mouse, printer, screen, stapler, telephone.* Explain the function of each item. For example, say: *The copy machine makes copies. A computer has a keyboard and a screen. The screen is sometimes called a monitor.*

b. Use learning strategies such as circumlocution Have students describe one of the items or act out using it. Have the class guess the answer. Model first, saying for example: *It is something you use to talk with someone far away. You put it to your ear and talk. What is it?* (telephone)

Listen, Speak, Interact

In the School Office

1 Listen and repeat. (Student Book, p. 53)

a. Use active listening to follow directions Have students find the activity and read the directions. Point to your ear and say the word *listen.* Then say the first word in the audio script: *calendar.* Now prompt the class and say: *Repeat the word calendar.* Gesture the class to repeat *calendar.*

b. Recognize phonological elements Play the audio or read the script. Give students visual cues when it is time for them to listen and to repeat.

c. Monitor oral production Encourage everyone to speak. Repeat the activity if necessary, but refrain from making corrections at this point.

Audioscript 🎧

1. Listen and repeat. Listen and repeat the words:
calendar, calendar / copy machine, copy machine / keyboard, keyboard / mouse, mouse / printer, printer /screen, screen / secretary, secretary / stapler, stapler / telephone, telephone

2 Listen and repeat. (Student Book, p. 53)

a. Listen to and extract meaning from audio Have students find the activity and read the directions. Refer to the guidelines in *Activity 1.*

b. Understand terms Draw a rough outline of a form and label it *Student Information Form.* Write in the form *Name, Address, Phone number,* each followed by a write-on line. Say: *This is a Student Information Form.* Then point to the form as it is mentioned in the audioscript.

Audioscript 🎧

2. Listen and repeat. Listen to the conversation.
Secretary: *Good morning. May I help you?*
Student: *Yes, please. I need a Student Information Form.*
Secretary: *Sure. Here's a Student Information Form.*
Student: *Thank you.*

Now repeat the conversation.
Secretary: *Good morning. May I help you?*
Student: *Yes, please. I need a Student Information Form.*
Secretary: *Sure. Here's a Student Information Form.*
Student: *Thank you.*

3 Pair work. (Student Book, p. 53)

a. Read through a dialogue Have students find the activity and read the directions. Pair students with a partner. First have students read the dialogue as it appears on the page. Then prompt them to use the photos for substitutions in the dialogue. Model this with several volunteers before students work in pairs.

b. Produce authentic discourse with peers Encourage students to make substitutions with other objects such as a *book* or *dictionary.*

Answer key

3. Pair work.
Secretary: Good morning. May I help you?
Student: Yes, please. I need a **pencil / pen / stapler.**
Secretary: Sure. Here's a **pencil / pen / stapler.**
Student: Thank you.

Culture Note

Share with students some more polite alternatives to *I need...* such as: *Can / Could / May I have...?*

VISIONS BASIC Teacher Resource Book • Copyright © Heinle

Build Vocabulary

The Calendar

4 **Listen and repeat.** (Student Book, p. 54)

a. Use prior knowledge Have students find the activity and read the directions. Refer to the guidelines in Activity 1. Students may already know some of the days of the week. Ask: *What day is today? What day was yesterday? What day is tomorrow?* You may want to introduce the terms *yesterday* and *tomorrow*.

b. Understand capitalization rules Explain that the first letter of each day must be capitalized, even in the abbreviated form. Write the abbreviated forms on the board. Explain that a period is necessary at the end of abbreviations.

c. Practice order of days Do a drill with the class by asking questions about the calendar such as: *What day comes before Sunday? What comes after Tuesday?*

5 **Listen and repeat.** (Student Book, p. 54)

a. Listen to and extract meaning from audio Have students find the activity and read the directions. Refer to the guidelines in *Activity 1*.

b. Understand capitalization rules Explain that the first letter of each month must always be capitalized, even in the abbreviated form. Write the abbreviated forms on the board. Emphasize that a period is necessary at the end of abbreviations. Point out that May, June, and July are not abbreviated.

c. Observe cultural variations Review how many days there are in each month. Point out that not all countries follow the Gregorian calendar with 365 days and 12 months. Other commonly used calendars are the Chinese, Islamic, and Hebrew calendars. Include seasons as part of the vocabulary and drill the months for each season.

Grammar Note

Teach the use of the following prepositions with reference to dates and the calendar:

on (days of the week)	on Wednesday
in (months)	in September
in (season)	in the winter
in (year)	in 2004

Culture Note

In the United States Monday marks the first day of the civic week, or workweek, and the school week is five days long. In many countries the school week is six days long. Explain that the days from Monday to Friday are called *weekdays,* and Saturdays and Sundays are called the *weekend.*

6 **Listen and point.** (Student Book, p. 54)

a. Use active listening to follow directions Have students find the activity and read the directions. Demonstrate by pointing to your ear and saying *listen.* Then say: *Listen to the dates on the calendar.* Point to the calendar and say: *Point to each date as you hear it.* Show your finger placement on the individual calendar squares.

b. Use nonverbal cues Play the audio or read the script. Give visual cues when it is time to listen and when it is time to point.

c. Chain drill For additional practice, starting in the front of the class, have each student say a date from the calendar, going in order. Start by saying: *January first.* You can also practice the current month if you have a calendar in the room.

d. Give information Put various events on the calendar such as: *dentist appointment, dance class, math test,* etc. Ask students questions such as: *On what day is the dentist appointment?* (Friday the sixteenth)

Audioscript 🎧

6. Listen and point. Listen to the dates on the calendar. Point to each date as you hear it.

Thursday, January first
Friday, January second
Saturday, January third
Sunday, January fourth
Monday, January fifth
Tuesday, January sixth
Wednesday, January seventh
Thursday, January eighth
Friday, January ninth
Saturday, January tenth
Sunday, January eleventh
Monday, January twelfth
Tuesday, January thirteenth
Wednesday, January fourteenth
Thursday, January fifteenth
Friday, January sixteenth
Saturday, January seventeenth
Sunday, January eighteenth
Monday, January nineteenth
Tuesday, January twentieth
Wednesday, January twenty-first
Thursday, January twenty-second
Friday, January twenty-third
Saturday, January twenty-fourth
Sunday, January twenty-fifth
Monday, January twenty-sixth
Tuesday, January twenty-seventh
Wednesday, January twenty-eighth
Thursday, January twenty-ninth
Friday, January thirtieth
Saturday, January thirty-first

7 Pair work. (Student Book, p. 54)

a. Ask for and give information Have students find the activity and read the directions. Before students work in pairs, model the activity with a volunteer.

b. Write numbers If students need practice writing numerals, make copies of the Numerals 1–20 Resource Master (pp. 161–162). Hand out to students and have them practice writing the numerals.

c. Calendar Make copies of the Calendar Resource Master (p. 163) and hand out to students. Write the current month on the board, underlining the capital letter. Have students label their calendars, making sure to capitalize the first letter of the month. Model filling in dates for the current month. Have students fill in their calendars. Note any special holidays. As a class or in pairs, practice saying the days and dates.

Activity Book, p. 33: What's in your school office?

Grammar Focus
Subject Pronouns and Possessive Adjectives

Grammar Notes

- Remind students that in English the second person *you* can be used as singular or plural.

- Nouns in Spanish have a masculine and feminine form. Therefore Spanish students will have a tendency of using the pronouns *he* and *she* instead of *it* when referring to inanimate objects. For example they may say: *The car— he is fast. The table—she is red.* Explain to students that in English we use the subject pronouns *he* and *she* only when referring to people and sometimes pets, and we use *it* to refer to animals, places, and things.

- Be sure to point out the indefinite articles *a* and *an*. Explain that both mean "one," and must be used before a general singular object. The article *a* is used before words that begin with consonant sounds such as *a house, a car,* etc., and *an* is used before words that begin with a vowel sound such as *an apple, an hour.* Emphasize that it is the sound, not the letter, that determines the article.

8 Read and find. (Student Book, p. 55)

a. Contrast grammatical components Have students find the activity and read the directions. Review the sentences in the table to demonstrate subject pronouns and possessive adjectives. Have a student read: *I am a student. My name is Mario.* Then say: *I, my.* You may want to repeat or have a student repeat the example in their native language. In Spanish it would be: *Soy un estudiante. Mi nombre es Mario.*

b. Infer meaning by making associations Practice several concrete examples as a choral activity to help reinforce understanding: *I am a teacher. You are a student. You are students. She is a student. He is a student. It is a book. This is my book. This is my pencil. This is my chair,* etc.

c. Identify grammatical function of words Work with the class as a whole to identify the subject pronouns and possessive adjectives in the letter.

VISIONS BASIC Teacher Resource Book • Copyright © Heinle

Answer key

8. Read and find.

To **my** teacher,

My name is John.

I'm new in class.

With **your** help,

I'm sure to pass.

John

Punctuation Note

Point out that although *its* is a possessive adjective, it does not take an apostrophe before the letter *s* (*'s*). Tell students that *it's* with *'s* is a contraction for *it is*.

---

9 **Choose.** (Student Book, p. 55)

a. Contrast grammatical components Have students find the activity and read the directions. Demonstrate the difference between subject pronouns and possessive adjectives with the following examples. Point to a student and say the student's name, for example, *Mario*. Shake hands with the student and say *friend*. Turn to the class and say *my friend* as you point to the student and then to yourself. Then say: *Mario is my friend.* Point to a boy in the class and ask: *Is Mario your friend?* Prompt the student to reply in the affirmative: *Yes, Mario is my friend.* Then point to the second student and say: *Mario is his friend.* Repeat the same with a girl, demonstrating *Mario is her friend.* Then elicit: *Mario is our friend; Mario is their friend.*

b. Identify grammatical function of words Work with the class to identify the subject pronouns and possessive adjectives in the sentences. Students may need to refer to the grammar chart for assistance.

c. Identify classmates For additional oral practice, have students do a chain drill identifying classmates. Start the drill by prompting a student to say: *My name is (Marco). I am a student.* Then say: *Your name is Marco. You are a student. My name is (Mr. Gonzalez). I am a teacher.* The next student will say: *His name is Marco. He is a student. Your name is Mr. Gonzalez. You are a teacher. My name is (Ana). I am a student.* Continue in the same way around the class, with each student identifying the two previous people in the chain.

Answer key

9. Choose.

1. Mario is (I / **my**) friend.
2. (**She** / Her) is new at school.
3. (You / **Your**) pen is on the floor.
4. (**They** / Their) are from Colombia.
5. (We / **Our**) class is in Room 311.
6. He is (we / **our**) teacher.

Activity Book, p. 34: Subject Pronouns
Activity Book, p. 35: Possessive Adjectives

Word Study

Short Vowels

10 **Listen and repeat.** (Student Book, p. 56)

Distinguish phonological elements of newly acquired vocabulary Have students find the activity and read the directions. Refer to the guidelines for *Listen and repeat* in *Activity 1*.

Audioscript 🎧

10. Listen and repeat. Listen to the short vowel. Then listen to the short vowel in each word. Repeat each word.

Short a:	bag, cap, man, map
Short e:	yes, bet, wet, ten
Short i:	his, hit, sit, pin
Short o:	hot, job, mop, jog
Short u:	bus, bun, gum, hug

---

11 **Group work.** (Student Book, p. 56)

a. Understand organizational structure of charts, columns, and rows Have students find the activity and read the directions. Review the format of the chart by drawing the same chart on the board. Point to each field in the top row and read the headings: *short a, short e, short i, short o, short u.* Point to the picture of the egg as an example. Then point to the first blank field in the second column and say: */e/: egg.* Write the word *egg* in the appropriate field.

b. Organize information into a chart Create flash cards with pictures of the following words: *egg, bus, lips, hat, fish, dog, pen, box, cat, sun.* Hold up one card at a time and have volunteers identify the card. Repeat the word and have a volunteer place the flash card in the correct column of the chart on the board. With help from the class have the volunteer write the word under the proper heading.

Answer key

11. Group work.

Short a	Short e	Short i	Short o	Short u
hat	egg	lips	dog	bus
cat	pen	fish	box	sun

Activity Book, p. 36: Short Vowels

Into the Reading (Student Book, p. 57)
Strategy: Use Prior Knowledge

Develop new learning strategies Point to the strategy box and have students follow along as you read it aloud. Say: *This reading is a form. Before we read, we think about what we already know. Look at the web here. We fill this in with our prior knowledge about forms.*

Use Prior Knowledge: Information About You (Student Book, p. 57)

Explain that schools need to have personal information about students. The information is part of each student's records. Write the web on the board and elicit ideas for other types of information. Students may suggest: date of birth, place of birth, telephone number, name of parent or guardian. Make copies of the Web Resource Master (p. 138) and hand out to students. Have them copy the web from the board.

Build Background: Parents and Guardians (Student Book, p. 57)

a. Develop new learning strategies Explain the concept of building background. *To learn new material sometimes we need to learn new words or ideas to build background about a subject.*

b. Understand new vocabulary Read the information aloud as students follow in their books. Ask volunteers to answer the questions *Do you live with your parents or a guardian? Who is your parent or guardian?* Be aware that these may be sensitive questions for some students.

Reading and Understanding
Text Structure: Form (Student Book, p. 58)

a. Understand the use of various documents Explain that a form is a paper with blank spaces for information. Brainstorm when students may need to fill out a form. List ideas on the board. Prompt with questions. For example, ask: *Do you fill out a form for school? For a sports team? For a library card?*

b. Choral reading Read the paragraph as students follow in their books. Then read again and have students read chorally with you.

Reading (Student Book, p. 58)

a. Read information in various formats Review the form with the class. Explain that the words appearing in capital letters followed by a colon (:) is the information requested on the form. The information in the boxes has been given by a student. Help students read the content from left to right. Clarify the difference between one's *grade* and one's *age.* Explain that *Last, First,* and *Middle* refer to various parts of a person's name.

b. Share prior knowledge to foster respect for others Ask volunteers to share their full name. Share with the class some naming conventions used in students' native countries.

Culture Note

Naming conventions vary greatly in different parts of the world. It will be very helpful for students if you can guide them in determining how their name best converts to the American standard of first, middle, and last name. For example, the typical Spanish name consists of four parts: the first name, the second first name, the father's last name, and the mother's last name. There can also be other additions such as middle names or married names. So most Spanish-speaking students would have a name with three to five words in it. You may want to research naming conventions of the cultures represented in you classroom to assist your students.

Beyond the Reading
Reading comprehension (Student Book, p. 59)

Participate in shared reading Introduce the words *birthday* and *date of birth.* Have students work in pairs to find the answers to the comprehension questions based on the Student Information Form on p. 58.

Answer key
Reading comprehension.
1. Is Ana a student? **Yes**
2. What is Ana's date of birth? **8/13/90**
3. Is Ana in the seventh grade or the eighth? **eighth**
4. Where does Ana live? **1450 West Street**
   Los Angeles, California

Strategy: Scan for Information (Student Book, p. 59)

> **Employ new reading strategies** Help students find the strategy box on the page. Then have students follow as you read aloud. Tell them that it is also helpful to look for bold text or headings that point out important information. Have students point to the heads and bold text on pp. 58 and 59.

Scan for information. (Student Book, p. 59)

> **Scan text to extract meaning** Read the directions. Have students look at the form again and scan for information. Tell them to scan using their eyes, not their fingers. Have them give answers orally.

Answer key

Scan for information.
  Ana's last name: **Vega**
  Ana's phone number: **(213) 555-1945**
  Ana's zip code: **90022**
  Ana's parent or guardian: **Miriam Vega**

Activity Book, p. 37: Social Studies: Holidays

From Reading to Writing
Filling Out a Form

Writing dates. (Student Book, p. 60)

a. **Distinguish between various writing conventions** Explain that there are two general ways to write the date. Both ways include the month, day, and year in that order. In the longhand form the month is spelled out. Point to the example: *September 13, 2004.* Sometimes the month may be written in abbreviated form such as: *Sept.* Emphasize that the first letter of a month must be capitalized even when abbreviated. Point out that the day and year need to be separated by a comma. Explain that the second way of writing a date is in numerical form. Point to the example: *9/13/04.* In this form the first set of numbers on the left represents the month. The number *9* in the example represents September, the ninth month of the year. The number between the slashes, */13/,* is the day.

The two-digit number on the right represents the year. Explain that the year must always include the last two digits of the year. However, the month and day may be written either as *9* or as *09* for single-digit numbers.

b. **Employ correct writing conventions** Call on a volunteer to write today's date on the board. Ask the student to write the date in two ways. Ask another volunteer to read the date.

c. **Write date of birth** Have students write their date of birth, using the two conventions. Circulate and check their work.

Culture Note

In most parts of the world the date is written as: day, month, year. This causes confusion for many students when writing the date in numerical form. Remind students that September 12, 2004 is written as 9/12/04, and 12/9/04 will be read as December 9, 2004.

Writing phone numbers (Student Book, p. 60)

a. **Become familiar with writing conventions** Explain to the class that a telephone number includes a three-digit area code that usually appears in parentheses and a seven-digit number that is divided by a dash into two parts. Point to the example: *(303) 555-1881.* Demonstrate how to read the numbers, pausing between segments: *area code three-zero-three, five, five, five, one, eight, eight, one.* This convention is less intuitive than you might suppose, and can lead to a great deal of confusion. You may want to introduce the following vocabulary pertaining to telephone use: *call, pick up, hang up, dial, local call, long distance, operator, leave a message, hold, cell phone, calling card,* etc.

b. **Look for patterns** Bring in pages from a local newspaper that contain phone numbers (advertisements, cultural listings). Model reading a phone number and have students copy it down. Then have them check their answers. Point to various phone numbers on the pages to help students locate them. Then have students practice reading telephone numbers to a partner. The other partner should copy down the number as it is read. Students should compare to see if the number was correctly read and copied.

c. Employ correct writing conventions Ask students to write their telephone number on an index card. Some students may not know their own number. Ask your office for a copy of a class roster with student phone numbers so that you can help students who may need to learn their own phone number. You may also have some students who do not have telephones in their homes. If you have students who do not have telephones, modify this activity and provide practice telephone numbers.

Culture Note

You may want to explain some telephone dialing procedures. For long-distance calls inside the U.S., dial 1 then the area code and number. To speak with a local operator, dial zero. To speak with an international operator, dial 00 and a long-distance company access code. For international calls, dial 011 then the country code, area code, and number.

You may want to explain that *eight hundred numbers* are *toll free calls,* which means that you do not pay for the telephone charges.

Writing addresses (Student Book, p. 61)

a. Become familiar with writing conventions Explain that an address has a building number, street name, city, state, and zip code. Point to the example: *126 Jansen Street, Denver, CO 33280.* Mention that an apartment number may follow the street name. Explain that mailing addresses are typically written on two lines. The first line includes the house number and street name. The second line is the name of the city, followed by an abbreviation of the state name and then a zip code.

b. Identify patterns and conventions Bring in some sample envelopes or labels. Help students identify various elements of an address.

c. Employ correct writing conventions Give students blank index cards and have them practice writing their addresses on the cards. Some students may not know their own address. Ask your office for a class roster with student mailing addresses so that you can help students who need to learn their own mailing addresses.

Activity Book, p. 39: Dates, Phone Numbers, and Addresses

Filling out a form (Student Book, p. 61)

a. Recognize organizational structure of a text Make copies of the Student Information Form Resource Master (p. 137). Point to the fields that need to be completed. Explain that some forms provide a line on which to fill in the information, others may have rectangular boxes, and others still may have small squares allocated for each letter. Bring examples of various types of forms for students to see. Demonstrate by filling out a sample form on the board or on an overhead projector. Explain that if information is not available for a field, it is best to indicate so by placing a dash in place of the information or by writing in *n/a*, which means "not applicable." This confirms that information was not accidentally skipped.

b. Fill out a form Have students fill out the form with their own information. Assist students with the various fields such as zip codes, postal abbreviations for states, and the spelling of street names and cities. You may want to make a list of abbreviations for types of streets such as: *Ave., Blvd., Cir., Ln., Pl., Rd., Rte., St.,* etc. Also mention where to put apartment numbers on addresses or other postal specifications that might apply in your community. You may want to explain about post office box addresses as well.

c. Proofread writing Explain that forms should be filled out with ink pens so that the information remains as a permanent record. Suggest that students can first fill in the information with lead pencil in case they make a mistake. After completing the form they should double-check it for accuracy and write over the correct answers in ink. Students can use the Editing Checklist to help check over their work.

Activity Book, p. 40: Filling Out a Form

Review (Student Book, p. 62)
Words

a. Put words in alphabetical order Write the words on the board. Have students work with a partner to copy the words on index cards and put them in alphabetical order.

VISIONS BASIC Teacher Resource Book   •   Copyright © Heinle

b. **Practice spelling and dictation** Have students take turns dictating the words to their partner. Have students check their own spelling.

c. **Make a personal dictionary** Make copies of the Personal Dictionary Resource Master (p. 136). Have students start compiling their own dictionaries, using one page for each letter of the alphabet. They can enter the words they have learned in this chapter.

d. **Classify words** Make copies of the Venn Diagram Resource Master (p. 139) and hand out to students. Draw a diagram on the board, labeling one circle *school office* and the other *classroom*. Have students help brainstorm things that they would find in the office, the classroom, or in both places. Write the words in the diagram on the board. Include additional vocabulary students have learned. Have students copy the words into their own diagrams.

Months of the year (Student Book, p. 62)

a. **Use rhyme to learn new vocabulary** Teach and explain the following rhyme:

> Thirty days has September,
> April, June, and November
> All the rest have thirty-one
> Excepting February alone:
> Which has but twenty-eight,
> Till leap year gives it twenty-nine.

b. **Sort months sequentially** Write the months on index cards and pass them out to students. Have students find their place sequentially in a line in front of the class. Ask each student: *How many days are in your month?* Then drill the class with questions such as: *What month comes before March? What month comes after August? What is the tenth month of the year?* etc.

Ordinal numbers (Student Book, p. 62)

Place numbers in sequential order Write out the ordinal numbers 1–31 on index cards and pass them out. Have students find their place in line in front of the class.

Word Study (Student Book, p. 62)

Short Vowels: a, e, i, o, u

Have students read the following tongue-twister and underline all the short vowel sounds. Then have them take turns reading it with a partner.

> *Betty Botter had some butter,*
> *"But," she said, "this butter's bitter.*
> *If I bake this bitter butter,*
> *it would make my batter bitter.*
> *But a bit of better butter—*
> *that would make my batter better."*

Assess
(Student Book, p. 63)

Answer key

Vocabulary

1. The first month of the year is _____.
   a. March   b. December   c. **January**   d. May
2. There are seven days in a _____.
   a. year   b. **week**   c. month   d. Saturday
3. My computer has a screen, a mouse, and a _____.
   a. telephone   b. street   c. **keyboard**
   d. stapler

Grammar

1. _____ is from Russia.   a. **She**   b. Her
2. You are _____ teacher.   a. me   b. **my**
3. _____ are students.   a. Their   b. **They**

Word Study

What is the vowel sound?

1. dog   a. short a   b. short e
         c. short i   d. **short o**

2. map   a. **short a**   b. short e
         c. short o   d. short u

Projects

Project 1: Make a Class Birthday Book
(Student Book, p. 64)

a. **Compile information for a book** Have the class make a class birthday book. Distribute index cards and have students write their name (last name first) and birthday as shown in the model. Collect all of the cards and have the class put the names in alphabetical order. Make one page for each letter group such as: *abc, def, ghi, jkl, mnop, qrst, uvw,* and *xyz.* Explain that not all letters of the alphabet will be represented. You may wish to organize the book by months of the year.

b. **Organize information alphabetically** Divide your class into groups and assign one page of the birthday book to each group. Sort and distribute the cards; have students copy the names and birthdays alphabetically on their assigned page.

c. **Produce visuals to support text** Have students decorate a front cover with the teacher's name and room number. Put the pages together and reproduce the book for the class. At the beginning of each month, have students identify who is having a birthday.

Project 2: Make a Class Calendar (Student Book, p. 65)

a. Brainstorm on a collaborative project
Divide the class into small groups and assign two or three months to each. Brainstorm a list on the board of school events and holidays for each month. Then have students check their ideas against a school calendar or list of holidays. Use small pictures or symbols for various holidays.

b. Organize information Make copies of the Calendar Resource Master (p. 163). Have each group decorate a page for their assigned months. They should include the name of the month, dates, and holidays, birthdays, or other important dates. Photocopy the calendars for each student. Encourage students to mark school assignments and tests on their calendar.

Viewing Activity

Interpret and evaluate visual images Bring in a variety of picture calendars, showing the class the photo or calendar image for the current month. Help students interpret the images, giving them key vocabulary. Discuss the choice of colors in the images. Have students "vote" on which calendar image they like the best. Help students verbalize why they like the image.

Chapter 2 About My Family

Materials

Student Book: pp. 66–79
Activity Book: pp. 41–48, Mini-Reader 2
Audio: Chapter 2
Student CD-ROM: Chapter 2
Teacher Resource Book
    Lesson Plan, pp. 49–56
    Resource Masters: Personal Dictionary, p. 136; Game Instructions, p. 164
Assessment Program: pp. 23–26
Transparencies

Themes

Family/Pets
Adjectives

Long Vowels: *a, i, o, u*
Present Tense Verb: *be*

Negatives and Contractions
Poem/Rhyme

Learning Strategies

Expand repertoire of learning strategies through deductive reasoning
Look for patterns in language
Monitor oral and written language production
Employ self-corrective techniques
Use semantic mapping to acquire new vocabulary
Use accessible language and learn new essential language

Listening

Use active listening comprehension to follow directions
Understand basic expressions and vocabulary
Recognize and distinguish phonological elements: long vowels *a, i, o, u*
Listen to and extract meaning from audio recording
Infer meaning from actions and visual context

Speaking

Identify people by the use of descriptive adjectives
Ask for and give information such as personal appearance
Initiate authentic discourse with peers
Produce phonological elements of newly acquired vocabulary: long vowels *a, i, o, u; voiced th*

Reading

Read authentic literature
Participate in shared reading of a poem

Develop basic sight vocabulary
Use verbal cueing strategies

Writing

Use graphic organizers to understand grammar
Demonstrate knowledge of the verb to be
Demonstrate knowledge of negatives and contractions
Construct correct sentences using present tense of the verb *be*
Use a pre-writing activity to prepare to write
Edit writing toward standard grammar

Viewing and Representing

Use visual cues to derive meaning
Produce visual to aid communication
Explore and describe media

Listen, Speak, Interact
That's My Mother

① Listen and repeat. (Student Book, p. 67)

a. Listen to and extract meaning from audio Have students find the activity and read the directions. Demonstrate by pointing to your ear and saying the word *listen*. Then say: *mother*. Now prompt the class and say *repeat*. Say: *Repeat the word mother*. Gesture the class to repeat. Play the audio or read the script. Give students visual cues to listen and repeat.

b. Produce phonological elements of newly acquired vocabulary Help students form the sound *th* as in *mother, father, brother, grandmother,* and *grandfather*. Demonstrate by placing the tip of the tongue at the front of the tooth ridge. Explain that this sound is voiced. Place your hand on your voice box while saying *th* as in *mother*. There should be a vibration. Now place your hand in front of your mouth as you make the sound again. Explain that there should be no air escaping.

c. Employ self–corrective techniques Have students work with partners to practice the new vocabulary. They should pay close attention to the *th* as in *mother* sound. Provide mirrors for students to watch their mouths and make self-corrective adjustments. Remind them to check for voiced articulation by putting a hand on their voice boxes to check for vibration and in front of their mouths to check that no air escapes.

Audioscript 🎧
1. Listen and repeat.

Listen and repeat the words.

mother, mother / father, father / sister, sister / brother, brother / grandmother, grandmother / grandfather, grandfather / bird, bird / cat, cat / dog, dog / fish, fish

Culture Note
Many students from traditional cultures consider the family to include extended members such as aunts, uncles, nieces, nephews, cousins, etc. You may want to teach these vocabulary words to your students as well. Explain, however, that in the United States the nuclear family is the most common family unit. Extended family members may live in other states. It is not uncommon for a person not to have met a cousin, aunt, or uncle. You may also want to mention other family structures such as step-families, adoptions, etc. Be aware that acceptable social norms will vary greatly with regards to family structure. In some cultures divorce, single parenthood, adoption, or same-sex partners may be frowned upon or entirely forbidden.

② Listen and repeat. (Student Book, p. 67)

Listen to and extract meaning from audio Have students find the activity and read the directions. Look at the guidelines in *Activity 1*.

Audioscript 🎧
2. Listen and repeat.

Listen to the conversation.

Student A:	*Who's that?*
Student B:	*That's my mother.*
Student A:	*Your mother is beautiful.*
Student B:	*Thanks.*

Now repeat the conversation.

Student A:	*Who's that?*
Student B:	*That's my mother.*
Student A:	*Your mother is beautiful.*
Student B:	*Thanks.*

③ Pair work. (Student Book, p. 67)

a. Read through a dialogue Have students find the activity and read the directions. Pair students with a partner. Have students read the dialogue as it appears. Then prompt them to use the photos for substitutions. Explain that *beautiful* describes a woman, *handsome* describes a man, and *cute* describes someone or something small such as a child or pet.

b. Initiate authentic discourse with peers Encourage students to make substitutions.

Answer key

3. Pair work.

Student A: Who's that?
Student B: That's my **brother / father / cat.**
Student A: Your **brother / father / cat** is **cute / handsome / beautiful.**
Student B: Thanks.

Culture Note

Some cultures may have a strict sense of modesty, and some students may not feel comfortable about giving or receiving personal compliments, particularly regarding physical appearance. This may be perceived as being forward. Also, open conversations between boys and girls may not be comfortable for some students. Help your students feel more at ease by explaining acceptable standards among boys and girls, men and women in general, and with regards to compliments.

④ Pair work. (Student Book, p. 67)

a. Produce visuals to aid in communication
Have students find the activity and read the directions. Look at the guidelines for *Activity 3.* Have students draw a picture of a family member or someone important to them. They don't need to show pictures of their family. Stress that artistic ability is not being judged.

b. Ask for and give information about personal appearance Have students work with partners to ask questions and describe the person they drew.

Build Vocabulary
Adjectives

⑤ Read and listen. (Student Book, p. 68)

a. Use visual cues to derive meaning Have students find the activity and read the directions. Explain that adjectives describe people, places, or things. Have students look at the pictures and read the adjectives. These adjectives describe how a person looks.

b. Understand basic vocabulary for units of measurement Measure each student's height and explain measurements in inches and feet as opposed to the metric system.

Audioscript

5. Listen and repeat.

Look at the pictures. Listen to the adjectives. Repeat the adjectives.

hair, hair
brown, brown / blond, blond / black, black / red, red / gray, gray / short, short / long, long / medium length, medium length / straight, straight / curly, curly / wavy, wavy
height, height
tall, tall / short, short / average height, average height
weight, weight
heavy, heavy / thin, thin / average weight, average weight

Language Transfer and Interference

Spanish: In Spanish many adjectives are placed after the noun. Emphasize that in English adjectives go before the noun they describe. Also, Spanish adjectives must match the gender and number of the noun being modified. Students may try to add an *s* to adjectives in an effort to make them plural.
Example: *The girls are talls. The shoes are blacks.*

⑥ Write. (Student Book, p. 68)

a. Write a description using new vocabulary Have students find the activity and read the directions. Cut out 10–15 magazine pictures of famous people with the various physical attributes mentioned in the vocabulary. Select people that have some common and some unique attributes. Circulate these among the class. Have students select one famous person to write about. Ask: *What adjectives best describe this person?* Have students write a description on a piece of paper.

b. Use semantic mapping to acquire new vocabulary Play a guessing game with the class. Write in columns on the board: *height, weight, hair color, hair length,* and *hair type.* Randomly select 5–10 pictures of famous people and place them in front of the class.

c. Identify people Tell the class: *The person I am thinking of is tall and thin, with long, wavy, red hair.* Have students guess who you are describing.

51

d. Use accessible language and learn new essential language Teach students additional vocabulary by using words they already know. For example: *The word for a man with no hair is bald. A person with gray hair is usually old. A person who is not old is young.*

7 **Pair work.** (Student Book, p. 68)

Describe a person Have students find the activity and read the directions. Look at the guidelines in *Activity 3*. Have students work with a partner.

Activity Book, p. 41: My Family

Grammar Focus
Simple Present of *be*

8 **Build the sentence.** (Student Book, p. 69)

a. Use graphic organizers to understand grammar Have students find the activity and read the directions. Review the sentences in the chart on p. 69 with your class.

b. Demonstrate knowledge of the verb *be* Have students work with partners to choose the correct form of the verb *be* in the activity. Then have partners take turns conjugating each sentence for all persons such as: *I am a student. You are a student. He is a student,* etc.

c. Monitor oral production Watch for agreement as students conjugate the verb with singular and plural subject pronouns such as: *She is a student. They are students.*

Answer key

8. Build the sentence. Add the verb.
1. She **is** a student.
2. I **am** from Mexico.
3. They **are** not teachers.
4. His eyes **are** not blue.
5. We **are** friends.
6. The dog **is** cute.

---

9 **Choose.** (Student Book, p. 69)

a. Demonstrate knowledge of negatives Have students find the activity and read the directions. Explain that the word *not* is used to make a sentence negative, or not true. Show students how to make a sentence negative. Explain that *not* must follow the verb *be* as in *I am not thin.*

Point to yourself and read the first sentence: *I am a student.* Shake your head to indicate that this is not true. Then say: *I am not a student.* Do the activity with the class. Have students make new sentences in the affirmative and then negate them.

b. Demonstrate knowledge of contractions Show the class how to change negative forms of *be* into contractions such as: *he / she / it isn't; we / you / they aren't.* Point out that the contraction for *I am not* is I*'m not.* Have students rewrite the sentences with negative contractions.

10 **Write.** (Student Book, p. 69)

a. Construct correct sentences Have students find the activity and read the directions. Review the example sentences. After students have written sentences, have volunteers write their sentences on the board.

b. Ask for and give information Play a modified game of Twenty Questions in which a student thinks of a classmate, then gives hints about the person, using simple present sentences until a classmate guesses the person's identity. Model this for students. Once the person has been identified, the class can combine the sentences into a unified description on the board. Help the class with sentence construction and punctuation.

Activity Book, p. 42: Simple Present: *be*
Activity Book, p. 43: Contractions: *be*

Word Study
Long Vowels: a, i, o, u

11 **Listen and repeat.** (Student Book, p. 70)

Listen to and extract meaning from audio. Have students find the activity and read the directions. Look at the guidelines in *Activity 1.*

Audioscript 🎧

11. Listen and repeat.

Listen to the long vowel. Then listen to the long vowel in each word. Repeat each word.

Long a:	face, cake, make, date
Long i:	like, kite, nice, white
Long o:	nose, note, phone, stove
Long u:	cute, June, rule, tube

VISIONS BASIC Teacher Resource Book • Copyright © Heinle

⑫ **Listen.** (Student Book, p. 70)

a. Recognize phonological elements such as long and short vowels Have students find the activity and read the directions. Review the short vowel sound *a* and the word *can*. Then demonstrate the long vowel sound in *cane*.

b. Look for patterns in language Play the audio or read the script. Have students listen to the contrasting vowel sounds in each word pair. Ask students to identify the difference between each pair. If they are unable to recognize the pattern, explain that the *e* at the end of each word changes the vowel before from a short vowel to a long one.

Audioscript 🎧
12. Listen.

Listen to the words. Which word has a long vowel sound? Can you find a pattern?

1. can **cane**
2. **kite** kit
3. **hope** hop
4. cut **cute**
5. mad **made**

Language Transfer and Interference

Haitian Creole: There are no sound transfers for short *e* and *u*.

Spanish: There are only approximate sounds for the short vowel sounds *a, i, o, u*. Students will have a tendency to substitute long vowel sounds.

Vietnamese: There are only approximate sounds for the short vowel sounds *a, e,* and *o* and for the long vowels *a* and *o*. There is no sound transfer for short *i*.

⑬ **Pair work.** (Student Book, p. 70)

a. Recognize phonological elements such as long and short vowels Have students find the activity and read the directions. Have them work in pairs to say the words on the list. Then have them copy the words on a piece of paper and add the letter *e* to the end of the words.

b. Monitor oral production Make sure students are using the short vowel sounds at first and the long vowel sounds after adding the *e* to the end of the word.

c. Expand repertoire of learning strategies through deductive reasoning You may want to introduce these other long-vowel spelling patterns:

long a: *ai* as in *paint, rain, nail*
     ei as in *eight, weight, sleigh*
     ay as in *day, play, gray*
long i: *ie* as in *lie, pie, tie*
     y as in *cry, fly, my*
     igh as in *high, light, fight*
long o: *oa* as in *boat, coat, soap*
     o as in *go, no, so*
     ow as in *grow, know, snow*
     o followed by two consonants as in *old, sold, most*
long u: *ue* as in *blue, sue, true*
     ui as in *fruit, suit, juice*
     ew as in *new, few, chew*

You may also want to teach the spelling rule: *i* before *e* except after *c*, except in words like *neighbor* and *weigh*.

Activity Book, p. 44: Long Vowels: a, i, o, u

Into the Reading (Student Book, p. 71)
Use Prior Knowledge: Describe a Baby

Pair students with partners and ask the class: *What adjectives describe a baby?* Have students brainstorm a list with their partners. Encourage them to use a dictionary to find new adjectives.

Build Background: Dimples (Student Book, p. 71)

Bring in magazine pictures of babies with dimples. Explain that many babies have dimples. Dimples are small marks on a face.

Strategy: Use a Dictionary (Student Book, p. 71)

Use resources Help orient students to dictionary use by pointing out organizational features such as alphabetical order, guide words at the top of each page, and alphabetical letter tabs. Hand out dictionaries to small groups of students and have them practice looking up definitions of words you write on the board. As an alternative, have groups work to see who can find the definition the fastest. Whoever finds it first stands up and reads the definition.

Reading and Understanding

Text Structure: Poem (Student Book, p. 72)

Develop understanding of literary structures Read or have a student read the explanation about poems. Ask: *What other examples can you think of that rhyme with cat?* Offer the examples *bat, sat, fat,* and *that.* You may want to elaborate on the concept of poems. For example, you can say that a poem is a descriptive and emotional piece of writing that often makes liberal use of adjectives.

Reading 🎧 (Student Book, p. 72)

a. Preteach vocabulary You may want to preteach the following words: *perfect, tiny, velvet, shiny, curled, tight, sharp, chews, laugh, show.*

b. Use verbal cueing strategies such as pauses and exaggerated intonation Read the poem aloud to the class, pausing appropriately to emphasize the rhythm of the poem. Use nonverbal cues such as facial expressions and gestures to enhance the reading experience. Then play the audio as students follow in their books.

c. Read authentic literature Reread the poem with the class as a choral reading. Bring attention to the rhythm of the poem. Then do a chain reading. Stop after each line to answer questions.

d. Recognize phonological patterns Have volunteers copy the poem on the board. Ask them to underline the rhyming words.

Beyond the Reading

Reading comprehension. (Student Book, p. 73)

Derive meaning from text Have students answer the questions based on the reading. Answers should be in complete sentences.

Answer key

1. **Is the baby large?**
   No, the baby is not large.
2. Is his hair brown or black?
   His hair is black.
3. How many teeth does he have?
   He has two teeth.
4. What adjectives in the poem describe the baby?
   beautiful, perfect, tiny; soft and *velvet brown* describe his skin; *dark* and *shiny* describe his eyes; *black* and *curled up tight* describe his hair; *two, new, sharp,* and *white* describe his teeth.

Language Transfer and Interference

Haitian Creole: The verb *be* is often omitted with adjectives: *I happy. She beautiful.*
—*Subject Pronoun:* There is no gender difference for third-person singular pronouns. Students may make mistakes such as: *It is a tall boy.*
—*Double Negatives:* These are routinely used.

Spanish: In Spanish, the subject is reflected by the inflection of the verb *be.* It is therefore not necessary to use a subject or subject pronoun in a sentence. Students may have a hard time remembering to put a subject or subject pronoun in a sentence.
—*Subject Pronouns:* Nouns in Spanish reflect a masculine or feminine gender. Students may make mistakes by using the wrong subject pronouns in third-person singular, saying such things as: *She is a red table. He is a fast car.*
—*Stating Age:* Spanish students may also have strong interference using the verb *be* for telling age. In Spanish the verb *have* is used to express states of being. For example: *She has 15 years.*
—*Double Negatives:* Double negatives are routinely used in Spanish and other Romance languages. For example: *This is not nothing.*

Vietnamese: The verb *be* is not used with adjectives. Students may have the tendency to say such things as: *She beautiful.*
—*Subject-Verb Agreement:* In Vietnamese, there is no plural form for nouns. Instead, plurality is expressed through an adjective quantifier. Students may therefore make such mistakes as: *There are three new student. I have many good idea.*
—*Subject Pronoun:* There is no gender difference for third-person singular pronouns. Students may make mistakes such as: *She is a tall boy.*

Find words that rhyme. (Student Book, p. 73)

Recognize phonological patterns Have students look at the last word in each line of the poem to find words that rhyme. Write the words on the board: *tiny-shiny; tight-white; toes-shows.* Then have students identify the vowel sound in the words that rhyme. Write the rhyming words on the board, noting the short or long vowel sound.

tiny-shiny; **long *i* sound**

tight-white; **long *i* sound**

toes-show; **long *o* sound**

Shared reading. (Student Book, p. 73)

Participate in shared reading Model paired reading with volunteers. Then have partners practice reading the poem, taking turns with each line.

Activity Book, p. 45: Science: Genes
Activity Book, p. 46: Reading Fluency

From Reading to Writing

Describing a Family Member (Student Book, pp. 74–75)

a. Use an organizational strategy for writing Read the sample writing in the text and review the writing steps: *Plan, Write, Edit,* and *Publish.* Explain what each step involves.

b. Use a pre-writing activity Have students choose a person in their family to write about. Give them the option of writing about someone other than a family member. Students may choose to write about a character in a TV family or about someone else they know. Have students draw a picture of the person.

c. Construct correct sentences Have students write four sentences about the person they drew. Ask questions to elicit sentences: *Who is the person? What does the person look like?* Have students brainstorm a list of descriptive adjectives to use in their sentences. They may also use a bilingual dictionary to find new adjectives.

d. Edit writing towards standard grammar Have students read their sentences. Ask if they can find any mistakes. Remind them to edit for correct subject-veb agreement, pronoun agreement and verb tense. Have them check their work using the Editing Checklist. Students should correct mistakes and write the sentences over. They may want to use a computer. Have students read their sentences to the class. Display student work in class, including drawings.

Activity Book, p. 47: Capitalization and End Punctuation
Activity Book, p. 48: Writing a Description

Review

Family members (Student Book, p. 76)

a. Use semantic mapping to review vocabulary Draw a family tree on the board and label it with appropriate vocabulary: *father, mother, sister, brother, grandfather,* etc. Explain that a family tree is a way of representing all the members of one's family. Have students make a family tree to present to the class. You may also include additional vocabulary such as *aunt, uncle, cousin, niece, nephew, step-brother,* etc. Under each word have students write the name of a family member. They may also add pictures to the family tree.

b. Initiate authentic discourse Have classmates ask questions using the following expressions: *Who's that? That's my...* If possible, have students bring in family photos to share and talk about.

Grammar (Student Book, p. 76)

Simple Present of *be*

Do an oral drill activity to have students make sentences about a person's age. Give an example sentence such as: *He is 15.* Have students make the sentence negative, or use a contraction such as: *He's not 15. He isn't 15.*

Word Study (Student Book, p. 76)
Long Vowels: a, i, o, u

Distinguish phonological elements Play a game of Word Bingo with your class using long vowel sounds *a, i, o, u* instead of B-I -N-G-O and the following words on cards: *bait, bite, boat, boot; say, sigh, sew, sue; fade, find; raid, ride, road, rude; sail, soul.* Use short vowel distracters such as: *bad, bed, bid, bat, bet, bit, but, fad, fed, fin, fun, pat, pet, pit, pot.* For a full description of how to set up or play the game see the Games Instructions Resource Master (p. 164).

Assess

Answer key

Vocabulary (Student Book, p. 77)

1. My father is _____.

   a. handsome   b. height   c. wavy   d. blue

2. My baby _____ is cute.

   a. mother   b. grandfather   **c. sister**   d. father

3. His eyes are _____.

   a. heavy   b. wavy   c. blond   **d. blue**

Grammar (Student Book, p. 77)

1. I _____ 15 years old.

   a. is   b. are   **c. am**

2. The dog _____ brown.

   a. are   b. am   **c. is**

3. We _____ friends.

   a. am   b. is   **c. are**

Word Study (Student Book, p. 77)

What is the vowel sound?

1. kite   a. long o   **c. long i**

            b. long a   d. long u

2. phone a. long a   c. long i

            b. long o   d. long u

Activity Book: Ch. 2 Mini-Reader

Projects

Project 1: Family Member Presentation (Student Book, p. 78)

a. Express ideas and feelings to an audience Have students give a presentation about a family member, a pet, or someone important to them. They may bring in a photograph or draw a picture.

b. Use graphic organizers as pre-writing activity Have students brainstorm a list of adjectives and examples of what makes their subject special.

c. Use a semantic map to organize ideas Make a semantic map on the board with the following *wh*-words: *who, what, where, when, why.* Encourage them to think of questions and answers about the person they will be presenting to the class. Questions may include: *Who is the person? Where does he/she live? What is a happy memory of this person? Why is this person important?* Give each student five index cards. Once students have some ideas, help them write note cards for their presentations.

d. Arrange phrases and clauses in meaningful patterns Have students practice giving their presentations by sorting their ideas on the note cards. Explain that one way of organizing ideas is to go from general to specifics. Another organizational structure is chronological order. Once each student has found the best order for the cards, have them put numbers on the cards to use for their presentations. Have them rehearse by reading through the cards several times.

e. Give information in an oral presentation Have each student give a short presentation in front of the class. Encourage them to use their note cards, but tell them not to read directly from the cards. They may display photographs and drawings or use any other props to help enhance the presentation. Make sure students know that they should speak clearly and slowly, making eye contact with peers.

f. Evaluate oral presentation Have students evaluate their own presentation using the checklist provided in the text.

Culture Note

In some cultures, making direct eye contact is considered impolite. It may be difficult for some students to look directly at people while speaking. Explain that direct eye contact shows interest, whereas lack of eye contact may convey distrust.

Project 2: Make and Organize Rhyme Cards (Student Book, p. 79)

Organize words into phonological groups Read the directions and make sure students understand the project. Then have students work in groups.

Viewing Activity

Explore and Describe Media Discuss with students how families are portrayed in the media, for example on television. Have students tell you about families in different popular TV shows, including the approximate ages and the relationships. Assist atudents as needed with new vocabulary.

Chapter 3 After School

Materials

Student Book: pp. 80–93
Activity Book: pp. 49–56, Mini-Reader 3
Audio: Chapter 3
Student CD-ROM: Chapter 3
Teacher Resource Book
    Lesson Plan, pp. 57–64
    Resource Masters: Personal Dictionary, p. 136; Web, p. 138; Game Instructions, p. 164
Assessment Program: pp. 27–30
Transparencies

Themes

Activities and Hobbies
Frequency Adverbs

Simple Present of Verbs
Poem: Free Verse

Learning Strategies

Look for patterns in language
Monitor oral and written language production
Employ self-corrective techniques
Use semantic mapping to acquire new vocabulary

Listening

Understand basic expressions and vocabulary
Recognize and distinguish phonological elements: long vowel *e*
Listen to and extract meaning from audio recording
Infer meaning from actions and visual context

Speaking

Ask for and give information about favorite activities
Initiate authentic discourse with peers
Produce phonological elements of newly acquired vocabulary: long vowel *e*

Reading

Read authentic literature
Participate in shared reading of a free verse poem
Develop basic sight vocabulary
Use verbal cueing strategies such as pauses and exaggerated intonation

Writing

Use graphic organizers to understand grammar
Demonstrate knowledge of the simple present tense of verbs
Demonstrate knowledge of negatives and contractions
Construct correct sentences using present tense of verbs
Use a pre-writing activity to prepare to write
Edit writing toward standard grammar

Viewing and Representing

Use visual cues to derive meaning
Produce visual to aid communication
Explore and discuss how artists influence the message

Listen, Speak, Interact
What Do You Do After School?

① **Listen and repeat.** (Student Book, p. 81)

a. **Listen to and extract meaning from audio**
Have students find the activity and read the directions. Point to your ear and say *listen*. Then say: *Listen to music.* Play the audio or read the script. Give visual cues.

b. **Use vocabulary in context** Provide the class with a few phrases to use with the vocabulary. For example: *It's fun to... I like to... I want to...* You may want to introduce specific phrases such as: *read a book, shop for new clothes, work for extra money, eat a snack, talk on the phone,* etc. You may want to point out some details in the pictures on page 80 and provide supplementary vocabulary such as: *headphones, CD player, wheelchair, guitar, soccer ball, book, clothes, fast food, uniform.* Students might enjoy discussing different styles of music. You may want to bring in some music to class such as jazz, country, rap, hip-hop, and pop, to expose students to diverse musical genres.

Audioscript 🎧

1. **Listen and repeat.**
Listen and repeat the words and phrases.
listen to music, listen to music / meet friends, meet friends / play an instrument, play an instrument / play a sport, play a sport / read, read / rent a video, rent a video / shop, shop / work, work / write e-mail, write e-mail

② **Listen and repeat.** (Student Book, p. 81)

Understand new concepts Have students find the activity and read the directions. List the following words in sequential order on the board: *always, usually, sometimes, never.* Draw a vertical arrow next to them marked 0%-100%. Say: *These words describe how often something happens.* Point to *always.* Say: *I speak English every day. I always speak English.* Point to *sometimes* on the scale. Say: *I sometimes speak Spanish.* Point to *never* on the scale. Say: *I never speak French. I don't know French.* Explain that *else* in *What else do you do?* means "more" or "other thing."

Audioscript 🎧

2. **Listen and repeat.**
Listen to the conversation.
A: *What do you usually do after school?*
B: *I usually work after school.*
A: *What else do you do?*
B: *I sometimes meet friends.*

Now repeat the conversation.
A: *What do you usually do after school?*
B: *I usually work after school.*
A: *What else do you do?*
B: *I sometimes meet friends.*

Culture Note
In some countries it is not as common for young people to have part-time jobs as it is in the United States. Explain that young people work part-time to earn pocket money. Describe typical odd jobs for young people such as baby-sitting, yard work, and delivering newspapers. See if students know about minimum age and minimum-wage laws.

③ **Pair work.** (Student Book, p. 81)

a. **Demonstrate knowledge of parts of speech: adverbs** Have students find the activity and read the directions. Review the frequency adverbs *always, usually, sometimes, never* with examples such as: *My brother reads every day. My mom and dad usually read the newspaper after breakfast.* Explain the different places frequency adverbs can appear in a sentence. Frequency adverbs generally come between the subject and the simple present tense of the verb, such as *I always read at night.* However, *usually* and *sometimes* can also come before the subject (*Sometimes I play soccer.*) or after the object of the sentence (*I rent videos sometimes.*). *Often* is also commonly used after the object. Emphasize that although frequency adverbs usually come before simple present verbs, they come after the verb *be.* For example: *I am never late.* Write examples on the board as you explain.

b. **Read through a dialogue** Have students work in pairs to practice the conversation and complete the sentences with information about themselves.

c. Initiate authentic discourse with peers
Divide the class into four or five groups. Have students interview members from other groups using the dialogue as a model. Encourage them to make substitutions using the new vocabulary words.

④ **Pair work.** (Student Book, p. 81)

Ask for and give information about yourself Have students find the activity and read the directions. Have students make a chart of their partner's responses.

Build Vocabulary

Activities

⑤ **Listen and Repeat.** (Student Book, p. 82)

a. Use visual cues to learn new vocabulary
Have students find the activity and read the directions. Have students look at the pictures. Call on volunteers to read the words. Play the audio or read the script. Have students listen to the words.

b. Produce phonological elements of newly acquired vocabulary Point out that the *w* in the word *write* is silent. Also mention that the *c* in *exercise* and *dance* has a soft *s* sound.

Audioscript 🎧

5. Read and listen.
Look at the pictures. Listen to the words. Repeat the words.
Sports, Sports
exercise, exercise / jog, jog / swim, swim / play soccer, play soccer / play baseball, play baseball
Arts, Arts
paint, paint / write, write / dance, dance / play guitar, play guitar / play drums, play drums

Culture Note

Mention that football and baseball are two of the most popular sports in the U.S. You may want to borrow some equipment from the gym teacher or invite the teacher as a guest speaker to explain the rules of the two sports to the class. As an alternative, you may have a student who can explain, drawing on the board.

⑥ **Pair work.** (Student Book, p. 82)

a. Ask for and give information Have students find the activity and read the directions. Pair students with partners. Have students write their partner's answers on a piece of paper.

b. Graph your responses Draw a bar graph on the board with 3 rows and 10 columns. Write *often, sometimes, never* from top to bottom on the vertical *y* axis. Write the vocabulary from *Activity 5* on the *x* axis. Show students how to fill in data on a graph. Have them copy the graph on a piece of paper and fill in their partner's answers. They can use colors to code the graph. Make sure they include a title such as: *Mario's Hobbies* or *Ana's Activities.* Explain that information presented in this way is called a graph. Display students' work.

Language Transfer and Interference

Spanish: In Spanish there are two different verbs for *play*: *jugar* (to play a sport or game) and *tocar* (to play an instrument). Point out to students that English has one verb for both kinds of activities.

⑦ **Organize.** (Student Book, p. 82)

a. Categorize ideas in a chart Have students find the activity and read the directions. Draw a chart on the board with three columns. Use these headings: *play baseball, write, paint.* Have students look at the objects. Call on volunteers to read the words: *pen, baseball, paint, bat, paintbrush, paper.* Ask: *Which activity uses a pen?* Confirm by writing *pen* under *write.* Have students copy the chart and put the words in the correct columns.

b. Use visuals to acquire new vocabulary
Provide a variety of magazines for students to find pictures related to hobbies and sports. Have them make large flash cards by cutting out pictures of activities. Help students label each activity correctly on the reverse side. You may want to refer students to a dictionary. Then have each student show and say an activity. Students can practice identifying the activities in small groups. They can also talk about what objects are used in each activity.

Answer key

7. Organize.

play baseball	write	paint
baseball	pen	paint
bat	paper	paintbrush

59

Activity Book, p. 49: Sports and Activities

Grammar Focus
Simple Present

Ask students to open their books to p. 83. Point to the chart in the book. Read through the chart with the class. Explain that verbs are action words. They tell us what someone or something is doing. Act out verbs such as: *swim, play, work.* Explain that the simple present tense tells about an action that usually happens or is happening now. Use several verbs in the simple present. *I swim. You play. He works.* Point out that with *he, she,* and *it,* we put an *s* after the verb: *He plays soccer. She meets friends.* Go over the spelling rules for third-person singular. You may want to write this information on a poster to display in the classroom.

Spelling Rules for Third-Person Simple Present

- Add *s* to the end of most verbs.
  - walk ➤ walks   She walks to school.
- For verbs that end in *y*, drop the *y* and add *ies:*
  - study ➤ studies   He studies English.
- For verbs that end in *ch, sh, x,* add *es:*
  - catch ➤ catches   He catches the ball.
  - brush ➤ brushes   She brushes her hair.
  - fix ➤ fixes   He fixes cars.

Write several verbs on the board and have students spell out the third-person form as you write on the board. Practice the verbs in an oral drill with the class.

Pronunciation Pointers

- The endings *s, es,* and *ies* used to mark third-person singular are pronounced with an */s/* or */z/* or */ez/* sound. The final sound of the verb determines the sound that the -s ending takes. Make it clear to students that it is the sound and not the letter that determines the sound of the final *s.* For example, *fix* ends with the sound */s/.*

- The sound */s/* is used after all voiceless consonants except */ch/, /s/,* and */sh/:*
  /s/: laughs, bakes, sips, sits

- The sound */z/* is used after all vowel sounds and all voiced consonants except */j/, /z/,* and */zh/:*
  /z/: grabs, reads, drags, calls, dreams, tans, hangs, tears, bathes, gives, tows, says, studies

- The sound */ez/* is used after the sounds */z/, /s/, /sh/, /ch/, /j/:*
  /ez/: catches, crosses, washes, judges, buzzes

- Voiced consonants are: *b, d, g, j, l, m, n, ng, r, th, v, w, y, z, zh*

- Voiceless consonants are: *f, h, k, p, s, sh, t, th, wh, ch*

8 Build the sentence. (Student Book, p. 83)

Demonstrate knowledge of the simple present tense Have students find the activity and read the directions. Have volunteers write the sentences on the board.

Answer key
8. Build the sentence.
1. I always **play** soccer on Saturday.
2. My mother **reads** the newspaper in the morning.
3. We sometimes **meet** our friends after school.
4. The dog **eats** all of his food.
5. The secretary **works** in the school office.

9 Choose. (Student Book, p. 83)

Demonstrate knowledge of negatives and auxiliaries Have students find the activity and read the directions. Create three flash cards for: *I, do not,* and *read.* Call up two students and ask them to hold the cards: *I, read.* Demonstrate for the class how a sentence is negated, by standing between the two volunteers and holding the card *do not.* Shake your head as you read the sentence: *I do not read.* Explain to the class that *do not* is an auxiliary. It must be placed in front of a verb to make the verb negative. Have students work with partners to say which sentences are true about them.

Activity Book, p. 50: Simple Present
Activity Book, p. 51: Simple Present Negative

Word Study
Long *e* sound: ee, ea

10 Listen and repeat. (Student Book, p. 84)

    a. Recognize phonological elements such as long vowel sounds Have students find the activity and read the directions. Review the long vowel sound *e* and the word *feet.* Explain to students that these vowels together make the sound of the letter *e: ee, ea.*

VISIONS BASIC Teacher Resource Book • Copyright © Heinle

b. Recognize phonological elements Play the audio or read the script. Have students listen to and repeat what they hear. Explain that the vowel combination *ee* and *ea* make the long vowel sound *e*. This is a general rule. You may want to mention that *feet* and *teeth* are the irregular plural forms for *foot* and *tooth*. Remind students of vocabulary words from earlier chapters that follow this spelling rule, such as: *green, read, teacher, week, year.* Other words you may want to introduce are: *clean, dear, each, east, easy, fear, feast, fee, feed, feel, hear, heat, keep, leaf, meal, near, need, real, scream, see, sleep, sneeze, sweet, tree, wheel.*

c. Look for patterns in language Introduce the word *meat* and point out that the meaning is different than *meet*. Explain that two words that sound the same but have different spellings and meanings are called homophones. Some other example of homophones with the long *e* sound are: *beach/beech, beat/beet, dear/deer, feat/feet, heal/heel, hear/here,* etc. You may want students to look up some or all of these in a bilingual dictionary.

Audioscript 🎧

10. Listen and repeat.
Listen to the long *e* sound. Then listen to the long *e* sound in each word. Repeat each word.

ee: feet, green, meet, teeth, street
ea: eat, ear, teach, team, seat

Pronunciation Pointer

Although the pronunciation of *ea* is relatively consistent, here are some exceptions you may want to keep in mind or bring to the attention of your students: *bear, beautiful, dead, deaf, early, earn, earth, head, health, heart, heavy, learn, measure, ready, search, sweater, tear, theater, treasure, wear, weather.*

⑪ Read and find. (Student Book, p. 84)

a. Recognize phonological elements such as long vowels Have students find the activity and read the directions. Then have them work in pairs to find words in the poem with the long *e* sound. Have them copy the poem on a piece of paper and underline the words with a long *e* sound.

b. Monitor oral production Listen to make sure that students are using the long *e* vowel sound appropriately. Show the class that they must smile broadly to make the long *e* sound. Have them practice this sound with exaggeration.

Answer key
11. Read and find.
After school, who do I **meet**?
I **meet** my friends down the **street**.
What do **we** do down the **street**?
We talk, **we** shop, and **we** always **eat!**

⑫ Pair work. (Student Book, p. 84)

Self monitor oral production Have students find the activity and read the directions. Have students take turns reading the poem. Give partners a mirror to observe themselves.

⑬ Read. (Student Book, p. 84)

Read new words Have students find the activity and read the directions. Read the words chorally with the class, and then have volunteers read the words aloud.

Activity Book, p. 52: Long e sound: ee, ea

Into the Reading (Student Book, p. 85)
Strategy: Preview Pictures

Use visuals to derive meaning Point to the strategy box and have students read it aloud. Say: *Pictures in books, magazines, and newspapers often give us hints, or clues, about what we are going to read. Look at the picture on page 86 and guess what we'll read.*

Use Prior Knowledge: Trying Something New (Student Book, p. 85)

a. Generate ideas Ask students: *What are some activities you are good at doing?* Have them think about when they first began learning the activity. Ask: *How did you feel?* Encourage students to use gestures to express their feelings. You can help provide some appropriate words. Here are some words that describe how someone might feel when first learning a new sport: *awkward, clumsy, confused, curious, determined, embarrassed, excited, exhausted, exhilarated, frustrated, proud, scared, shy, tired.*

b. Use a semantic map to learn new vocabulary Make copies of the Web Resource Master (p. 138) and hand them out to students. Ask students to brainstorm a list of words that express how they might feel when first learning a new sport. Students may work in pairs and use a bilingual dictionary. Have students share their webs with the class. Display the students' work in the class. Explain that learning a new sport is in many ways like learning a new language. You might experience many of the same feelings you noted in the web. Encourage students that with a positive attitude, practice, and perseverance, we can learn to master any new skill.

Build Background: Roller Skating (Student Book, p. 85)

a. Use visual cues to derive meaning Ask students to explain what a roller skate is. Point to the wheels on the bottom of the skates. Ask if anyone in class has roller-skated before. Ask students about other forms of skating such as ice skating and roller blading. Explain that roller skating is difficult at first. Demonstrate that at first a person feels clumsy. Use gestures and facial expressions to elicit more ideas about this activity from the class.

b. Understand new vocabulary Ask the class: *What equipment might you need to learn roller skating?* Point to different parts of your body as you introduce the words for various safety gear: *helmet, knee pads, elbow pads, wrist guards.* Explain that this is safety equipment so that people don't get hurt while learning this sport. Tell students that, like many other sports, roller skating requires a lot of practice before being able to skate well.

Reading and Understanding

Text Structure: Free Verse Poem (Student Book, p. 86)

Develop understanding of literary structures

Explain that a poem is a form of writing that sometimes has words that rhyme. Point out that this poem does not rhyme. It is called a free verse poem. You may want to explain that although this form of poetry has no obvious rhyme, it describes images and emotions. Read or have a volunteer read the explanation at the top of p. 86.

Reading 🔊 (Student Book, p. 86)

a. Preteach vocabulary You may want to preteach some or all of the new vocabulary: *put on, stand up, hop, backward, stick out, fall down, smack, grab, slide, inches, skin (a knee), brush off, dirt, blood, spit.*

b. Use verbal cueing strategies such as pauses and exaggerated intonation Read the poem aloud, pausing appropriately to emphasize its rhythm. Use nonverbal cues such as facial expressions and gestures to enhance the reading experience. Have students listen as you play the audio.

c. Read authentic literature Reread the poem as a choral reading. Then do a chain reading. Stop after each line to answer questions.

d. Recognize grammatical patterns Have students copy the poem on a piece of paper and look for verbs. Ask them to underline verbs and circle the *-s* endings. Pair students with partners and have them compare their work.

Beyond the Reading
Reading Comprehension

Answer the questions (Student Book, p. 87)

a. Derive meaning from text Have students answer the questions based on the poem. Challenge them to answer the questions in complete sentences.

b. Derive a sentence from a question Write on the board: *Does the girl hurt her knee or her foot?* Ask the class for the correct response. Then cross out or erase the words *or her foot.* Next cross out the word *Does.* Remind students that does is an auxiliary used for making a question. When making a question, it comes before the verb. Sometimes other question words such as *what* come in front of *do/does.* Then point to the word *girl.* Ask the class: *Do we say girl hurt or girl hurts?* Confirm that the correct inflection of the verb is *hurts* and add the *-s* ending. Ask the class: *Do we have a complete sentence now?* (no) Say: *A sentence needs to begin with a capital letter and end in a period.* Erase the lowercase *t* in the and replace it with an uppercase letter. Finally replace the question mark with a period. Say: *We just changed a question into a sentence—The girl hurts her knee.*

VISIONS BASIC Teacher Resource Book • Copyright © Heinle

c. Ask for and give information Suggest that students come up with more questions based on the picture. Have them work with partners to ask and answer more questions about the reading.

Answer key

1. Does the girl hurt her knee or her foot?
   She hurts her knee.
2. How many times does she fall?
   She falls two times. / She falls twice.
3. What does she grab?
   She grabs a step.
4. What does the little girl do after she falls?
   The little girl hits her hand. She grabs a step. She falls again and cuts her knee. She cleans herself. She tries to roller skate again.

Organize pictures (Student Book, p. 87)

Recognize sequence Have students look at the six pictures and place them in order. Remind students that the pictures should be placed in sequence from left to right as if being read.

Answer key

Organize pictures.
1. A girl putting on roller skates.
2. She is falling down and smacking her hand.
3. She is grabbing a step to balance herself.
4. She skins her knee as she gets up.
5. The girl with a cut knee brushes dirt off her clothes.
6. The girl, a bit dirty and with a cut, sticks out her foot trying to skate again.

Retell the story. (Student Book, p. 87)

Work with a partner Have students work in pairs and use the pictures to tell the events in the poem.

Act out the poem. (Student Book, p. 87)

Work with a partner Pair students. Have one read the poem and the other do the action. Walk around the classroom and monitor their speaking.

Activity Book, p. 53: The Arts: The Statue of Liberty
Activity Book, p. 54: Reading Fluency

From Reading to Writing
My Favorite Activity (Student Book, pp. 88–89)

a. Use an organizational strategy for writing Read over the model paragraph on p. 88 and review the four steps of writing: *Plan, Write, Edit,* and *Publish.*

b. Use a pre-writing activity to prepare to write Have students write about their favorite activity. Say: *Think about the activity you enjoy the most. What is your favorite activity? When do you do it? Do you need special objects or equipment?* Have students draw a picture of the activity.

c. Construct correct sentences Have students write a paragraph of three or four sentences about their favorite activity. Say: *Give a title to your writing.* Have them brainstorm a list of descriptive adjectives.

d. Edit writing towards standard grammar. Have students read their paragraphs. Ask if they can find any mistakes. Have them check their work using the Editing Checklist. They should correct mistakes and rewrite their work. They may want to use a computer. Have students read their paragraphs to the class. Display the work in the classroom.

Activity Book, p. 55: Combining Sentences and Using Quotation Marks
Activity Book, p. 56: Describing an Activity

Review
Vocabulary (Student Book, p. 90)

a. Use visual cues to review vocabulary Make large flash cards with the new vocabulary words for activities. Divide the class into two teams and have students play a game of Charades. For a detailed description of how to set up or play the game, see the Games Resource Master (p. 164).

b. Develop basic sight vocabulary: Objects Make large flash cards with the new vocabulary words. Divide the class into two teams. Have the class play a game of Picture Dictionary. For a description of how to play the game, see the Games Resource Master (p. 164).

c. Initiate authentic discourse Give the class one minute to interview as many students as possible about various activities they perform. Have them take notes on the people they interview. Those answering should use frequency words. Ask volunteers to report what they found out to the class.

Grammar (Student Book, p. 90)

Simple Present

Employ increasingly complex grammar Have students finish the free verse poem below by adding six or seven lines describing how they might feel about trying something new at the beach. Tell them to use the simple present tense in each sentence. Encourage them to use negatives and contractions.

> We go to the beach.
> The waves crash.
> I stop...

Word Study (Student Book, p. 90)

Long *e* sound: *ee, ea*

Distinguish phonological elements Divide the class into groups of four or five. Start the class off with two words that have the long *e* sound such as: *teacher/speak.* Have students build upon the base by making other words with the long *e* sound.

Assess (Student Book, p. 91)

Answer Key

Vocabulary
1. I _____ soccer every Saturday.
   a. eat   b. dance   **c. play**   d. listen
2. He always _____ the newspaper.
   a. reads   b. listens   c. rents   d. speaks
3. I want to play baseball. I need a baseball and a_____.
   a. pen   **b. bat**   c. paintbrush   d. soccer ball

Grammar
1. We_____ at the gym.
   a. exercise   b. exercises
2. My mother_____ beautiful pictures.
   a. paint   **b. paints**
3. _____ listens to music.
   a. She   b. We   c. They

Projects
Activity Book, Ch. 3 Mini-Reader
Project 1: Activities Collage (Student Book, p. 92)

a. **Produce communication using appropriate media** Have students work with small groups to make a poster of their favorite activities. Have students discuss their favorite activities with the group. Have the groups make a list of the various favorite activities. Then have the class choose a word or words that the activities may have in common. Have students find and cut out pictures and words from magazines and newspapers that show the activities. Students may also draw pictures.

b. **Explore and describe how color shape and line influence a message** Have the class paste the pictures on a poster board. Have students point to and identify the different colors, shapes, and lines in the composition. Hang the poster up in your classroom.

Project 2: Favorite Activity Presentation (Student Book, p. 93)

a. **Give an oral presentation** Go over the directions carefully with students. Then brainstorm topics for their presentations. Encourage the class to use a bilingual dictionary. Model each step for the students, including making note cards and giving the presentation.

b. **Use note cards as an organizational tool** Have students write notes for their presentation. Supply them with note cards, or paper cut to that size.

c. **Prepare for an oral presentation** Have students practice their presentation. Encourage them to ask you for help with pronunciation. After the presentation have students evaluate their presentation with the checklist.

Viewing Activity

Explore and discuss how artists influence the message Bring in examples of paintings or drawings depicting young people in various leisure time activities. You may want to include art from different time periods. Discuss what is shown in each image, and identify the predominant colors. Explore how colors and shapes help convey the message.

Chapter 4 Home

Materials

Student Book: pp. 94–107
Activity Book: pp. 57–64, Mini-Reader 4
Audio: Chapter 4
Student CD-ROM: Chapter 4
Teacher Resource Book
    Lesson Plan, pp. 65–72
    Resource Masters: Cluster Map p. 140; Sense Chart, p. 143
Assessment Program: pp. 31–34
Transparencies

Themes

Rooms in the House
Compound Words
Simple Present Tense

Learning Strategies

Expand repertoire of learning strategies through inductive reasoning
Look for patterns in language such as in compound words
Use nonverbal cues to acquire new vocabulary
Use accessible language and learn new essential language

Listening

Understand basic expressions and vocabulary
Recognize and distinguish phonological patterns: *-s / -es / -ies* endings
Listen to and extract meaning from audio recording
Infer meaning from actions and visual context

Speaking

Identify places by the use of descriptive adjectives
Ask for and give information such as immediate surroundings
Initiate authentic discourse with peers
Describe immediate surroundings such as: classroom, home, school

Reading

Read authentic literature: vignette
Develop basic sight vocabulary
Decode words by identification of cognates in compound words
Use verbal cueing strategies such as pauses and exaggerated intonation

Writing

Use graphic organizers as pre-writing activity
Apply spelling rules such as: *-s / -es / -ies* endings
Construct correct sentences using subject-verb agreement
Edit writing toward standard grammar

Viewing and Representing

Use visual cues to derive meaning
Produce visuals to aid communication
Distinguish purposes of various media forms
Analyze and respond to print presentations

Listen, Speak, Interact
I Study in the Living Room

① **Listen and repeat.** (Student Book, p. 95)

Listen to and extract meaning from audio
Have students find the activity and read the directions. Point to your ear and say *listen*. Then say: *house*. Now prompt the class to repeat. Say: *Repeat the word—house*. Gesture the class to repeat. Play the audio or read the script. Give visual cues.

Audioscript 🎧

1. **Listen and repeat.**
Listen and repeat the words.
house, house / bedroom, bedroom / bathroom, bathroom / kitchen, kitchen / living room, living room / apartment building, apartment building / apartment, apartment

② **Listen and repeat.** (Student Book, p. 95)

Listen to and extract meaning from audio
Have students find the activity and read the directions. Look at the guidelines in *Activity 1*.

Audioscript 🎧

2. **Listen and repeat.**
Listen to the conversation.
A: *What do you do in the living room?*
B: *I watch TV in the living room.*
A: *What else do you do in the living room?*
B: *I study in the living room.*

Now repeat the conversation.
A: *What do you do in the living room?*
B: *I watch TV in the living room.*
A: *What else do you do in the living room?*
B: *I study in the living room.*

③ **Pair work.** (Student Book, p. 95)

a. **Read through a dialogue** Have students find the activity and read the directions. Pair students with a partner. Have them practice the conversation and complete the sentences based on the pictures. Ask students to take turns.

b. **Initiate authentic discourse with peers** Encourage students to make substitutions with rooms such as: *dining room, laundry room, garage,* etc.

Answer key
3. **Pair work.**
A: What do you do in the **bathroom**?
B: I **take a shower** in the **bathroom**.
A: What else do you do in the **bathroom**?
B: I **brush my teeth** in the **bathroom**.

A: What do you do in the **bedroom**?
B: I **sleep** in the **bedroom**.
A: What else do you do in the **bedroom**?
B: I **read** in the **bedroom**.

A: What do you do in the **kitchen**?
B: I **cook** in the **kitchen**.
A: What else do you do in the **kitchen**?
B: I **eat** in the **kitchen**.

④ **Group work.** (Student Book, p. 95)

Ask for and give information Have students find the activity and read the directions. You may want to repeat the activity with *living room*. However, do not use *bathroom* or *bedroom* in order to avoid uncomfortable or offensive responses.

Build Vocabulary
What's in the Room?

⑤ **Listen and repeat.** (Student Book, p. 96)

a. **Use visual cues to learn new vocabulary** Have students find the activity and read the directions. Have students look at the pictures. Call on volunteers to read the words. Play the audio or read the script.

b. **Learn to use synonyms** You may mention that *couch* is a synonym for *sofa*. Say: *Synonyms are two words that mean the same thing. In different regions of the country one word may be used more than the other.* Other synonyms: *cupboard / cabinet; range / stove; cushion / pillow; icebox / refrigerator / fridge; rug / carpet; drapes / curtains.*

Audioscript 🎧

5. **Listen and repeat.**
Look at the pictures. Listen to the words. Repeat the words.
living room, living room
bookcase, bookcase / lamp, lamp / rug, rug / sofa, sofa
kitchen, kitchen
oven, oven / refrigerator, refrigerator / sink, sink / table, table
bedroom, bedroom
bed, bed / closet, closet / curtain, curtain / dresser, dresser / pillow, pillow
bathroom, bathroom
bathtub, bathtub / mirror, mirror / shower, shower / toilet, toilet

6 **Find the word.** (Student Book, p. 96)

a. Look for patterns in language Have students find the activity and read the directions. When students have finished, have them give answers, spelling the words aloud.

b. Identify new words Divide the class into small groups. Give each group a copy of a picture of a room. Say to each group: *See how many items you can identify in one minute.* Afterwards have groups use a dictionary to look up new words.

c. Use media to convey meaning Have students draw a picture of a room in their home. They should label objects in their pictures with correct words from the vocabulary. Another option is to cut out pictures from magazines and catalogs to create a collage of a room.

d. Words to know Build a supplementary vocabulary list with the class based on their drawings. Some additional vocabulary words are: *alarm clock, blanket, sheets, bedspread, lamp, stove, dishwasher, microwave, pantry, sink, toilet, soap, towel, razor, medicine cabinet, bath mat, coffee table, love seat, armchair,* etc.

Answer key
6. Find the word.

1. **a**	deb	**bed**
2. **d**	aofs	**sofa**
3. **b**	nksi	**sink**
4. **c**	erfrigtrearo	**refrigerator**

Activity Book, p. 57: Rooms at Home

Grammar Focus
There is / There are

7 **Build sentences.** (Student Book, p. 97)

a. Look for patterns in language Explain that *there is* may be contracted (*there's*), but *there are* should not be contracted. Write the contraction on the board. Remind students of the indefinite articles *a/an*. Explain that the indefinite article is necessary after the singular *there is*. Also explain to the class that to make most nouns plural, they need to add an *s* to the end of a noun: *chair / chairs, window / windows.*

b. Construct correct sentences First explain that a phrase is a part of a sentence. It is made of two or more words, but it does not express a complete idea. For example, *in the kitchen* is a phrase, but we don't know anything more about the kitchen. The phrase is not complete. By combining two or more phrases we can explain a complete idea. A complete sentence would be: *There is an oven in the kitchen.* Have students find the activity and read the directions. Then have them look at the pictures on p. 96. Guide the class to make a true sentence with phrases from each of the columns.

Answer key
7. Build sentences.
There is an oven in the kitchen.
There are two pillows in the bedroom
There are two sofas in the living room.
There is a shower in the bathroom.

Language Transfer and Interference

Haitian Creole: Plural forms are not used after a number. Therefore, students may say: *There are four window in the room.* They may also add an additional word after the noun as a plural marker in place of *-s / -es / -ies* endings.

Spanish: To form the plural in Spanish, *-es* is added to nouns that end in *y* or in any consonant. Therefore, students may have a tendency to spell *walls* as *walles* or *rays* as *rayes.* They may also pronounce the ending as a separate syllable: *wal'ez* or *rey'ez.* Emphasize to students who make such mistakes that in English, *-es* is only added after the following consonants: *ch, s, sh, ss,* and *x.* Also remind students that in English the *y* is changed to an *i* before adding *-es.*

Vietnamese: There are no plural noun forms in Vietnamese, Chinese, Hmong, or Korean. Instead, plurals are expressed through adjective quantifiers. Therefore, these students may have a tendency to disregard the plural endings *-s / -es / -ies.* Vietnamese students may have a tendency to substitute *have* for *is* in the expressions *there is / there are* such as: *There have many windows in the room.*

8 **Pair work.** (Student Book, p. 97)

a. **Initiate authentic discourse with peers** Have students find the activity and read the directions. As students work in pairs, circulate and assist as needed.

b. **Describe immediate surroundings** For more challenging practice, give one partner a blank piece of paper and the other a picture of a room to describe. As one describes the position of objects in the picture, the partner must sketch what is being described. Have partners compare the sketch to the original picture. Model the activity with a volunteer before students work in pairs.

Language Transfer and Interference

Indefinite articles are not used in Vietnamese or in other Asian languages such as Chinese, Hmong, and Korean. Native speakers of these languages may have difficulty remembering to use the indefinite articles *a/an* or instead they may substitute the word *one* as in: *He reads book. or He reads one book.*

English grammar uses the Subject-Verb-Object word order in sentences. Not all languages follow the same grammatical structure. For example, in Spanish, the verb often precedes the subject, such as *Comes the bus.* In Korean, verbs are always placed at the end of a sentence. Students may construct sentences such as: *In the kitchen, an oven there is.* Help students become more aware of the correct sentence structure in English.

Activity Book, p. 58: There is / There are
Activity Book, p. 59: Is there? / Are there?

Word Study
Compound Words (Student Book, p. 98)

Explain to the class that a compound word is made when two words are joined to form a new word. You may want to mention that there are three forms of compound words. Sometimes the two words are written as one word such as *classroom*. Sometimes a hyphen is used to connect the two words as in *twenty-one*. Sometimes the words are written separately but read as one word such as *living room.*

Strategy: Word Recognition
Use prior knowledge to learn new vocabulary
Point to the strategy box and have students read it aloud.

9 **Read and find.** (Student Book, p. 98)

Using prior knowledge Have students find the activity and read the directions. Tell the class: *There are compound words you already know, such as classroom: class + room.* Have the class find the two words that form each compound word in the activity.

Answer Key
9. Read and find.

1. classroom	class	room
2. backpack	back	pack
3. bathtub	bath	tub
4. bedroom	bed	room
5. football	foot	ball
6. notebook	note	book

10 **Listen.** (Student Book, p. 98)

a. **Recognize compound words** Have students find the activity and read the directions. Have students break a compound word such as *classroom* into its separate components and repeat the two words with a pause: *class... room.*

b. **Look for patterns in language** Play the audio or read the script. Have students listen for the two words that are combined in each compound word.

c. **Use prior knowledge** Ask: *What other compound words can you think of with the word room?* Elicit these words from the vocabulary: *bathroom, bedroom, living room,* etc. Start a class list of compound words on a large sheet of paper. Post it in the classroom and add words to it as they come up in class.

d. **Infer meaning** Ask students to think about the following: What does a person do in these rooms: *laundry room, waiting room, operating room?*

VISIONS BASIC Teacher Resource Book • Copyright © Heinle

Audioscript 🎧
10. Listen.
Listen to the smaller words in the compound word. Then listen to the compound word.

1. class	room	classroom
2. back	pack	backpack
3. bath	tub	bathtub
4. bed	room	bedroom
5. foot	ball	football
6. note	book	notebook

11 **Read and understand.** (Student Book, p. 98)

a. Recognize compound words Have students find the activity and read the directions. Then have them work in pairs to match the words with the corresponding pictures. Ask students to copy the words on a piece of paper and write the correct letter next to each word.

b. Use imagery memorization to acquire new vocabulary Bring to class the following objects or other household items that are compound words: *toothbrush, toothpaste, nail file, hair spray, pencil sharpener, toothpick,* etc. Demonstrate the function of each item. For example, hold a toothbrush in front of your mouth and say: *This brush is for cleaning teeth. What is it called?* Have students think of compound words they could call each object. Tell the class the actual word for each item. Ask students to draw a picture that represents the compound word. Follow up by playing a game of Picture Dictionary with the class. Refer to the Game Instructions Resource Master (p. 164).

Answer key
11. Read and understand.
1. **f** armchair
2. **e** birdhouse
3. **b** mailbox
4. **c** waterfall
5. **a** hairbrush
6. **d** headphones

Activity Book, p. 60: Compound Words

Into the Reading (Student Book, p. 99)
Strategy: Predict (Student Book, p. 99)

Use inductive reasoning Point to the strategy box and have students read it aloud. Have students predict what the reading will be about based on the title and picture.

Use Prior Knowledge: Feelings About Home (Student Book, p. 99)

a. Use the five senses Make sure students understand the five senses. Create a poster of a face and label the eyes, ears, nose, and tongue with their corresponding senses. Then explain the sense of touch. You may want to introduce modifiers for sights, sounds, smell, tastes, touch such as: *bright, dark, dim, loud, soft, sweet, bitter, sour, sharp,* etc.

b. Use sensory observations to describe surroundings Have students look at the model in the text. Make copies of the Sense Chart Resource Master (p. 143) and hand it out to students. Help students as needed while they fill in the chart.

Build Background: Petunias (Student Book, p. 99)

Become familiarized with new words Ask students: *What are some other flowers that you know?* Examples can be: *rose, daisy, tulip,* etc. If possible, have on hand for reference a magazine or gardening catalog.

Reading and Understanding
Text Structure: Vignette (Student Book, p. 100)

Develop understanding of literary structures Review the explanation about the structure of a vignette with the class. Explain that a vignette is like a quick sketch. It uses words and phrases to create glimpses into an idea or emotion. It has similarities to a poem, but it is also like a very short story.

Reading 🎧 (Student Book, p. 100)
a. Pre-teach vocabulary You may want to pre-teach some or all of the new vocabulary in the reading: *flat, porch, beside, shake a stick at, nobody, garbage, quiet, snow, space, clean.*

b. Read authentic literature Read the vignette with the class as a choral reading. Bring attention to the mood and tone of the piece. Ask: *Is the poem happy or sad?* Then do a chain reading. Stop after each line to answer questions about the content.

Culture Note

Mention that the word *flat* is a British term. You may also wish to mention that there are also variations in vocabulary, spelling, and pronunciation of some words in American English versus British English.

Beyond the Reading

Reading Comprehension. (Student Book, p. 101)

a. **Derive meaning from text** Have students answer the questions from the reading. Ask them to answer in complete sentences. Have volunteers write answers on the board.

b. **Ask questions** Suggest that students come up with more questions based on the picture. Have them work with partners to ask and answer more questions about the reading.

Answer key

1. Does the author have a home of her own?
   Yes, she has a home of her own.
2. Does she have an apartment or a house?
   She has a house.
3. What does she have in her home?
   She has a porch, pillows, petunias, books, and her shoes in her home.
4. What adjectives in the poem describe her home?
   Her house is quiet and clean.

Think about the picture. (Student Book, p. 101)

Discuss the questions with the class. Suggest that a vignette is like a sketch with words.

Compare with words. (Student Book, p. 101)

Use contrastive analysis Have a volunteer read the explanation. Explain that this kind of comparison is called a simile. Help students brainstorm other comparisons and write them on the board.

Activity Book, p. 61: Social Studies: The White House
Activity Book, p. 62: Reading Fluency

From Reading to Writing

My Future Home (Student Book, pp. 102–103)

a. **Use writing strategies** Review the four writing steps: *Plan, Write, Edit,* and *Publish.* Explain each step. Remind students: *In a paragraph, the sentences are about the same subject. The first line must be indented.*

b. **Use pre-writing graphic organizers** Make copies of the Cluster Map Resource Master (p. 140) and hand them out to students.

c. **Construct correct sentences** Read through the steps with students, making sure they understand the directions. Have students write a paragraph of three or four sentences about their future home. Encourage them to use similes. They may also use a bilingual dictionary to find new words.

d. **Edit writing toward standard grammar** Have students read their paragraph. Ask if they can find any mistakes. Have them check their work with the Editing Checklist. You may have students exchange papers and correct one another's work. At this early level, students may often miss their own mistakes. Encouraging students early on to have others look at their work will help reduce anxiety over sharing their writing.

Activity Book, p. 63: Use of Commas
Activity Book, p. 64: Describing a House

Review

Vocabulary (Student Book, p. 104)

Write for various purposes Have students write a brief description of a house for rent. You may want to bring examples for students to review before writing their own. Have students read their description to the class.

Word Study (Student Book, p. 104)
Compound words

Divide the class into groups of three or four. Give each group a base word such as: *room, house, machine,* etc. and have the class brainstorm a list of compound words they already know. Then have them try to invent at least five new compound words. Have them check in the dictionary to see if their invented words already exist in the English language.

Assess

Answer key

Vocabulary (Student Book, p. 105)

1. I cook in the _____.
   - a. bathroom
   - **c. kitchen**
   - b. living room
   - d. bedroom
2. The _____ is on the bed.
   - a. bookcase
   - **c. pillow**
   - b. couch
   - d. stove
3. The _____ is in the bathroom.
   - a. couch
   - c. bed
   - b. refrigerator
   - **d. toilet**

Grammar (Student Book, p. 105)

1. There _____ five rooms in my home.
   - a. is
   - **b. are**
2. There _____ a pillow on the bed.
   - **a. is**
   - b. are
3. There are two _____ in the kitchen.
   - a. window
   - **b. windows**

Word Study (Student Book, p. 105)

1. **b** haircut   2. **a** handbag   3. **c** earring

Activity Book: Ch. 4 Mini-Reader

Projects

Project 1: Create Your Dream House (Student Book, p. 106)

a. **Distinguish the purposes of various forms of media** Bring to class several floor plans from popular magazines. Explain that a floor plan is a diagram. It is like a map to help a person understand the space in a room. Pass out a large sheet of poster paper for students to use to make a floor plan of their dream home.

b. **Initiate authentic discourse with peers** As students discuss their plans with partners and complete their projects, circulate and offer assistance as needed.

Project 2: Match Compound Noun Cards (Student Book, p. 107)

a. **Learn basic sight vocabulary** After students have made the word cards, have them put the cards next to each other to find the matching compound nouns. They should talk it out to decide if they think a combination might be a word.

b. **For a challenge, give students a new word.** Ask them to think of compound words with it. For example: *house* (birdhouse, doghouse, housefly, housework, houseboat).

Answer key

The following compound words can be made by matching the cards so that all the cards are used: *backpack, birthday, paintbrush, notebook, classmate, bathroom, football, blackboard.*

Viewing Activity

Analyze and respond to print presentations
Bring in photos of homes in different cultures. An excellent resource in *Material World* by Peter Menzel. This is a photo essay documenting homes and families of different world cultures. Each family is shown in front of the home with all of the contents of their home outside with them. Discuss differences and similarities.

Chapter 5 The Community

Materials

Student Book: pp. 108–121
Activity Book: pp. 65–72, Mini-Reader 5
Audio: Chapter 5
Student CD-ROM: Chapter 5
Teacher Resource Book:
    Lesson Plan, pp. 73–80
    Resource Masters: Web, p. 138; Sunshine Organizer, p. 141; Games Instructions, p. 164
Assessment Program: pp. 35–46
Transparencies

Themes

Community Buildings
Transportation
Time
Present Continuous
Newspaper

Learning Strategies

Monitor oral and written language production
Employ self-corrective techniques
Use contrastive analysis to acquire new vocabulary

Listening

Understand basic expressions and vocabulary
Recognize and distinguish phonological elements: digraphs *ch, sh, th, wh, ng*
Listen to and extract meaning from audio recording

Speaking

Identify places and the use of prepositions with transportation vehicles
Ask for and give information, such as time
Initiate authentic discourse with peers in interviews
Produce phonological elements of newly acquired vocabulary: *ch, sh, th, wh, ng*

Reading

Read authentic literature
Participate in shared reading of a newspaper article
Develop basic sight vocabulary
Use reading strategies such as scanning

Writing

Use graphic organizers as a pre-writing tool
Construct correct sentences using the present continuous tense
Edit writing toward standard grammar

Viewing and Representing

Use visual cues to derive meaning
Produce visuals to aid communication
View and interpret ideas from art

Listen, Speak, Interact

How Do You Get There?

❶ Listen and repeat. (Student Book, p. 109)

a. Listen to and extract meaning from audio Have students find the activity and read the directions. Point to your ear and say: *listen.* Then say: *hospital.* Say: *Repeat the word— hospital.* Gesture to the class to repeat. Play the audio or read the script. Give students visual cues to listen and repeat.

b. Produce phonological elements of newly acquired vocabulary Help students form the sound of voiceless *th* as in *theater.* Place the tip of the tongue at the top of the tooth ridge as you say *th.* Explain that this sound is voiceless. Put your hand on your voice box while saying *th.* There should be no vibration. Put your hand in front of your mouth as you say *th.* Explain that there should be air escaping. Remind students that this is in contrast to the voiced *th* sound in words such as *mother* or *father* in Chapter 2.

c. Employ self-corrective techniques Have students work with partners to practice the new vocabulary. They should pay close attention to the *th* sound. Remind them to check for voiceless articulation by putting a hand on their voice boxes to check for no vibration and in front of their mouths to check for air.

Audioscript 🎧

1. Listen and repeat.
Listen and repeat the words.
hospital, hospital / library, library / movie theater, movie theatre / park, park / post office, post office / supermarket, supermarket / video store, video store / car, car / bus, bus / train, train / walk, walk

❷ Listen and repeat. (Student Book, p. 109)

a. Listen to and extract meaning from an audio Have students find the activity and read the directions. Explain the meaning of the expression *How do you get to...?*

b. Words to know Point out the vocabulary in the Words to Know box. Model the use of *take* with public transportation vehicles such as *bus, plane, subway, taxicab, train: I take the subway to the library.* Introduce the verb *drive,* giving an example sentence: *I drive a car.* You may also

mention the prepositions *on / off* as used in the expression *to get on / get off* vehicles.

Audioscript 🎧

2. Listen and repeat.
Listen to the conversation.
A: *How do you get to the library?*
B: *I take the bus. How about you?*
A: *I walk.*

Now repeat the conversation.
A: *How do you get to the library?*
B: *I take the bus. How about you?*
A: *I walk.*

❸ Pair work. (Student Book, p. 109)

a. Read through a dialogue Have students find the activity and read the directions. Model asking and answering questions with a volunteer before having students work in pairs.

b. Initiate authentic discourse with peers Have students make substitutions with other locations such as *supermarket, park,* etc. Then have them look at the various community places. Students should ask their partner how he/she gets to each place: *How do you get to school? I walk to school.*

c. Field trip Organize a field trip with your class to the public library, museum, or zoo. Many students are unfamiliar with the various public facilities available in their local community. Some may have never had the opportunity to go to such places. Encourage students to get a public library card, and explain the procedure for checking out material.

Build Vocabulary

Time

❹ Listen and repeat. (Student Book, p. 110)

a. Use visual cues to learn new vocabulary Have students find the activity and read the directions. Then have them look at the clocks, listen to the audio or script, and repeat the times. You may want to introduce alternatives such as: *quarter of two, five after one,* etc. Point out the Words to Know box at the top of the page and explain that 12:00 can be daytime or nighttime.

b. Expand vocabulary Write some supplementary vocabulary words for the class such as: *hour, minute, second, face, hand, digital, clock, watch.*

Audioscript 🎧
5. Listen and repeat.
Look at the clocks. Listen and repeat the times.
1. one o'clock
2. one oh five
3. one fifteen
4. one thirty
5. one forty-five
6. one fifty-five

5 Pair work. (Student Book, p. 110)

a. Follow directions Have students find the activity and read the directions. Hand out to each student a paper plate, a brad fastener, and two thin strips of cardboard paper, one short and one long. Give directions for students to make a clock with these materials. Show them how to number the face of the clock. They can decorate their clocks if they like. Then have students attach the hands with the brad fastener. They may need to use a hole-puncher or a pair of scissors.

b. Listen for information Have students work with partners. One should call out the time and have the other set the clock to the time. Students should then hold up their clocks to check if they have the right time. Alternatively, you can draw a clock on the board and show the correct time once everyone has set their clocks.

6 Read and answer. (Student Book, p. 110)

Have students find the activity and read the directions. Explain that AM refers to the time between midnight and noon, and PM refers to the time between noon and midnight.

Answer key
7. Read and answer.
1. It's 7:00 AM. What time is the next bus?
   The next bus is at **7:15 AM.**
2. It's 8:45 AM. What time is the next bus?
   The next bus is at **9:00 AM.**
3. It's 10:30 AM. What time is the next bus?
   The next bus is at **11:00 AM.**
4. It's 5:10 PM. What time is the next bus?
   The next bus is at **5:15 PM.**
5. It's 6:30 PM. What time is the next bus?
   The next bus is at **7:05 PM.**

Activity Book, p. 52: Places and Times

Grammar Focus
Present continuous (Student Book, p. 111)

Review the present continuous chart and have students read the explanation in the text. You may also want to model the contractions for the present continuous: *I'm, you're, he's, she's, it's, we're, they're.* Review the spelling rules with the class.

7 Read and find. (Student Book, p. 111)

a. Using visual cues to derive meaning Have students find the activity and read the directions. Then teach the following verbs by acting them out: *dance, leap, skip, gallop, grin, giggle, shout, swing, sing, wiggle, run.*

b. Read authentic literature Read the poem as students follow along in their books. Then read the poem once with the class as a choral reading and again as a chain reading.

c. Use contrastive analysis Have students copy the poem on a sheet of paper. Discuss how the present continuous and simple present tense sentences are different.

d. Write with more proficient orthographic patterns Use the poem as a cloze activity. Photocopy the poem and remove some or all the verbs using white correct ink. Then photocopy the template to pass out to students. Read the poem aloud and have students fill in the missing verbs.

e. Demonstrate knowledge of verb tenses Write the poem on the board and remove all the verbs. Have students rewrite the poem using different verbs. You may suggest that students try to change the tone or mood of the poem.

Answer key
7. Read and find.

present continuous:	I'm dancing, I'm leaping, I'm skipping, I'm swinging, I'm singing
simple present tense:	I gallop, I grin, I giggle, I shout, I wiggle, I run

Language Transfer and Interference

The /ng/ sound does not occur in many languages. Practice the articulation of this nasal sound with students: *sing, swing, thing.*

8 Write. (Student Book, p. 111)

a. Using prior knowledge Have students find the activity and read the directions. Ask the class for various action verbs that describe different things students may be doing such as: *listening, sitting, reading, talking, using, writing,* etc. You may want to write the verbs on the board.

b. Use contrastive analysis Review the *-ing* spelling rules with the class. Draw a chart on the board with three columns marked: *most verbs; verbs ending in e; one-syllable consonant-vowel-consonant verbs.* Write the words the class mentions in the chart on the board, placing each verb into one of the three spelling categories.

c. Demonstrate knowledge of verb tenses Give students five minutes to write as many present continuous sentences as possible such as: *Sam is talking.* Stop the class and have students compare sentences with their classmates.

Activity Book, p. 66: Present Continuous
Activity Book, p. 67: More About Present Continuous

Word Study

Digraphs: *ch, sh, th, wh, ng*

Produce phonological elements Have students read the explanation of digraphs and look over the words in the chart. Practice pronouncing the words with the class. Explain that all verbs in the present continuous have the *ng* sound at the end.

9 Listen and repeat. (Student Book, p. 112)

a. Produce phonological elements of newly acquired vocabulary: ch, sh Have students find the activity and read the directions. Help students form the voiceless sounds of *ch* as in *cheek* and *sh* as in *she.* To make the *ch* sound, direct students to push the front of their tongue up front against the roof of the mouth. Have students force air out with open lips to make the

sound *ch.* Explain that this sound is voiceless. Put your hand on your voice box and say *ch.* There should be no vibration. Now put your hand in front of your mouth as you say *ch.* Air should be escaping.

To make the *sh* sound, have students relax their tongue instead of pushing it up against the roof of their mouth. Have them force air out to make the sound *sh.* Explain that the air should be escaping the mouth with less force than with *ch.* Have students confirm that this is a voiceless sound by putting their hand on their voice box as they say *sh.* There should be no vibration. Have them put their hand in front of their mouth as they say *sh* to feel the air escaping.

b. Produce phonological elements of newly acquired vocabulary: th Help students form the sound of the voiceless *th* as in *bath.* Explain that this sound is voiceless. Have students put their hand on their voice box and say *th.* There should be no vibration. Now have them put their hand in front of their mouth as you say *th.* There should be air escaping. Remind students that this is in contrast to the voiced *th* sound in words such as *mother* or *father* that they learned in Chapter 2.

c. Produce phonological elements of newly acquired vocabulary: wh Help students form the sound of the voiceless *wh* as in *white.* Remind students that this sound is voiceless unlike the sound *w.* There should be no vibration when they put their hand on their voice box, but there should be air escaping.

d. Produce phonological elements of newly acquired vocabulary: ng Help students form the sound of the voiced nasal *ng* as in *wing.* Explain that this sound is voiced and nasal. There is vibration but no air.

e. Look for patterns in language Play the audio or read the script. Then have students practice repeating the words several times.

f. Employ self-corrective techniques Have students work with partners to practice the five digraphs and their corresponding sounds. If possible, pair students from different linguistic backgrounds so that they may better identify the particular pronunciation challenges of their peers. Students should pay close attention to the

VISIONS BASIC Teacher Resource Book • Copyright © Heinle

sounds that are most difficult for them. If available, provide mirrors so students can watch their mouths and make self-corrective adjustments. Make sure they check for voiceless articulation in *ch, wh,* and *ng* by putting a hand on their voice box to check. For voiced sound in *sh* and *th,* students should feel vibration in their voice box but no air escaping.

g. **Use contrastive analysis** For additional practice, use any of these pronunciation contrast pairs that target the needs of your students. Model these pair sounds for the class. You may want to have students make personalized pronunciation cards. This activity helps students locate the correct positioning of their tongue, jaw, etc. through contrastive exercises.

ch: talk / chalk, tap / chap, tart / chart

sh: self / shelf, sell / shell, sue / shoe

th: thick / sick, think / sink, mouth / mouse

wh: where / hair, white / height, why / hi

ng: ham / hang, clam / clang, ran / rang

Audioscript 🎧
9. Listen and repeat.

Listen to the sound the two consonants make together. Then listen to the sound in each word. Repeat each word.

ch: **ch**eek, **ch**ild, **ch**in, por**ch**

sh: **sh**e, **sh**op, fi**sh**, book**sh**elf

th: ba**th**, **th**ank, **th**ree, tee**th**

wh: **wh**ite, **wh**en, **wh**ere, **wh**y

ng: wi**ng**, fi**ng**er, si**ng**, readi**ng**

Language Interference and Transfer

Spanish:

ch: The voiceless sound /ch/ does occur in Spanish, but its variant *tch* as in *kitchen* or *match* does not.

sh: The counterpart /sh/ does not occur in Spanish. Spanish speakers will substitute /ch/ for /sh/. For example, they will say /cher/ for *share.* Help students form the voiceless /sh/ sound by lowering their tongue instead of pushing it up against the roof of the mouth.

th: The digraph *th* does not appear in Spanish. However, the voiced sound /th/ does occur. *D* will have the /th/ sound wherever possible. *Z* and *c* have the /th/ sound before the vowels *e* or *i* as in *gracias* or *estación.*

wh: Does not appear in Spanish.
ng: Does not appear in Spanish.

Vietnamese:

ch: Vietnamese does not have the sound /ch/.

sh: The sound /sh/ does occur. However, /sh/ is written with the *ch* digraph. This may lead to spelling errors such as: *chell* instead of *shell* and pronunciation errors such as /sheek/ instead of /cheek/.
To help these students produce the *ch* sound have them first make the *t* sound. Explain that this is where the tongue needs to be to say *ch.*

th: Vietnamese has an approximate sound transfer for voiceless /th/ as in *bath* but none for voiced /th/ as in the word *this.* Voiceless initial *th* can become *t* or *s* for these speakers. Therefore *think* can be pronounced /tink/ or /sink/. The voiced initial *th* can become *z,* making that sound like /zat/.

wh: Does not occur in Vietnamese.
ng: Does not occur in Vietnamese.

⑩ Write. (Student Book, p. 112)

Distinguish phonological elements Have students find the activity and read the directions. Then have them copy it on a piece of paper and write in the missing letters.

Answer key
11. Write.

1. **sh** irt	3. mou **th**	5. **sh** oe
2. **ch** air	4. **wh** eel	6. ri **ng**

⑪ Listen and choose. (Student Book, p. 112)

Distinguish phonological elements Have students find the activity and read the directions. You may want to introduce additional consonant digraphs: *ph, gh.*

Audioscript 🎧
11. Listen and choose.

Look at the pair of words. Listen. Which word do you hear?
1. chin 2. math 3. think 4. when 5. choose 6. shop

Activity Book, p. 68: Digraphs: ch, sh, th, wh, ng

Into the Reading

Use Prior Knowledge: Newspapers (Student Book, p. 113)

Bring a local newspaper to class. Go over the various sections of the paper such as the front page, sports, community, classified, editorial, horoscope, advice, etc. Make copies and hand out the Web Resource Master (p. 138). Have students fill in their ideas.

Build Background: Community Service (Student Book, p. 113)

Have students read over the community service explanation in the text. Point out the three pictures and discuss the kind of help shown in each. Write useful new vocabulary words on the board.

Culture Note

Explain to the class the importance of volunteerism in communities. In many cultures such help is either done within the extended family network or else relegated to religious or government institutions. Emphasize that in the U.S. there is a strong value for volunteerism and helping individuals that one may not personally know. There are many organizations where one can either volunteer or get help. Explain that volunteers don't get paid for what they do, but the rewards they gain are from helping others and learning new things in the process. You may want to invite some volunteers from local organizations to speak with the class, or take the class on a field trip to a local organization or community center.

Reading and Understanding

Text Structure: Newspaper Article (Student Book, p. 114)

Develop understanding of literary structures Have a student read out the explanation about newspaper articles. Go over the Words to Know box with the class. Show the class a newspaper and point the headlines. You may want to explain that headlines are usually written in the present tense, and are not written as complete sentences. Sometimes headlines may be difficult for students to understand. Practice reading headlines and predicting the subject of an article.

Reading 🎧 (Student Book, p. 114)

a. Pre-teach vocabulary You may want to pre-teach some or all of the potentially new vocabulary in the reading: *elderly, residents,*

bringing, appointments, showing, care, exciting, tickets, Town Hall, free, senior citizens, mall, hurry, manager, customers.

b. Read authentic literature Play the audio or read the text. Then read the three articles with the class as a choral reading. Bring attention to the headlines and photos. Then do a chain reading. Stop to answer questions.

Beyond the Reading

Reading Comprehension (Student Book, p. 115)

a. Derive meaning from text Have students answer the questions based on the newspaper articles. Challenge students to answer the questions in complete sentences.

b. Higher order thinking Have students answer more challenging questions based on the reading. Below are some questions students could answer.

1. How do you know that kids in Brookdale care about their community? (Students from the high school are doing community service for the elderly. They are reading to the residents and helping them shop.)

2. Read the article about the Brookdale soccer team. What are some facts in the article? What are some opinions in the article? (The team plays every Saturday is a fact. Tickets are free for students, senior citizens, and children under 12 is a fact. Brookdale loves its soccer team is an opinion. The Bears always play an exciting game is an opinion.)

3. Why is the manager of the mall giving away free T-shirts? (He wants many people to come to the new mall. He hopes if they come for the T-shirts they will shop at the mall. The free T-shirts probably have information printed on them about the mall. When people wear the free T-shirts, others will find out about the mall.)

Answer key

1. Are Brookdale students helping the elderly?
   Yes, they are helping the elderly.
2. Do the Brookdale Bears play soccer on Saturday or Sunday?
   They play soccer on Saturday.
3. What is the manager of the Brookdale Mall giving away today?
   The manager is giving away free T-shirts.
4. Which article is most interesting to you? Why? (Answers will vary.)

Scan for information. (Student Book, p. 115) Remind students that this strategy was introduced in a previous chapter. Ask students to copy the chart, then look at the questions to get an idea of what information they need to find. Then have them scan for the information and fill out the chart.

Answer key

Brookdale Soccer Team Always Scores a Goal
Who is the article about? **Brookdale Soccer Team**
What is the article about? **the next soccer game**
When is the event happening? **Saturday at 1:00 PM**
Where is the event happening? **Clark Park**

Brookdale Mall Opens
Who is the article about? **Brookdale Mall**
What is the article about? **opening of new mall**
When is the event happening? **today**
Where is the event happening? **300 Main Street**

Activity Book, p. 69: Social Studies: The Government and Elections
Activity Book, p. 70: Reading Fluency

From Reading to Writing
Informational Paragraph (Student Book, p. 116)

a. **Use a graphic organizer for pre-writing** Review the four writing steps: *Plan, Write, Edit,* and *Publish.* Explain what each step involves. Then remind students that the sentences in a paragraph are about the same subject and the first sentence that introduces the general idea of the paragraph must be indented. Make and hand out copies of the Sunshine Resource Master (p. 141) for students to use.

b. **Construct correct sentences** Have students draft three or four sentences about their subject. Then have them write an introductory sentence. Ask students to use ideas from their organizer. Encourage them to use a bilingual dictionary to find new words. Remind them to give their paragraph a title.

c. **Edit writing toward standard grammar** As students check their work, circulate and assist as needed.

d. **Prepare to publish a piece of writing** Discuss with students how they would like to display their writing in class.

Activity Book, p. 71: Arranging Phrases Correctly
Activity Book, p. 72: A Community Event

Review
Vocabulary (Student Book, p. 118)

a. **Demonstrate knowledge of correct spelling of new words** Teach students the game of Hangman. You can refer to the Games Instructions Resource Master (p. 164). Have students play the game with a partner or with the class as a whole using the community places and transportation words.

b. **Initiate authentic discourse** Have students discuss their schedules with classmates answering questions such as *who, what, where, when, why.*

c. **Ask for and give information** Create a simple map of the students' community. Have students ask one another how to get to various places.

Grammar (Student Book, p. 118)
Present continuous

Express ideas, opinions, and feelings Have students write a poem using verbs in the present continuous tense. Alternatively, have them write a newscast of a breaking event, explaining things as they are happening. Some ideas may be a play-by-play sports broadcast, a natural disaster, an exciting public event, a rescue in progress, a police chase, etc.

Word Study (Student Book, p. 118)

Digraphs: *ch, sh, th, wh, ng*

Produce phonological elements Have students practice the five digraphs by saying these tongue-twisters or making some of their own:

ch: How much wood would a woodchuck chuck if a woodchuck could chuck wood?

sh: She sells seashells by the seashore, and the seashells that she sells are seashore shells I'm sure.

th: The thirty-three thieves thought that they thrilled the throne throughout Thursday.

wh: Why do you cry, Willy? Why do you cry? Why, Willy? Why, Willy? Why, Willy? Why?

ng: Singing Sammy sung songs on sinking sand.

Assess

Vocabulary (Student Book, p. 119)

1. My mother buys food at the _____.
   - a. post office
   - **c. supermarket**
   - b. park
   - d. hospital

2. I get books at the _____.
   - a. supermarket
   - c. park
   - b. police station
   - **d. library**

3. _____ is the next bus?
   - **a. When**
   - c. How
   - b. Why
   - d. Who

Grammar (Student Book, p. 119)

1. My teacher _____ the computer now.
   - a. are using
   - c. uses
   - b. use
   - **d. is using**

2. I _____ the bus every day.
   - a. are taking
   - c. takes
   - **b. take**
   - d. am take

3. We are _____ the book.
   - a. read
   - **c. reading**
   - b. reads
   - d. are reading

Word Study (Student Book, p. 119)

Say these nonsense words.

chim / wheg / shob / lang / thrib

Activity Book: Ch. 5 Mini-Reader

Projects

Project 1: Make a Transportation Graph (Student Book, p. 120)

a. **Ask for and give information** Divide the class into four groups and have students work together to create a bar graph of how all the class members get to school. Assign each group one of the four questions. Give students time to survey their classmates.

b. **Produce visuals** After groups have compiled their data, have the class draw a bar graph on a large piece of poster paper and each group fill the appropriate column with data from their research.

c. **Discuss information with a group** Talk about the graph. Have students discuss questions such as: *How many students take the bus to school? How many students walk? How do most students get to school? What is the most/least common way of getting to school?*

Project 2: Create a School Newspaper (Student Book, p. 121)

a. **Develop drafts by categorizing ideas into sentences and paragraphs** Divide the class into various teams such as news, editorial, sports, art and cultural events, etc. Have each group brainstorm subjects for news articles with their teammates.

b. **Edit writing toward standard grammar** Have students check their articles for mistakes. Then show articles to the other groups and ask them to look for mistakes or problems in the article.

c. **Present information in an appropriate format** Bring in sample newspapers and have students establish a layout template based on actual papers. Help students finalize and copy their papers.

Viewing Activity

View and interpret ideas from art Bring in examples of famous American artists' portrayals of communities and neighborhoods. Include examples from early America. Help students identify places and buildings in the art. Compare the different styles and colors used by artists of different times.

Chapter 6 Food

Materials

Student Book: pp. 122–135
Activity Book: pp. 73-80, Mini-Reader 6
Audio: Chapter 6
Student CD-ROM: Chapter 6
Teacher Resource Book:
    Lesson Plan, pp. 81-88
    Reading Fluency, p. 130
    Resource Masters: Web, p. 138; Paragraph, p. 144;, Step-by-Step Instructions, p. 146
Assessment Program: pp. 47–50
Transparencies

Themes

Food/Diet   Plural of Count Nouns   Writing About a Dish
Count/Noncount nouns   Informational Text   Science

Learning Strategies

Look for patterns in language
Use prior knowledge to understand meaning
Use contrastive analysis to acquire new vocabulary
Make connections across content areas
Use accessible language and learn new essential language

Listening

Use active listening comprehension to follow directions
Understand basic expressions and vocabulary
Listen to and extract meaning from audio recording
Infer meaning from actions and visual context

Speaking

Identify objects such as food
Share prior knowledge with peers to foster respect for others
Ask for and give information
Initiate authentic discourse with peers
Express ideas, opinions, and needs

Reading

Read authentic text   Read silently
Participate in shared reading   Use print from environment to derive meaning
Develop basic sight vocabulary

Writing

Use graphic organizers to gather new information
Demonstrate knowledge of plural forms
Construct correct sentences
Edit writing toward standard grammar

Viewing and Representing

Use visual cues to derive meaning
Produce visual for other kinds of communication
Assess how medium and presentation contribute to the message

Listen, Speak, Interact

What Do You Eat for Breakfast?

❶ Listen and repeat. (Student Book, p. 123)

Listen to and extract meaning from audio
Have students find the activity and read the directions. Point to your ear and say *listen*. Play the audio or read the script. Give students visual cues to listen and repeat.

Audioscript 🎧

1. Listen and repeat.
Listen and repeat the words.
breakfast, breakfast
cereal, cereal / eggs, eggs / bacon, bacon / toast, toast
lunch, lunch
sandwich, sandwich / soup, soup / pizza, pizza / hamburger, hamburger / salad, salad
dinner, dinner
chicken, chicken / peas, peas / steak, steak / potatoes, potatoes / rice, rice / beans, beans

❷ Listen and repeat. (Student Book, p. 123)

Use active listening comprehension Have students find the activity and read the directions. Remind students that the preposition *at* is used with time.

Audioscript 🎧

2. Listen and repeat.
Listen to the conversation.
A: *What time do you eat breakfast?*
B: *I eat breakfast at 7:30.*
A: *What do you usually eat for breakfast?*
B: *I usually eat cereal for breakfast.*

Now repeat the conversation.
A: *What time do you eat breakfast?*
B: *I eat breakfast at 7:30.*
A: *What do you usually eat for breakfast?*
B: *I usually eat cereal for breakfast.*

❸ Group work. (Student Book, p. 123)

a. Use graphic organizers to learn new vocabulary Draw a Venn diagram on the board with three overlapping circles. Label the circles *breakfast, lunch,* and *dinner.* List food items in the various categories. Say: *We usually eat cereal or pancakes only at breakfast.* Write these words in the appropriate area on the diagram. Say: *We eat sandwiches for lunch. We eat pizza for lunch or dinner.* Place *sandwiches* and *pizza* in the different sections of the *lunch/dinner* circles. Explain that these are not absolute rules, but

customs. Say: *In Japan, for example, people eat fish and rice for breakfast. It is a typical breakfast in that culture.*

b. Initiate authentic discourse with peers Have students find the activity and read the directions. Point to the pictures in the text and say: *In the morning we eat breakfast. Pancakes, cereal, waffles, French toast, and eggs are some foods we eat for breakfast.* Have students work in small groups to brainstorm about the various meals.

c. Share prior knowledge Ask students to share eating conventions from their own culture. For example: *What do you think is the most important meal of the day? Why? What foods do you eat with your hands? Do you use a fork or knife to eat pizza, a hamburger, or French fries? What time do you eat dinner?* Students are often quite surprised to discover cultural differences for routines that they may have taken for granted. Be sure to remind them to be respectful of cultural diversity.

Culture Note

Explain that in the U.S. dinner is traditionally the largest meal of the day. Dinner is eaten earlier in the U.S. than in some other countries. Dinnertime is usually between 6:00 and 7:00 PM. However, eating habits have been changing rapidly in today's fast-paced life. Breakfast and lunch have become less significant meals and are sometimes skipped or eaten on the run. Even dinnertime, which was once a set family event, is becoming less formal. For example, it is not uncommon for families these days to eat dinner while watching TV.

❹ Pair work. (Student Book, p. 123)

Ask for and give information about yourself Have students find the activity and read the directions. Model the conversation with a volunteer before students work in pairs.

Build Vocabulary

Setting the Table

❺ Listen and repeat. (Student Book, p. 124)

a. Use active listening comprehension to follow directions Bring to class some disposable utensils, plates, bowls, cups and napkins. Show students how tables are set in the U.S. Pass out tableware to the class. Instruct students where to place each item. Say: *Put the plate in the middle of your*

VISIONS BASIC Teacher Resource Book • Copyright © Heinle

desk. *Place your fork on the left side of the plate.* Provide students with terms such as: *left, right, next to, above, beside, under,* etc.

b. Share prior knowledge with peers to foster respect If you have Asian students in class, invite them to demonstrate the use of chopsticks. Have the other students try using chopsticks. You may want to have an international banquet and ask students to each bring a special food from their native country to share with the class.

Audioscript 🎧

5. Listen and repeat.
Listen and repeat the words.
knife, knife / fork, fork / spoon, spoon / plate, plate / bowl, bowl / glass, glass / napkin, napkin / tablecloth, tablecloth

6 Listen. (Student Book, p. 124)

a. Infer meaning Read or play the audio for the poem twice as students read the poem in their books. Call on students to repeat the words: *bite, chin, core, lick, pit, rind, ripe, seed, skin,* and *stem.* Explain that these words all refer to eating a fruit. Ask: *Why do you think all these words compare a poem to a fruit? How do you usually eat a fruit? What is a polite way of eating fruit? What do you think is a difficult fruit to eat politely? Why?*

b. Compare and contrast Ask students: *What are some polite eating habits? What are some impolite eating habits?* Draw a two-column chart on the board and have the class list some polite and impolite habits. Compare and contrast cultural norms, and subtly teach what behavior is considered impolite in the United States. For example, in Asian culture it is polite to burp at the table, but this is highly impolite in the U.S.

Audioscript

6. Listen. Listen to the poem.
How to Eat a Poem by Eve Merriam
Don't be polite.
Bite in.
Pick it up with your fingers and lick the juice
that may run down your chin.
It is ready and ripe now, whenever you are.
You do not need a knife or fork or spoon or
plate or napkin or tablecloth.
For there is no core
or stem

or rind
or pit
or seed
or skin
to throw away.

7 Pair work. (Student Book, p. 124)

a. Use new vocabulary Have students find the activity and read the directions. Model the activity with a volunteer before students work in pairs.

b. Use circumlocution to learn new vocabulary Have students ask you for new vocabulary words by explaining or demonstrating the objects. List new words on the board such as: *cup, saucer, teaspoon, mug, pot, pan,* etc.

Activity Book, p. 73: Breakfast, Lunch, and Dinner

Grammar Focus (Student Book, p. 125)
Count and Noncount Nouns

Review the explanation of count and noncount nouns in the text. Explain that noncount nouns are sometimes items that are too small or numerous to count such as granules of rice, salt, sugar, and flour, or they may be liquids that make it impractical to count by drops. We therefore consider these nouns as a single unit. In order to count these substances, we need to place them in a container and count the containers. For example: *two spoons of sugar, three cups of coffee,* etc. If students grasp the concept of concrete noncount nouns easily, expand upon the definition to include abstract noncount nouns such as names of academic subjects, sports, and words such as *information, homework,* and *love.* Note that some concrete nouns may be considered as noncount in one context and countable in another. Say: *We had some chicken for dinner. Chicken (meat) is a noncount noun. There are many chickens in the barn. Chickens (animals) is a count noun.*

8 Pair work. (Student Book, p. 125)
Demonstrate knowledge of grammatical structures Have students find the activity and read the directions. After students have completed the chart, have several students put their work on the board.

Answer key

8. Pair work.
   Count: hamburger, potato, banana
   Noncount: rice, soup, fruit

Activity Book, p. 74: Count and Noncount Nouns
Activity Book, p. 75: Expressing Quantity

Word Study
Plural Count Nouns: Spelling and Pronunciation

Review the spelling rules for plural count nouns. Remind students of the rules for the *-s* verb ending. Explain that the same rules apply for the plural form. Then point out that nouns that end with a vowel + *y* keep the *y*: *boys, toys, monkeys,* etc.

9 Write. (Student Book, p. 126)

  a. Write with proficient use of orthographic patterns and rules Have students find the activity and read the directions. After students have written the plural forms, have them spell their answers aloud.

  b. Look for patterns in language Have students try to explain the spelling rules for plural count nouns.

Answer key

9. Write.
1. bowl **bowls**
2. class **classes**
3. window **windows**
4. baby **babies**
5. tomato **tomatoes**
6. city **cities**
7. glass **glasses**
8. chair **chairs**

10 Listen and repeat. (Student Book, p. 126)

Look for patterns in language Have students find the activity and read the directions. Introduce to students the three different ways to pronounce the *s* in plural nouns. Draw three columns on the board and label them */s/, /z/,* and */iz/* In the first column, write *forks;* in the second column, write *eggs;* in the third column, write *glasses.* Pronounce each of the words. Say: *There are three different ways to pronounce the -s or -es in plural nouns. It is pronounced /s/ after voiceless sounds p, t, f, k, and th. It is pronounced /z/ after voiced sounds b, d, g, v, m, n, l, r, and vowels. The final -es is pronounced /iz/ after s, z, sh, and ch sounds.* Play the audio for the activity.

Audioscript 🎧
10. Listen and repeat.
Listen to the different ways to pronounce the last sound in plural nouns. Repeat each word.
s like in *books: cups / forks / steaks / tablecloths*
s like in *beds: eggs / oranges / hamburgers / spoons*
es like in *classes: dishes / sandwiches / glasses*

Activity Book, p. 76: Plural Count Nouns: Spelling and Pronunciation

Into the Reading
Use Prior Knowledge: What Foods Are Healthy? (Student Book, p. 127)

Use a semantic map to learn new vocabulary
Make and hand out to students two copies each of the Web Resource Master (p. 138). Encourage students to use a bilingual dictionary or ask for help.

  Build Background: Pyramids (Student Book, p. 127)

Refer to the diagram in the text to explain the meaning of the words *top, middle,* and *bottom.*

Reading and Understanding
Text Structure: Informational Text (Student Book, p. 128)

Understand various text structures Go over the explanation for informational text with the class. Make sure students understand what *topic* means.

Reading 🎧 (Student Book, p. 128)

  a. Pre-teach vocabulary Pre-teach some or all of the new words in the reading: *diet, fats, yogurt, cheese, meat, poultry, nuts, oils, serving, sweets.* Point to the box that introduces *should.* Give examples of its use in the affirmative and negative forms.

  b. Read silently Have students silently read the paragraph. Remind them to think about the questions introduced in the Text Structure section as they read.

  c. Participate in shared reading Play the audio or read the text. Ask a volunteer to read the paragraph aloud. Then call on students to read a few sentences at a time. Ask students to paraphrase parts of the reading.

Beyond the Reading

Reading comprehension. (Student Book, p. 129) Have students work independently to find answers to the questions. Then prompt students to work with partners to think about answers to the more challenging higher order thinking skills questions listed below.

1. What is the main idea of the paragraph?

2. Why should we eat fewer sweets?

3. Why is the food guide made in the shape of a pyramid?

Answer key

1. Should you eat a lot of sweets? **no**
2. Is bread at the top of the pyramid or the bottom of the pyramid? **bottom**
3. How many servings of fruit should you eat each day? **2–4**
4. What foods are very important for a healthy diet? **bread, cereal, rice, and pasta**

Analyze your diet. (Student Book, p. 129)

a. **Use graphic organizers to analyze information** Have students work with a partner.

b. **Compare and contrast information** Bring in several food packages and have students read the content labels. Explain that sodium is salt. Have students compare the sodium, sugar, fat, protein, and calories for the various packaged food items. Ask: *Are you surprised about what is in the food we eat?* You may also want to have students do a comparison of the nutritional content of various fast-food menus. This information should be readily available on the Internet.

Compare your diet to the Food Guide Pyramid. (Student Book, p. 129)

Use charts to compile and analyze data You may want to give students examples of what constitutes a serving of each food group. Bring in various containers as examples. Other helpful words include: *pint, quart, gallon, ounces, pound, half, quarter, slice, piece, dozen,* etc. You may have students create an alternative meal plan for a healthy diet. Have students list foods they would like to eat to better balance their diet.

Activity Book, p. 77: Social Studies: Where Do Foods Come From?
Activity Book, p. 78: Reading Fluency

From Reading to Writing
My Diet (Student Book, p. 130)

a. **Use an organizational strategy for writing** Review the four writing steps: *Plan, Write, Edit,* and *Publish.* Do a shared reading of the steps. Have students paraphrase the instructions in their own words. Have students refer to the chart they created on page 129 for supporting details.

b. **Use a pre-writing activity to prepare to write** Ask students to talk to a partner about their diet. Have them write notes to help them remember important details.

c. **Construct correct sentences** Make and hand out copies of the Paragraph Resource Master (p. 144). Remind students to use count and noncount nouns in their details. Students may use a bilingual dictionary for new words and to help check spelling.

d. **Edit writing toward standard grammar** Have students check their work with the Editing Checklist and ask their partner to use the Peer Editing Checklist.

e. **Publish work for presentation** Have students explain to their partners the changes that they made. Students can read their paragraphs to the class. Display students' work.

Activity Book, p. 79: Arranging Phrases
Activity Book, p. 80: Food and Nutrition

Review
Vocabulary (Student Book, p. 132)

Spell words aloud Do a Spelling Bee with your class, using the vocabulary words on this page. For more challenge, you can include other words they have learned in this chapter. Divide the class into two teams, and have each team line up on opposite sides of the room. Say the word, and have the student spell it aloud. If it is correct, the team gets a point. The student who just answered goes to the back of the team line.

Assess

Vocabulary (Student Book, p. 133)

1. I eat _____ at 7:30 AM.
   a. lunch   c. morning
   b. breakfast   d. dinner
2. _____ is his favorite meat.
   a. Milk   **c. Chicken**
   b. Rice   d. Soup
3. We cut steak with a _____.
   a. fork   **c. knife**
   b. spoon   d. napkin

Grammar (Student Book, p. 133)

1. We want _____.
   a. a rice   b. two rices   **c. rice**
2. Bananas are my favorite _____.
   a. fruit   b. fruits   c. a fruit
3. He gives the children _____.
   a. milks   **b. milk**   c. three milks

Word Study (Student Book, p. 133)

1. spoon   **a. spoons**   b. spoonz   c. spoones
2. potato   a. potatos   **b. potatoes**   c. potatohs
3. baby   a. babys   **b. babies**   c. babeis

Activity Book: Ch. 6 Mini-Reader

Projects

Project 1: Make a Food Pyramid Poster (Student Book, p. 134)

a. Paraphrase Have volunteers read the steps aloud. Make sure students understand the directions. Ask students to paraphrase what they have to do.

b. Use illustrations to convey a message Provide old magazines, newspapers, or supermarket flyers for students to use.

Project 2: Make a Class Recipe Book. (Student Book, p. 135)

a. Use graphic organizers to prepare to write Brainstorm with students dishes and recipes they could write about. Encourage them to select a simple recipe. Make and hand out copies of the Step-by-Step Resource Master (p. 146).

b. Ask for information Assign Steps 1–3 as homework so that students can gather information for their recipes. Help students with step 4. Allow students to take notes in their native language.

c. Share responsibilities to foster respect for others In many cultures children, especially boys, are discouraged from participating in food preparation activities. Pay close attention to the reaction of students and help establish a positive atmosphere about the activity. You may want to explain that in the United States both boys and girls participate from an early age in various household activities. Explain that this kind of behavior is encouraged because it promotes both cooperation and self-reliance.

d. Give directions Provide helpful verbs such as: *chop, cut, dice, peel, slice, boil, fry,* etc.

e. Produce visuals to enhance presentation Have students figure out how to assemble the recipe book, who will do the cover, and how to make copies.

f. Make connections across content areas Challenge students to practice their math skills by taking a recipe and modifying it for double or half the original quantity.

Viewing Activity

Assess how medium and presentation contribute to a message Bring to class magazines containing advertisements for foods. Have students cut out different food ads. Spread out all the clippings on a table, and talk about what foods are shown and if they are healthy foods. Talk about how advertising makes foods look appealing.

Chapter 7 Money

Materials

Student Book: pp. 136–149
Activity Book: pp. 81–88; Mini-Reader 7
Audio: Chapter 7
Student CD-ROM: Chapter 7
Teacher Resource Book:
    Lesson Plan: pp. 87–94
    Reading Fluency: p. 131
    Resource Masters: Web, p. 138; Paragraph, p. 144
Assessment Program: pp. 51–54
Transparencies

Themes

Money and Prices
Comparative Adjectives
The Prefix *re-*
Myths
Opinion Paragraph
Math

Objectives

Use contrastive analysis
Use accessible language to acquire new vocabulary
Make connections across content areas

Listening

Listen to and extract meaning from audio recording
Infer meaning

Speaking

Ask for and give information
Share prior knowledge with peers
Initiate authentic discourse with peers
Express feelings and opinions

Reading

Read authentic literature
Retell or role-play the order of events
Develop basic sight vocabulary

Writing

Use graphic organizers as a pre-writing tool
Construct correct sentences using comparative adjectives
Edit writing toward standard grammar

Viewing and Representing

Use visual cues to derive meaning
Produce visuals to aid communication
Assess how medium and presentation contribute to a message

Listen, Speak, Interact
Money and Prices

1 Listen and repeat. (Student Book, p. 137)

a. Listen to and extract meaning from audio Have students find the activity and read the directions. Play the audio or read the script. Give students visual cues to listen and repeat.

b. Further information Mention to students that some less commonly used coins in circulation are the half-dollar and the silver dollar. Other bills in circulation are the $50 and $100 bills.

c. Proverbs and sayings You may want to teach a few idioms and expressions related to money such as: *Money doesn't grow on trees; to have money to burn; Penny for your thoughts; Flip a coin - heads or tails.*

Audioscript 🎧
1. Listen and repeat.
Listen and repeat the words and phrases.
coins, coins

> *a penny, a penny / one cent, one cent*
> *a nickel, a nickel / five cents, five cents*
> *a dime, a dime / ten cents, ten cents*
> *a quarter, a quarter / twenty-five cents,*
> *twenty-five cents*

> *bills, bills*

> *a dollar bill, a dollar bill / one dollar, one*
> *dollar*
> *a ten dollar bill, a ten dollar bill / ten dollars,*
> *ten dollars*
> *a five dollar bill, a five dollar bill / five*
> *dollars, five dollars*
> *a twenty dollar bill. a twenty dollar bill /*
> *twenty dollars, twenty dollars*

Culture Note
Bank notes in most countries vary in size and color to help differentiate between denominations. This makes U.S. currency quite challenging for people from other countries. Point out that currently all U.S. bills are the same size and the same color. Therefore, students need to pay close attention to the numeric values in the corner of each bill or to the portraits. You may want to discuss the portraits of the famous American figures on each bill. It may also be worthwhile to discuss recent changes in the look of bank notes. For example, the portraits on newer bills have been enlarged, and the Treasury will be adding background colors to $20, $50, and $100 bills. That means that students may come across both old and new versions of bills.

2 Pair work. (Student Book, p. 137)

a. Use math skills Have students find the activity and read the directions. After students have discussed the answers in pairs, have students give the answers orally.

b. Initiate authentic discourse You may want to bring in play money and have students practice counting money and making change.

c. Share prior knowledge with peers Invite students to bring currency from other countries to show the class. You may want to bring in some of the U.S. state quarters currently being minted and discuss the symbols chosen for each state.

Answer key
2. Pair work.
1. (T-shirt for $5.50)
   b. one $5 bill, one quarter, two dimes, one nickel
2. (pants for $20.75)
   d. two $10 bills, three quarters
3. (shoes for $45.00)
   a. two $20 bills, one $5
4. (socks for $2.15)
   c. two $1 bills, one dime, one nickel

3 Listen and repeat. (Student Book, p. 137)

a. Listen to and extract meaning from audio Have students find the activity and read the directions. Play the audio or read the script.

b. Words and expressions to know Explain the expression *How much...?* Point out that the word *much* refers to money. Explain that the noun *money* as a counting unit is considered to be a noncount noun even though the coins and bills are individually countable. Also point out that *pants, shoes,* and *socks* are plural and take the plural form, *are: How much are the pants?*

Audioscript 🎧
3. Listen and repeat.
Listen to the conversations. Repeat the conversations.
1. **A:** *How much is the T-shirt?*
   B: *The T-shirt is $5.50*
2. **A:** *How much are the pants?*
   B: *The pants are $20.75*
3. **A:** *How much are the shoes?*
   B: *The shoes are $45.00*

4. **A:** *How much are the socks?*
   B: *The socks are $2.15.*

Now repeat the conversations.
1. **A:** *How much is the T-shirt?*
   B: *The T-shirt is $5.50.*
2. **A:** *How much are the pants?*
   B: *The pants are $20.75.*
3. **A:** *How much are the shoes?*
   B: *The shoes are $45.00.*
4. **A:** *How much are the socks?*
   B: *The socks are $2.15.*

④ **Listen.** (Student Book, p. 137)

Listen for information Have students find the activity and read the directions. Then have them look at the pictures of the objects and their price tags. Explain to students how prices are represented with decimal points as shown on the item 1 price tag. In some countries a comma is used in place of a period to mark a decimal. Teach the dollar sign ($) as well as the sign for cents (¢). Have students listen for the price of each object, and write the price on the right price tag.

Audioscript 🎧
4. **Listen.**
   What prices do you hear?
   1. *The cup is $1.15. / The cup is $1.15.*
   2. *The dish is $1.50. / The dish is $1.50.*
   3. *The bowl is $1.75. / The bowl is $1.75.*
   4. *The napkins are $3.99. / The napkins are $3.99.*
   5. *The tablecloth is $12.50. / The tablecloth is $12.50.*

Build Vocabulary
How Do You Pay for It?

⑤ **Listen and repeat.** (Student Book, p. 138)

a. Use visual cues to learn new vocabulary Have students find the activity and read the directions. Then have them look at the various ways of paying for a purchase such as cash, credit card, check, and ATM card. Play the audio or read the script.

b. Use accessible language to learn new words and expressions Write additional vocabulary for the class such as: *bargain, bucks, discount, sale, sales tax, store manager,* etc. Introduce the following idiomatic expressions that relate to money or shopping: *on sale, window shopping, shopping around, stock up, rain check,* etc.

Audioscript 🎧
5. **Listen and repeat.**
   Listen and repeat the words.
   customer, customer / salesperson, salesperson / price, price / cash, cash / credit card, credit card / check, check / ATM card, ATM card

⑥ **Listen and repeat.** (Student Book, p. 138)

a. Listen to and extract meaning from audio Have students find the activity and read the directions. Play the audio or read the script and have students listen to the conversation and repeat it.

b. Learn new phrases Point out the vocabulary in the *Ways to pay* box. Explain that the prepositions *with* and *by* are used when saying how something is being paid for. Also discuss the three paying options mentioned in the box.

Audioscript 🎧
6. **Listen and repeat.** Listen to the conversation.
   A: *How do you pay for CDs?*
   B: *I pay with a check. How about you?*
   A: *I pay with cash.*

Now repeat the conversation.
   A: *How do you pay for CDs?*
   B: *I pay with a check. How about you?*
   A: *I pay with cash.*

⑦ **Pair work.** (Student Book, p. 138)

Initiate authentic discourse with peers Have students find the activity and read the directions. As students practice in pairs, circulate and help as needed.

Culture Note
Credit card use is not as prevalent in many other countries. Explain to students how credit cards work. In simple terms, when a purchase is made with a credit card, the credit card company pays the store. Then once a month the credit card company sends you a bill. If you don't pay the full amount, the credit card company will charge you interest on the purchase. Bring to class sample credit card applications.

89

Culture Note

Students could benefit from learning various concepts associated with making purchases in the United States. For example you may want to explain about return policies, layaway, hold, sales, coupons, etc. You may also want to touch upon the sensitive but important topic of store security and shoplifting and its legal consequences. Also discuss other venues for shopping other than stores such as flea markets, farmers' markets, garage sales, auctions, television shopping channels, telemarketing, mail order, online shopping, etc.

Activity Book, p. 81: Dollars and Cents

Grammar Focus
Comparative Adjectives

Read over the explanation about comparative adjectives with the class. Point out the spelling rules associated with the *-er* ending. Also discuss the meaning of the words *cheap* and *expensive* in the Words to Know box. Practice the pronunciation of the vowel sound in the word *cheap,* particularly with Spanish speakers.

⑧ Choose. (Student Book, p. 139)

Demonstrate knowledge of comparative adjectives Do the activity orally, and have students tell how they decided on the answer.

Answer key
8. Choose.

1. tall	**a. taller**	b. more tall
2. thin	a. thiner	**b. thinner**
3. happy	**a. happier**	b. happyer
4. important	**a. more important**	b. importanter

⑨ Compare. (Student Book, p. 139)

Initiate authentic discourse Have students find the activity and read the directions. After working in pairs, have volunteers read their answers aloud. Then invite students to compare the prices of other common objects.

Answer key
9. Pair work.
1. The milk is **cheaper** than the juice.
2. The juice is **more expensive** than the milk.
3. The pants are **more expensive** than the shirt.
4. The shirt is **cheaper** than the pants.

Activity Book, p. 82: Comparative Adjectives
Activity Book, p. 83: More About Comparisons

Word Study
The Prefix *re-*

Have a volunteer read the explanation about the prefix *re-*. Point to the Strategy box and review the information with the class. Explain to students that many words in English are formed by adding prefixes to root words. You may want to explain that many such words have either a Latin or Greek origin. You may want to have students search in the dictionary for other words with the *re-* prefix such as: *reheat, rename, renumber, reopen, reorder, resell, reunite, reword.* You may also want to introduce other common prefixes such as: *dis-, non-, over-, pre-,* and *un-.*

Language Interference and Transfer

Spanish speakers can often rely on similar root words to guess the meaning of many English words. Encourage students to look for such similarities.

⑩ Write a definition. (Student Book, p. 140)
   a. Recognize word roots and affixes Have students find the activity and read the directions. Then have them copy the list and do the activity. Have students use an English-only dictionary to check their work.

Answer key
10. Write a definition.

1. reread: **read again**	3. review: **view again**
2. retell: **tell again**	4. rewrite: **write again**

⑪ Unscramble. (Student Book, p. 140)
   a. Use visual cues to derive meaning Have students find the activity and read the directions. Do the activity as a class, having students spell out each word.
   b. Compare and contrast meanings Students often have difficulty distinguishing between the words *borrow* and *lend*. Make the contrast explicit through demonstrations and even an oral drill activity. You may want to compare these two words with the words *give* and *take*.

Answer key

11. Unscramble.

1. perya **repay**
2. pnrteai **repaint**
3. friell **refill**

Activity Book, p. 84: Prefix: *re-*

Into the Reading (Student Book, p. 141)

Strategy: Preview Questions

Develop new learning strategies Point to the Strategy box and review the information with the class. Then have students look at the questions in Beyond the Reading (p. 143) to help them identify what they should look for in the reading.

Use Prior Knowledge: What Do You Wish For? (Student Book, p. 141)

Use a graphic organizer Make and hand out copies of the Web Resource Master (p. 138). Brainstorm a list of possible wishes with students. Then have students fill in their webs. You may have students share their wishes in small groups.

Build Background: Gold (Student Book, p. 141)

a. Infer meaning by making associations Have students look at the pictures to help them understand the definition for gold. Confirm that students understand the words *gold* and *valuable*. Ask: *Is gold valuable? What else is valuable?*

b. Make connections across content areas You may want to make a connection to social studies by briefly discussing the California Gold Rush and how the discovery of gold influenced the state's history. In this discussion you may want to make reference to fool's gold or otherwise allude to illusions and unfulfilled dreams.

Reading and Understanding

Text Structure: Myth

a. Develop understanding of literary structures Have a student read the description of a myth. Explain to the class that there are four types of literature based on the art of storytelling, or oral tradition. They are: myths, folktales, fables, and legends. Like a fable, a myth is a story that tries to explain or teach about life in a supernatural way. You may want to explain that the word *myth* itself comes from the Greek word *mythos,* which originally meant "speech" but later came to mean "fable" or "legend."

b. Learn new literary terminology Point to the box that defines *character.* Remind students that in myths some characters will have special powers to help overcome challenges.

Reading 🎧 (Student Book, p. 142)

a. Pre-teach vocabulary You may want to pre-teach some or all of the potentially new vocabulary in the reading: *powers, thankful, golden, turn, hungry, piece of, starve, river, tears, wash away, relieved.*

b. Read authentic literature Play the audio or read the selection. Then do it as a choral reading with the class. Next, do a chain reading, stopping after each line to answer any questions. You may want to talk a bit about the origin of western drama from Greek mythology. Explain that myths were acted out on stage to teach important civic and religious lessons. Then ask three volunteers to pantomime the story of "King Midas and the Golden Touch" as you narrate it.

d. Share prior knowledge with peers Invite students to give examples of myths from their culture. You may want to make a chart of the stories students share to show the elements they have in common.

Beyond the Reading

Reading Comprehension. (Student Book, p. 143)

a. Derive meaning from text Give students time to silently read and answer the questions.

b. Infer meaning Help students discuss the difference between wants and needs. Introduce the term *greed* to the class. Encourage students to express their personal opinions and values about these concepts.

Answer key

1. Does Midas wish for the golden touch? **yes**
2. Does Midas turn a chair or a bed to gold? **a chair**
3. What does Midas turn to gold? **a chair, table, food, and his daughter**
4. Why doesn't he want the golden touch at the end of the fable? **Because it was not practical; also, some things are more valuable than gold.**

Make a story timeline. (Student Book, p. 143)

Put events in proper sequence Have a volunteer read the events. Then orally have students discuss the events and determine the correct order.

Answer key

Make a story timeline.

 2 The man tells Midas to make a wish.

 6 Midas washes away the golden touch with his tears.

 3 Midas wishes for the golden touch.

 5 Midas turns food and his daughter to gold. He is not happy.

 1 Midas helps a man with special powers.

 4 Midas turns objects to gold. He is happy.

Retell the story. (Student Book, p. 143)

a. **Express ideas in a new way** Have students work with a partner and use the story map to tell the events in the story. Students should tell the story in as much detail as they can. Explain that in the oral tradition, a storyteller, or narrator, often adds details to a story. Encourage students to add their own details as they retell the story without changing the basic premise.

b. **Produce communication using appropriate media** Have students act out the story of "King Midas and the Golden Touch" in groups of three students. One student should play each character: King Midas, the man with special powers, and King Midas's daughter. You may want to have students create props, masks, or puppets to use in their performance. Have groups practice their play and prepare to perform it for the class.

Activity Book, p. 85: Social Studies: The European Union and the Euro
Activity Book, p. 86: Reading Fluency

From Reading to Writing

Is Money Important? (Student Book, pp. 144-145)

a. Have volunteers read the explanation and sample paragraph aloud. Point out the box of phrases for expressing opinions. Help students prepare to write an opinion paragraph about money by discussing the question, *Do you think money is important?* Hand out copies of the Paragraph Resource Master (p. 144).

b. **Use a graphic organizer for pre-writing** Review the four writing steps: *Plan, Write, Edit,* and *Publish.* After students have done their charts, have volunteers write their ideas in a chart on the board.

c. **Construct correct sentences** Have several students write their topic sentences on the board. Have them explain which details they will use in their supporting sentences. Encourage students to use a bilingual dictionary.

d. **Edit writing toward standard grammar** Remind students to use the Editing Checklist. Then have them ask a partner to review their writing with the Peer Editing Checklist.

e. **Prepare to publish a piece of writing** After students have corrected their mistakes, have them show their paragraph to their partner and explain changes they made. Ask students to read their paragraphs to the class.

Activity Book, p. 87: Clauses

Review

Vocabulary (Student Book, p. 146)

Have students find as many vocabulary words as they can in the word puzzle. Explain to students that words may be found horizontally from left to right or vertically from top to bottom.

e	b	a	q	d	h	h	h	x	r	q	u	t	e	r
h	n	i	t	i	h	c	h	e	c	k	w	y	s	s
a	w	u	e	m	h	h	h	y	o	w	d	c	p	d
r	q	r	n	e	c	e	e	a	e	y	i	r	e	o
a	u	w	p	j	c	a	s	h	r	e	t	e	l	l
c	a	e	y	d	k	p	r	i	c	e	q	d	m	l
t	r	n	a	v	p	n	e	d	u	x	u	i	t	a
e	t	e	n	e	h	e	c	i	v	p	s	t	u	r
r	e	f	i	l	l	t	n	p	e	e	h	c	e	q
h	r	e	c	h	e	n	s	n	x	n	i	a	p	r
e	z	i	k	t	w	e	n	t	y	s	o	r	i	k
s	o	m	e	d	f	e	r	e	w	i	f	d	b	w
h	a	c	l	h	q	w	e	f	i	v	e	n	i	a
e	h	k	h	c	u	s	t	o	m	e	r	s	e	r
s	a	l	e	s	p	e	r	s	o	n	i	k	l	t

Answer key

Horizontal: twenty, customer, cash, check, price, five

Vertical: quarter, ten, nickel, dime, cheap, expensive, credit card, dollar

Expressions (Student Book, p. 146)

Bring in several prints of modern art to display in the class. Invite students to analyze the art and give their opinions using the expressions: *I think..., I believe..., I feel that..., In my opinion...*

Assess

Vocabulary (Student Book, p. 147)

1. We get cash from the _____.
   - a. store
   - **c. ATM machine**
   - b. salesperson
   - d. police officer

2. The _____ of the shirt is $15.99.
   - a. money
   - c. check
   - b. cash
   - **d. price**

3. Three _____ is $.75.
   - a. a quarter
   - **c. quarters**
   - b. five dollars
   - d. a dime

Grammar (Student Book, p. 147)

1. I am _____ than my sister.
   - a. short
   - **c. shorter**
   - b. more short
   - d. shortter

2. The kitchen is _____ than the living room.
   - a. more big
   - c. biger
   - b. more bigger
   - **d. bigger**

3. The sofa is _____ than the table.
   - a. expensiver
   - c. expensive
   - **b. more expensive**
   - d. very expensive

Word Study (Student Book, p. 147)

1. In the word *review,* what is the prefix?
   - a. review
   - **b. re**
   - c. view
   - d. ew

2. In the word *review,* what is the root word?
   - a. re
   - b. review
   - **c. view**
   - d. noun

Activity Book: Ch. 7 Mini-Reader

Projects

Project 1: Make a Menu (Student Book, p. 148)

Have students work in small groups to make a restaurant menu. First go over the steps and make sure students understand the directions. Bring in sample menus from different ethnic restaurants. The groups should brainstorm a list of foods for their menu, making sure to include soups, salads, desserts, beverages, and a variety of dishes, and decide on the price of each item. When students have finished the menus, you can have them role-play ordering at different restaurants.

Project 2: Create a Store (Student Book, p. 149)

Start by having volunteers read the steps aloud. Make sure students understand the instructions. Talk about different types of stores. Then have students work in small groups to create a store. Have students "open their stores" and take roles as customers and salespeople.

Viewing Activity

Assess how medium and presentation contribute to a message Cut out and bring to class advertisements for different credit card companies. Discuss the advertisements. Talk about the images used and the information given. Compare how the ads are similar or different. Have students select the most effective ad.

Chapter 8 Jobs

Materials

Student Book: pp. 150–163
Activity Book: pp. 89–96; Mini-Reader 8
Audio: Chapter 8
Student CD-ROM: Chapter 8
Teacher Resource Book:
>   Lesson Plan, pp. 95–102
>   Reading Fluency, p. 132
>   Resource Masters: Step-by-Step Instructions, p. 146; Friendly letter, p. 147
>   Assessment Program: pp. 55–58

Transparencies

Themes

Jobs
Object Pronouns

The Suffix -er
Reading/Writing "How-to" Narration

Learning Strategies

Use prior knowledge
Use learning strategies such as circumlocution
Make connections across content areas

Listening

Use active listening comprehension to follow directions
Understand basic expressions and vocabulary
Listen to and extract meaning from audio recording
Infer meaning from actions and visual context

Speaking

Identify people, places, and basic concepts such as occupations
Initiate authentic discourse with peers
Express ideas and feelings such as gratitude, needs, and opinions
Arrange phrases, clauses, and sentences into correct and meaningful patterns

Reading

Read authentic text
Participate in shared reading of a "How-to" Narration
Develop basic sight vocabulary
Use a combination of skills to decode words such as identification of root words and suffixes
Read silently with increasing ease for longer periods

Writing

Use graphic organizers as pre-writing activity
Edit writing toward standard grammar
Demonstrate knowledge of object pronouns
Construct correct sentences

Viewing and Representing

Tell important events and ideas gleaned from video segments
Distinguish the purpose of various media forms
Produce visual for other kinds of communication
Interpret and evaluate how artists convey meaning

Listen, Speak, Interact
What's the Job?

1 **Listen and repeat.** (Student Book, p. 151)

Listen to and extract meaning from audio
Have students find the activity and read the directions. Point to your ear and say *listen.* Then say: *cashier.* Now say: *Repeat the word—cashier.* Play the audio or read the script. Give students visual cues to listen and repeat.

Audioscript
1. Listen and repeat.

Listen and repeat the words and sentences.
cashier, cashier
A cashier takes money and gives change.
A cashier takes money and gives change.
doctor, doctor
A doctor takes care of sick people.
A doctor takes care of sick people.
firefighter, firefighter
A firefighter puts out fires.
A firefighter puts out fires.
hairstylist, hairstylist
A hairstylist cuts hair.
A hairstylist cuts hair.
child-care worker, child-care worker
A child-care worker takes care of children.
A child-care worker takes care of children.
chef, chef
A chef prepares food.
A chef prepares food.

2 **Listen and identify.** (Student Book, p. 151)

Use active listening comprehension
Have students find the activity and read the directions. Ask students to listen to the dialogues. Then have them identify each person's job. Remind students that either men or women can do any of these jobs.

Audioscript
2. Listen and identify.

What job do you hear?
1. OK. The shirt is $16.00 and the pants are $25.00. That will be $41.00. Are you paying with cash or credit card?
2. Do you want to keep your hair long or cut it short? I think it would look very nice short. And how about color? Do you want to keep it brown? Or should we try blond this time?
3. She is still such a small baby. She sleeps most of the day. She usually cries when she's hungry. I feed her every two or three hours.
4. This is my special dish. I always make the pasta with tomato sauce, meat, and three different kinds of cheese. Then I put it in the oven for 20 minutes. It's delicious!
5. So, you are very tired and have a cough? Please open your mouth wide. I want to look at your throat. Aha. Your throat is very red. It looks like you have a cold. You should get a lot of sleep, take two aspirin, and call me if you still feel sick in a few days.

3 **Pair work.** (Student Book, p. 151)

a. **Identify people** Have students find the activity and read the directions. Model the activity, acting out several jobs for the class.

b. **Use circumlocution to learn new vocabulary** Have students ask for names of other occupations by explaining what the person does. You may want to introduce a range of other occupations such as: *tailor, gardener, accountant, lawyer, engineer,* etc.

4 **Group work** (Student Book, p. 151)

Share prior knowledge Have students find the activity and read the directions. Ask students to list some traditional jobs for men (soldier, firefighter, president, mechanic, etc.). Ask: *What are some traditional jobs for women?* (teacher, nurse, stewardess, maid, etc.) Ask: *How do you feel about a person of a different gender performing these jobs? Are there any jobs today that you think only men should do? Are there any you think only a woman should do? Why?* Encourage students to express their opinions openly, and remind students to respect differences in opinions.

Culture Note
Although traditionally some jobs were filled only by men or women, today many of those gender stereotypes have been broken. Explain that a stereotype is a false or incorrect over-generalization. For example, it is a stereotype that all nurses are women. It is not unusual to find male nurses or female firefighters today. Our language has changed to reflect this progress. For example, we now use terms such as *police officer* instead of *policeman, firefighter* instead of *fireman, mail carrier* instead of *mailman,* and *flight attendant* instead of *stewardess.* While work opportunities have broadened significantly, at times men and women still encounter prejudice and discrimination.

Build Vocabulary
Job Tools and Objects

⑤ **Listen.** (Student Book, p. 152)

a. Brainstorm Have students find the activity and read the directions. Have students close their books. Play the audio or read the poem. Call on students to name the jobs they remember; write them on the board. Then have students open their books again and silently read the poem. Point out the expression: *I'd like to be.* Explain that the verb *like* with the infinitive *to be* means you want to have a kind of job. Do a Round Robin asking students: *What would you like to be?* List a variety of jobs on the board or let students use a bilingual dictionary. Explain the differences between part-time, full-time, temporary, and permanent jobs.

b. Compare and contrast Have students work in groups of four or five. Have each student choose one of the jobs mentioned in the poem. Ask students to draw a two-column chart on a piece of paper. Have them list the pros and cons of the job. Say: *Pro means "what is good about something" and con means "what is bad" about something.* Then have students share their lists with the group. Do students agree with all the points on the lists? Remind them that one person's likes may be another person's dislikes.

c. Express feelings and opinions Have students work independently to list their personal likes and dislikes on a two-column chart. For example: *I like to fix things. I don't like to sit at a desk. I like to meet new people. I don't like to do the same thing all day.* Then have students exchange lists with a classmate. Have students review their partner's list and recommend some good jobs based on the person's likes and dislikes. Model and write on the board some possible expressions such as: *I think you'd like to be a.../ In my opinion, you should be a .../ I think you would be a good....*

d. Role Play As an expansion activity you may want to have students conduct a mock job interview. You may want to copy a real application from a local business and have students complete the application. Then discuss some questions commonly asked at job interviews such as: *Why do you think you would be good for this job? What skills do you have for this job?* etc. Mention to students that speaking a second language is often a valuable skill for many jobs. Have one student be the recruiter and one the applicant. Interviews can be video taped, and the class can vote on the person they think seems best qualified for the job.

Audioscript 🎧

5. Listen.
Listen to the poem.

Choices
By Jill Korey O'Sullivan

There are so many things I'd like to do.
I'm considering some jobs. Here are a few:

I'd like to be an astronaut and wear a special suit.

I'd like to be a musician. Perhaps I'll play the flute.

Maybe I'll be a waiter and serve food on a tray.

Maybe I'll be an artist and work with paint or clay.

I'd like to be a mechanic and fix cars with a wrench.

Or perhaps I'll teach English. Or maybe even French.

I could be a carpenter and use a hammer and nails.

Or a grocery store clerk who weighs things on scales.

Hey, I know what I should be. I know the perfect job for me:

A job that's interesting every day—president of the USA!

Culture Note

Explain to students that in the United States most jobs are open to both all legal residents. However, some sensitive jobs in the government and private industry require workers to be U.S. citizens. Of course, immigrants who become naturalized citizens are then able to work in most of these positions. In fact, positions as high as congressmen and congresswomen can be held by naturalized citizens. The only government position that requires a person to be born a U.S. citizen is the job of the president.

6 **Categorize.** (Student Book, p. 152)

a. Use organizational charts Have students find the activity and read the directions. Have students reread the poem silently. Then have them copy and fill in the chart.

b. Infer meaning from lyrics For added cultural interest, you may want to play for the class some folk or pop songs about work. You can make cloze activities with the lyrics or have students learn parts or all of a song. Some songs to consider include: "Get a Job," "Nine to Five," "Sixteen Tons," "Working in a Coal Mine," etc.

c. Make connections across content areas This may be a good opportunity to discuss the contributions of immigrants and African-Americans in the building of this nation. You may want to bring in pictures of African-American, Asian, and Irish railroad workers, farmers, miners, and modern entrepreneurs. In simple terms, discuss the hopes, difficulties, and achievements of immigrants whose work contributions helped build American history.

Activity Book, p. 89: Jobs and Tools

Grammar Focus

Object Pronouns (Student Book, p. 153)

Review the explanation of object pronouns in the text. Make large flash cards for each of the object pronouns. Write sample sentences on the board and use the flash cards to demonstrate substitution of direct and indirect objects with object pronouns. Practice this concept with some oral drill substitution activities. For example: *I gave the pencil to Maria. I gave it to her.*

7 **Complete the sentence.** (Student Book, p. 153)

Demonstrate knowledge of grammar Have students find the activity and read the directions. Do the activity orally before having students write out the sentences.

Answer key

7. Complete the sentence.

1. She is my best friend. I really like **her.**
2. My parents cook every night. Sometimes I help **them.**
3. John and I are in the same class. He usually sits next to **me.**
4. This is my favorite TV program. I watch **it** every week.
5. My grandfather lives in Florida. I visit **him** every summer.

Activity Book, p. 90: Object Pronouns

Activity Book, p. 91: More Practice with Object Pronouns

Word Study

The Suffix -er (Student Book, p. 154)

Decode words using roots and suffixes Have students look over the Strategy box and the explanation of a suffix. Remind students of root words and how adding a prefix changes the meaning. Explain that a suffix often changes a word's grammatical function. For example, the -er suffix changes a verb such as *paint* to the noun *painter,* a person who paints. You may want to introduce other words with the -er suffix such as: *construction worker, housekeeper, reporter, homemaker, bank teller, waiter, mail carrier, gardener.* You may also want to introduce other suffixes that have the meaning "someone who does something," such as: *-ist (florist, manicurist, dentist, pianist, receptionist, journalist, scientist); -or (doctor, actor, editor, director, author, tailor, sailor, janitor, mayor); -ess (waitress, seamstress, actress); -ian (librarian, politician),* etc. Other common suffixes you may want to teach include: *-ly, -ion / -tion / -ation / -tition, -ible / -able, -ness, -ity / -ty, -ment, -ful,* and *-less.*

8 **Write a definition.** (Student Book, p. 154)

Decode words using roots and suffixes Have students find the activity and read the directions. Go over the items orally before students write their answers. Students can look in a dictionary if necessary. Encourage them to note other words with the same root in the dictionary.

Answer key

8. Write a definition.
1. painter: **someone who paints**
2. writer: **someone who writes**
3. gardener: **someone who gardens**
4. manager: **someone who manages**

9 **Match** (Student Book, p. 154)

Use root *re-* to make new words Have students find the activity and read the directions. Go over the items orally and have students spell out their answers.

Answer key

9. Match.
1. **singer**
2. **teacher**
3. **painter**
4. **dancer**

Activity Book, p. 92: The Suffix -er

Into the Reading

Use Prior Knowledge: How Do You Order Fast Food? (Student Book, p. 155)

Learn new vocabulary Elicit from students useful vocabulary and write it on the board. Have them include some or all of this vocabulary in their lists. Encourage students to use a bilingual dictionary or ask for help.

Build Background: Cash Registers (Student Book, p. 155)

Have a volunteer read the explanation. Ask if any of the students know how to use a cash register. Refer to the pictures of cash registers in the text and explain (or have a student explain) the function of a cash register and how it operates.

Reading and Understanding

Text Structure: "How-To" Narration (Student Book, p. 156)

Understand various text structures Go over the explanation of a "how-to" narration with the class. Make sure students understand what the word *sequence* means. Distinguish between the word *order* as in the context of a sequence and *order* as in the context of placing one's request. Explain to students that these two words are homonyms: *They are words that sound the same, but mean different things.*

Reading (Student Book, p. 156)

How to Take a Fast-Food Order

a. **Preteach vocabulary** Pre-teach some or all of the new words in the reading: *behind, counter, press, buttons, cost, coworkers.*

b. **Read silently** Have students silently read the paragraph. Ask that they think about this question as they read: *What are the different things Alex does at work?*

c. **Participate in shared reading** Play the audio or read the text aloud. Ask a volunteer to read the paragraph aloud. Then call on students to read a few sentences at a time. Ask students to paraphrase the portion that they read.

Beyond the Reading

Reading comprehension (Student Book, p. 157)

Higher Order Thinking Skills Questions

Have students work independently to find answers to these questions in the reading. Then prompt students to work with partners to think about answers to the more challenging questions below.

1. What responsibilities does Alex have at work? (be polite, take money and give correct change, speak with customers)

2. What are some advantages and disadvantages of Alex's job? (advantages: busy, meet people, not difficult, free food; disadvantages: standing a long time, too busy, low pay)

3. What are three useful skills that Alex is learning at this job? (how to use a cash register, how to deal with customers, and how to work with others)

Answer key

1. Does Alex work in a fast-food restaurant? **yes**

2. Does Alex cook or take orders at the counter? **He takes orders.**

3. Who brings the food to the counter? **coworkers**

4. How does Alex feel about his job? **He likes it.**

Illustrate the order of events. (Student Book, p. 157)

Create a storyboard to visually illustrate the order of events Have a volunteer read the instructions. Have students reread the article and think about the order of events. Talk about which steps would be good to illustrate. Remind students to draw the pictures from left to right as they would if they were writing a description. For more challenge, students can write sentence captions under each picture. For example: *First, the customer says what he wants.*

Retell the sequence of events (Student Book, p. 157)

Recall information Have students work with a partner to retell the sequence of events for taking a fast-food order. Encourage students to use their own words and not look at the text.

Act out the sequence of events (Student Book, p. 157)

Role-play the order of events Have students work with a partner to role-play a customer and a fast-food worker. Offer students some possible expressions such as: *May I take your order? How can I serve you today? What would you like today? Would you like anything else? Your total is…That'll be…Have a nice day. Please come back soon.*

Activity Book, p. 93: Science: How Much Do You Sleep?

Activity Book, p. 94: Reading Fluency

From Reading to Writing

A "How-To" Paragraph (Student Book, pp. 158–159)

a. **Use an organizational strategy for writing** Review the four writing steps: *Plan, Write, Edit,* and *Publish.*

b. **Tell important events and ideas viewed in video segments** Show the class some video segments from TV programs such as: cooking shows, art and craft shows, home improvement and gardening programs, etc. Pause and rewind segments and discuss with the class how the information is being presented. For example, Ask: *Does the speaker repeat the steps? How are visual aids used? Are the demonstrations clear? Does the speaker talk slowly and clearly? Is the presentation interesting?* Have students think about these questions as they prepare to write their paragraphs.

c. **Use a pre-writing activity to prepare to write** Ask students to first perform the activity they will write about in front of a partner. Have the partner take notes to help remind the student of all the steps. Then have students draw a storyboard about their activity and include a caption for each step.

d. **Construct correct sentences** Remind students to use the sequence words to help the flow of ideas from one sentence to the next. Encourage students to also use a bilingual dictionary.

e. **Edit writing toward standard grammar** Have students check their work with the Editing Checklist and ask their partner to use the Peer Editing Checklist.

f. **Publish work** Have students read their paragraphs to the class and do a demonstration for the class. Collect all students' paragraphs to make a class "How-to" book.

Activity Book, p. 95: Arranging Clauses

Activity Book, p. 96: How Do You Do It?

Review
Vocabulary (Student Book, p. 160)

a. **Occupations** Divide the class into groups of four or five. Have each group create two decks of flash cards. In the first deck have students write the following occupations: *artist, astronaut, carpenter, cashier, chef, child-care worker, doctor, firefighter, grocery store clerk, hairstylist, mechanic, musician, waiter.* For the second deck have students write words for job tools and objects: *clay, flute, hammer, nail, scales, scissors, thermometer, tray, wrench.* Have the students shuffle the cards and play a matching card game similar to Go Fish. The object of the game is for players to match a job with an appropriate object to get rid of all the cards in their hand. Students may match unlikely pairs, but they need to offer a reasonable explanation to the other players. For example, clay is a natural match for an artist, but a child-care worker may use clay as well if the player can explain why. He/She might say: *The children want to do an art project with clay.*

b. **Sequence words** Teach students a modified version of the "Hokey Pokey":

First, you put your left foot in.
Then, you put your left foot out.
Next, you put your left foot in
and you shake it all about.
After that, do the Hokey Pokey.
Finally, you turn yourself around.
That's all you need to do!

Grammar

Object pronouns (Student Book, p. 160)

Introduce a Round Robin game that helps students review object pronouns. Assign one of the object pronouns to each student. For the plural forms you may want to pair two students to be *us* and *them*. Have the first seven or nine students come to the front of the class and stand in a circle. Have them call out their object pronoun names making sure they remember which one they are. Then start the round by saying: *I'll give the hot potato to her* as you hand a prop to the student with the object name *her*. The student should say: *Why did you give it to me? Give it to them.* The student needs to remember who has the object name *them* and needs to pass the prop along quickly. The round continues until someone makes a mistake. You can either wait until the last person left wins before you start a new circle with new students or you can make substitutions so that all students have a turn.

Assess

Vocabulary (Student Book, p. 161)

1. The _____ takes orders and brings food to the tables.
   a. cashier   **c. waiter**
   b. chef   d. farmer

2. The _____ fixes cars.
   a. carpenter   c. police officer
   b. mechanic d. hairstylist

3. The hairstylist cuts hair with _____.
   a. scissors c. scales
   b. a wrench   d. a tractor

Grammar (Student Book, p. 161)

1. He's a friendly person. I like _____.
   a. her   c. you
   b. him   d. me

2. The movie is great. You should see _____.
   a. them   **c. it**
   b. us   d. her

3. We are going to a movie. Do you want to come with _____?
   a. us   c. it
   b. them   d. him

Word Study (Student Book, p. 161)

1. In the word *singer*, what is the suffix?
   a. si   **c. er**
   b. singer   d. ger

2. In the word *singer*, what is the root?
   a. si   c. er
   b. sing   d. ger

Activity Book: Ch. 8 Mini-Reader

Projects

Project 1: Invite a Guest Speaker to Class (Student Book, p. 162)

a. **Identify people and places in the community** Have students brainstorm some interesting jobs in the community such as: *police officer, firefighter, mayor, reporter, nurse, social worker, artist, musician, coach, principal,* etc. Have students vote on the jobs that most interest them. You may consider a panel of speakers. You may consider inviting guests that have either similar or diverse backgrounds in relation to your students.

b. **Share prior knowledge to foster respect** Prior to the visit from a guest speaker, contact the person to explain the language limitations and demographics of the student body. Provide as much information as possible so that the experience will be positive for both students and your guest. Also provide students with a brief background history of the guest speaker.

c. Express ideas and feelings such as gratitude in a friendly letter After the presentations, have students individually write a short thank you letter. In the letter they should mention at least three new things they learned from the speaker. Hand out copies of the Friendly Letter Resource Master (p. 147).

Project 2: Give a "How-To" Presentation
(Student Book, p. 163)

a. Use graphic organizers to prepare for a presentation Make and hand out copies of the Step-by-Step Instructions Resource Master (p. 146). Have students choose an activity they know how to do. Ask: *What are the steps for doing this activity?* Bring in some sample instruction manuals or "how-to" books to help students visualize how they can present their ideas. Consider showing some video segments from such programs as: cooking shows, art and craft shows, home improvement and gardening programs, etc. Have students perform the steps for a partner, pausing from time to time to make sure that all the steps are documented. Have students write notes on the sequence of the steps. Allow students to take these notes in their native language if helpful. Help students understand what is considered a necessary step to list and what is self-evident.

b. Distinguish purpose of various media Students should also make a list of any objects that would be helpful for a demonstration. Have them create a visual display of the material. Ask students to think of how to best display the visual material. Students may also wish to draw a storyboard of the necessary steps.

c. Give verbal instructions Provide students with some helpful sequencing words such as: *First, then, next, before, while, during, as, after, finally,* etc.

d. Retell, role-play, or visually illustrate the sequence of events Have students practice their presentations by reading over their note cards and using the props so that they can foresee any difficulties. You may want to video tape the presentations to provide students the opportunity to view themselves. Have students evaluate their presentation with the checklist.

Viewing Activity

Interpret and evaluate how artists convey meaning Bring in books showing art from various periods in the U.S. Have students go through and find illustrations of different types of jobs and occupations. Have students show the art to the class. Help students talk about how colors and styles convey meaning about the job shown.

VISIONS BASIC Teacher Resource Book   • Copyright © Heinle

Chapter 9 Holidays

Materials

Student Book: pp. 164–177
Activity Book: pp. 97–104; Mini-Reader 9
Audio: Chapter 9
Student CD-ROM: Chapter 9
Teacher Resource Book:
Lesson Plan, pp. 103–110
Reading Fluency, p. 133
Resource Masters: Personal Dictionary, p. 136; Venn Diagram, p. 139; Cluster Map, p. 140;
    Timelines, p. 142
Assessment Program: pp. 59–62
Transparencies

Themes

Holidays
Past Tense: *be* and regular verbs
Consonant Clusters: *s* blends

Biography/Autobiography
Social Studies

Learning Strategies

Look for patterns in language
Use prior knowledge

Use contrastive analysis to acquire new vocabulary
Make connections across content areas

Listening

Use active listening comprehension to follow directions
Recognize and distinguish phonological elements such as consonant clusters
Listen to and extract meaning from a variety of media in various content areas
Infer meaning from actions and visual context

Speaking

Share prior knowledge with peers to foster respect for others
Initiate authentic discourse with peers
Express ideas and feelings such as opinions
Arrange phrases, clauses, and sentences into correct and meaningful patterns
Produce phonological elements of newly acquired vocabulary such as consonant clusters: *s* blends

Reading

Read authentic text
Participate in shared reading of a biography
Read silently with increasing ease for longer periods
Retell the order of events

Writing

Use basic capitalization and punctuation correctly
Use graphic organizers as pre-writing activity
Write with more proficient use of orthographic patterns: consonant doubling, dropping final *e,* and
    changing *y* to *i*
Edit writing toward standard grammar
Demonstrate knowledge of past tense and auxiliary *do*
Construct correct sentences
Develop a draft by categorizing ideas, organizing them into sentences, paragraphs, and larger units

Viewing and Representing

Describe how illustrations support text or tell a story
Tell important events and ideas gleaned from video segments
Distinguish the purpose of various media forms
Explore and describe how color, shape, and line influence the message
View and interpret illustrations

Listen, Speak, Interact
What's the Holiday?

1 **Listen and repeat.** (Student Book, p. 165)

Listen to and extract meaning from audio
Have students find the activity and read the
directions. Play the audio or read the script.
Give students visual cues to listen and repeat.

Culture Note

Explain that young children usually give cards to
their friends and teachers for Valentine's Day.
However, Valentine's Day has a romantic
connotation for teenagers and adults. It is therefore
less appropriate for older students to give cards to
their teachers.

2 **Listen and identify.** (Student Book, p. 165)

a. **Listen to and extract meaning from
audio** Have students find the activity and
read the directions. Play the audio or read
the script.

b. **Make connections across content areas**
You may want to discuss the history of
the Fourth of July and Thanksgiving.
For example, explain that: *The Fourth of
July is also called "Independence Day"
because it is the day the Declaration of
Independence was signed.* Students may
also enjoy learning about Thanksgiving.
Explain that: *The first Thanksgiving took
place in 1621 when Pilgrims held a
harvest meal to give thanks for having
survived their first year in America.*

Audioscript 🎧

1. **Listen and repeat.** Listen and repeat the
words.
*Fourth of July, Fourth of July: fireworks,
fireworks / parade, parade / barbecue,
barbecue*
Thanksgiving, Thanksgiving:
turkey, turkey / stuffing, stuffing / pie, pie
Valentine's Day, Valentine's Day:
*heart, heart / flowers, flowers / chocolates,
chocolates / card, card*

Audioscript 🎧

2. **Listen and identify.** What holiday do you
hear?

1. **Woman:** *Are these flowers for me?*
   Man: *Yes! Do you like them?*
   Woman: *They're beautiful. I love them!*
   Man: *And on this special day, I want you
   to know that I love you.*

2. **Woman:** *Do you want some more turkey?*
   Man: *I'm full. I can't eat another thing.*
   Woman: *Not even a little pie?*
   Man: *Well, maybe just a little. I love this
   holiday. It brings together the two
   things I love most—family and food!*

3. **Man:** *Do you want a hamburger or a hot
   dog?*
   Boy: *A hot dog, please.*
   Man: *Look up at the sky. The fireworks
   are beginning.*
   Boy: *Wow! Look at that one—it's red,
   white, and blue. Just like the flag!*

Answer key
2. Listen and identify.
1. Fourth of July / Thanksgiving / **Valentine's Day**
2. Fourth of July / **Thanksgiving** / Valentine's Day
3. **Fourth of July** / Thanksgiving / Valentine's Day

3 **Group work.** (Student Book, p. 165)

Use prior knowledge Have students find the
activity and read the directions. Write
holidays the students suggest on a large piece
of paper to hang up in the classroom. Refer to
these holidays as you go through the chapter.

4 **Pair work.** (Student Book, p. 165)

a. **Read through a dialogue** Have students
find the activity and read the directions.
Start by having the class ask you
questions. Then pair students with a
partner and have them ask each other
about their favorite holiday.

b. Initiate authentic discourse with peers
As an alternative, do this as a timed activity, giving students five minutes to mingle and take notes. You might have students ask one another: *When and how do you celebrate the new year? What are some special holiday foods and traditions?*

c. Compare and contrast Hand out copies of the Venn Diagram Resource Master (p. 139). Then have students compare and contrast an American holiday to a similar holiday from their culture.

Build Vocabulary

Holidays Throughout the Year

⑤ Listen and repeat. (Student Book, p. 166)

a. Have students find the activity and read the directions. Then have students look at the timeline, listen to the information, and repeat it.

b. Make connections across content areas
Give students information about the origin of Presidents' Day. Say: *Two of the greatest American presidents were born in February—George Washington and Abraham Lincoln. In 1971, Congress combined the two dates into one holiday. Today, Presidents' Day honors all past presidents.*

Audioscript 🎧

5. Listen and repeat. Listen and repeat the holidays.
January first: New Year's Day
February fourteenth: Valentine's Day
the third Monday in February: Presidents' Day
April twenty-second: Earth Day
the second Sunday in May: Mother's Day
the third Sunday in June: Father's Day
July fourth: Independence Day
the second Monday in October: Columbus Day
October thirty-first: Halloween
the fourth Thursday in November: Thanksgiving

Culture Note

The Federal government recognizes ten days when Federal government offices are closed: New Year's Day, Martin Luther King Jr. Day, Presidents' Day, Memorial Day, Independence Day, Labor Day, Columbus Day, Veterans Day, Thanksgiving, and Christmas.

⑥ What's missing? (Student Book, p. 166)

a. Use a timeline to learn about new events
Have students find the activity and read the directions. Hand out copies of the Timelines Resource Master (p. 142). Help students think of other holidays celebrated in the United States.

b. Share prior knowledge to foster respect
Explain that people often come up with ideas for new holidays. For example, many Americans would like to see Election Day declared a holiday to make it easier to vote. There are also minor holidays with a fun spirit such as Groundhog Day, February second, which is based on the legend that if a groundhog sees its shadow when it emerges from its winter home, winter will last six more weeks. Ask: *Are there other days that you think should become holidays?*

Answer key

6. What's missing? (Possible answers)
Jan.	Martin Luther King Jr. Day (third Monday)
Feb.	Groundhog Day (2/2)
Mar.	St. Patrick's Day (3/17)
Apr.	April Fools' Day (4/1), Easter, Arbor Day
May	May Day (5/1), Memorial Day (last Monday)
June	Flag Day (6/14)
July	Parents' Day
Aug.	(none)
Sept.	Labor Day (first Monday)
Oct.	United Nations Day
Nov.	Veteran's Day (11/11)
Dec.	Christmas (12/25), Kwanzaa (12/26)

⑦ Pair work. (Student Book, p. 166)

a. Use prior knowledge Have students find the activity and read the directions. Ask: *What other holidays do you have in your home country? How do you think these holidays began?*

b. Share prior knowledge to foster respect
Ask: *Do you know any holidays from other cultures?* Have students tell their partners about any other holidays, and have them add these to the timeline.

Activity Book, p. 97: Holidays in the U.S.

Grammar Focus
Past Tense: *be* **and Regular Verbs**

a. Demonstrate knowledge of the past tense
Point to the chart in the text and review the information about the past tense. Explain that in the example *"It was sick yesterday,"* it could refer to a pet. Animals are sometimes referred to as *it*. Do a substitution oral drill with the class to have students practice the past tense.

b. Distinguish phonological elements Students may confuse the words *where* and *were*. Practice the pronunciation of these words with the class. Do some drill work using flash cards. Give an index card to each student. On one side have students write the word *where*, and on the other side write *were*. Have students hold up the correct word as you say sentences using either *where* or *were*. Point out that since *where* is a question word, students can listen for the rise in intonation at the end of sentences beginning with *where*.

c. Understand time phrases You may want to teach time phrases used with the past tense: *a long time ago, yesterday, the day before yesterday, last week, last month, last year, two days ago, a week ago, a month ago.*

d. Recognize patterns in language Review the following spelling rules with the class and have students take note of the spelling changes in the past tense of regular verbs.

Spelling rules for past tense *-ed*
Add *-ed* to the end of most verbs:
want ➔ *wanted*
For verbs ending in *e*, drop the e and add *-ed*:
like ➔ *liked*
For verbs ending in vowel + consonant, double the last consonant and add *-ed*:
stop ➔ *stopped*
For verbs ending in a consonant + *y*, change *-y* to *i* and add *-ed*:
study ➔ *studied*

Pronunciation Notes

- Explain to students that the *-ed* ending is pronounced with a *d* sound with all words ending with a voiced consonant (except *d*) such as: *planned /pland/.*

- The *-ed* ending is pronounced with a *t* sound in all words ending with a voiceless consonant (except *t*) such as: *wished /wisht/.*

- The *e* in the *-ed* ending is pronounced as a separate syllable in words that end in *t* or *d* such as: *wanted, needed.*

8 **Complete the sentences.** (Student Book, p. 167)

Have students find the activity and read the directions. Then have them read the sentences and add *was* or *were* to form the past tense.

Answer key
8. Complete the sentences.
Our Fourth of July barbecue ¹· **was** fun. We ²· **were** with all of our friends. Maria ³· **was** there with her brother. Thomas ⁴· **was** the cook. The fireworks ⁵· **were** beautiful. It ⁶· **was** a great day!

9 **Rewrite.** (Student Book, p. 167)

a. Use the correct verb tense Have students find the activity and read the directions. Pair students with partners to make the sentences past tense.

b. Produce correct phonological elements Review the three possible pronunciations of the *-ed* ending in past regular verbs: /t/ as in *asked*, /d/ as in *played*, and /id/ as in *wanted*.

Answer key
9. Rewrite.
1. My parents **cooked** Thanksgiving dinner.
2. I **ordered** an apple pie from the bakery.
3. We **finished** the pie.
4. My parents **asked** for the recipe.

VISIONS BASIC Teacher Resource Book • Copyright © Heinle

Language Transfer and Interference

Spanish: Students have a tendency to pronounce the *e* for all regular past tense verbs.

Vietnamese: There is no tense inflection since tense is usually indicated through context words expressing time. Students will have the tendency to use the present tense at all times and including a time phrase such as: *She go to store yesterday.*

Activity Book, p. 98: Past Tense: *be* and Regular Verbs

Activity Book, p. 99: Past Tense: Negative of Regular Verbs

Word Study

Consonant Clusters: *s* blends

Review with the class the explanation and examples of words with the *s* blend consonant clusters.

10 Listen and repeat. (Student Book, p. 168)

a. **Recognize and distinguish phonological elements** Have students find the activity and read the directions. Play the audio or read the script and have students listen for the consonant clusters *st, sk, sp.*

b. **Look for patterns in language** Have students work with partners and skim through the *s* section of a dictionary to find other English words beginning with the consonant clusters: *sk, sp, st.* Have students write the words on the board in three columns.

c. **Produce phonological elements** You may explain that words can end in these consonant clusters such as: *ask, mask, task, desk, brisk, disk, risk, dusk, husk, tusk; clasp, grasp, crisp; fast, last, past, east, best, nest, pest, rest, test, vest, west, fist, wrist, cost, host, lost, most, post,* etc.

d. **Infer meaning by making associations** Review the comparative adjectives from Chapter 7. Then briefly explain the superlative form of adjectives, and demonstrate the use of the *-est* ending. Provide students with a list of comparative adjectives such as: *bigger, smaller, happier,* etc., and have students derive the superlative form.

Audioscript

10. Listen and repeat. Listen to the sounds the two consonants make separately and together. Then listen to the blend in each word. Repeat each word.

s p sp:	speak, **sp**ell, **sp**end, **sp**ort
s t st:	**st**udent, **st**art, **st**udy, **st**ory
s k sk:	**sk**ate, **sk**ip, **sk**i, **sk**in

Language Transfer and Interference

The sounds of these consonant blends *(sp, st, sk)* do not occur in many languages. Students will have a tendency to insert a vowel sound before the *s.* Practice the articulation of these blends with your class.

11 Read and listen. (Student Book, p. 168)

Distinguish phonological elements Have students find the activity and read the directions. Have students read the poem silently. Then ask a volunteer to read the poem aloud. Play the audio or read the script.

Audioscript

11. Read and listen. Read and listen to the poem. Then find the words in the poem with the *sp, st,* and *sk* blends.

Fourth of July Night
by Eleanor Dennis

The fireworks are a lot of fun.
I watch each giant spark
As it goes streaking up the sky—
Then lights up all the dark
In a lovely splashing splatter
Of a thousand silver stars,
In a tumbling, rumbling clatter
That goes echoing off to Mars.

Answer key

11. Read and listen.

sp-	spark, splashing, splatter
st-	streaking, stars
sk-	sky

12 Pair work. (Student Book, p. 168)

Using prior knowledge You may wish to expand on the list of *s* consonant clusters: *sc, sk, sl, sm, sn, sq, sw.* Provide a few example words for each: *scream, slide, smear, snore, squeeze, swim,* etc. Have students work in small groups and search in a dictionary for other *s* consonant cluster words. Hand out copies of the Personal Dictionary Resource Master (p. 136) for students to use.

⑬ What is the missing blend? (Student Book, p. 168)

Look for patterns in language Have students find the activity, read the directions, and then fill in the missing consonant clusters.

Answer key

13. What is the missing blend?

1. star   3. stairs
2. spoon   4. skirt

Activity Book, p. 100: Consonant Clusters: s blends

Into the Reading

Use Prior Knowledge: Leader (Student Book, p. 169)

a. **Use prior knowledge** Bring in pictures of various world leaders to display in the classroom. Consider your class demographics when making your selections. Try to include both men and women from various backgrounds. A good source might be winners of the Nobel Peace Prize such as: Jimmy Carter, former U.S. President; Kofi Annan, UN Secretary General from Ghana; Kim Dae Jung, South Korean president; Nelson Mandela, South African leader; Rigoberta Menchu Tum, Guatemalan human rights leader; the Dalai Lama, leader of the Tibetan people; Alfonso Garcia Robles, Mexican diplomat; Mother Theresa, leader of missionaries of charity in India, etc.

b. **Make connections across content areas** Ask students if they can identify any of the people mentioned above. Explain that these people have all worked at achieving peace in our world. Then introduce the word *leader* and have a volunteer read the information in the text.

Build background: Peaceful protest (Student Book, p. 169)

a. **Make connections across content areas** Ask a volunteer to read the background information about peaceful protest. Discuss what *freedom of speech* means. Explain that freedom of speech is a right of all U.S. citizens, guaranteed by the Bill of Rights in the Constitution. Give students a bit of background information on segregation. This could also be an opportunity to talk about the structure of the U.S. government.

b. **Tell important events and ideas gleaned from video segments, graphic arts, or technology presentation** Present students with a variety of historic resources to help contextualize the biography of Dr. Martin Luther King Jr. Show pictures, slide shows, or video clips of the struggles for civil rights in the U.S.

Reading and Understanding

Text Structure: Biography (Student Book, p. 170)

Use active listening comprehension Have students listen to the biography of Dr. Martin Luther King Jr. Replay the audio and ask students to take notes on important dates in Dr. King's life. Repeat the reading and ask students to take notes about important people in his life.

Reading 🎧 (Student Book, p. 170)

a. **Pre-teach vocabulary** You may want to pre-teach some or all of the potentially new vocabulary in the reading: *minister, graduate, equal, rights, treated, organize, successful, accept, gunshot, honor.*

b. **Read authentic literature** Read the passage with the class as a choral reading. Bring attention to the dates before you begin the reading. Then do a chain reading with the class. Stop after each paragraph and ask students to recall what they read in their own words.

c. **Recognize rhetorical patterns** If possible, play an audio or video segment of Dr. King's famous "I Have a Dream" speech. Explain that this speech was delivered in Washington, D.C. on August 28, 1963. Tell students that you don't expect them to understand all of the speech. Point out the use of pauses and exaggerated intonations, and the repetition of key words and phrases such as: *Go back to…I have a dream, every valley…mountain…hill…plain…Let freedom ring.*

Beyond the Reading

Reading comprehension (Student Book, p. 171)

a. **Derive meaning from text** Have students answer the questions based on the article. Have students work with partners to ask and answer more questions about the reading.

VISIONS BASIC Teacher Resource Book • Copyright © Heinle

b. **Answer higher order thinking questions**
After going over the comprehension questions in the text, you may wish to discuss these questions with your class.

    1. Compare and contrast a leader and a dictator. *(Leaders and dictators are both in charge of things. Both are strong. Both might protect their followers. A leader may convince or inspire people to do something, but a dictator uses fear or force to make people follow.)*

    2. What influences in Dr. King's youth may have shaped his personality? *(his religious upbringing; his mother's love for learning; maybe his sense of fair play from sports or his experiences as a young African-American during the Great Depression)*

Answer key
Reading comprehension.
1. Was Martin Luther King Jr. born in 1928? **no**
2. Was his father a minister or teacher? **minister**
3. What prize did Dr. King accept? **Nobel Peace Prize**
4. What did Dr. King believe? **Everyone's equal.**

Fill in a timeline. (Student Book, p. 171)

Use a graphic organizer Have a student read the box about timelines. Have students scan the reading. Point out that students' eyes should look for numbers, stop, backtrack and read the sentence for information. Hand out copies of the Timelines Resource Master (p. 142).

Answer key
1948	**graduated from college**
1953	**married Corretta Scott**
1954	staffed work as a minister
1964	**accepted the Nobel Peace Prize**
1968	killed

Draw a picture. (Student Book, p. 171)

a. **Distinguish purposes of various media forms**
Discuss with students the various purposes of communication such as: information, entertainment, persuasion, etc. Talk about a single event from Dr. King's life and ask students to think about how this information might be represented visually if it were to

inform as opposed to persuade someone. Divide the class into small groups and assign groups the task of illustrating an event from Dr. King's life for either the purpose of informing or persuading the viewer.

b. **Select an appropriate type of media for communication** Bring in examples of various types of media such as photographs, political cartoons, murals, collage, oil paintings, etc. Discuss the advantages and disadvantages of each medium. Ask: *Would a cartoon or a photograph be more effective in persuading a viewer?* Have students choose the best medium for their picture.

Activity Book, p. 101: Social Studies: Two Holidays That Help the Earth
Activity Book, p. 102: Reading Fluency

From Reading to Writing
Write an Autobiography (Student Book, pp. 172–173)

a. **Use prior knowledge to infer meaning**
Write the word *autobiography* on the board. Point out that *auto-* is a prefix that means "self." Have students guess what the word means. Ask a volunteer to read the information in the text about *autobiography*.

b. **Use a graphic organizer for pre-writing**
Review the four writing steps: *Plan, Write, Edit,* and *Publish.* Students should be encouraged to record the year of important events, even if they don't know the full date.

c. **Construct correct sentences** Have students write a sentence about each event on their timelines. Then have students compose the sentences into one or two paragraphs, using transition words.

d. **Edit writing toward standard grammar.**
Have students check their work with the Editing Checklist. Ask partners to use the Peer Editing Checklist.

e. **Publish your writing** Ask students to read their autobiographies to the class. Display student work in class.

Activity Book, p. 103: Arranging Sentences

Activity Book, p. 104: Write a Biography

Review

Vocabulary (Student Book, p. 174)

Categorize holidays Review the seasons with students, writing the seasons and months on the board. Have students draw a large circle on a piece of paper and divide it into four sections. Have them write a season in each section. Demonstrate this on the board. Then have students work in pairs or groups to fill in the holidays for each season. When they are finished, go over their answers orally. Ask: *What holidays are in the summer? When (what season) is Thanksgiving?* Review how major holidays are celebrated.

Assess

(Student Book, p. 175)

Answer key

Vocabulary

1. I always give my sister a _____ on her birthday.

   a. stuffing   c. parade

   b. card   d. Thanksgiving

2. Most countries celebrate _____ on January 1.

   a. Earth Day   **c. New Year's Day**

   b. Mother's Day   d. Columbus Day

3. _____ is my favorite meat.

   a. Pie   c. Pizza

   b. Stuffing   **d. Turkey**

Grammar

1. They _____ home yesterday.

   a. is   c. was

   b. are   **d. were**

2. I ____ dinner last night.

   a. was   c. were

   b. cook   **d. cooked**

3. My friend _____ in Mexico last year.

   a. lives   c. live

   b. lived   d. liveed

Word Study (Student Book, p. 175)

Which consonant cluster does the object begin with?

1. skirt   a. st   b. sp   **c. sk**   d. s
2. spoon   **a. sp**   b. st   c. so   d. st

Activity Book: Ch. 9 Mini-Reader

Projects

Project 1: American Holiday Presentation (Student Book, p. 176)

Have a volunteer read through the instructions and paraphrase them. Then have students come up with a schedule and timeline for completing their presentations. Give students a fixed time limit of two or three minutes for presentations. Model a presentation of the subject for the class, using props and pictures to enhance the presentation. You may want to allow students to work cooperatively on a group presentation. Have students create holiday posters for their presentation. You may want to keep these and display them throughout the year as each holiday approaches. Video tape or tape record the presentations and allow students to view and critique their own work.

Project 2: Timeline of a Famous American's Life (Student Book, p. 177)

Before the project, check with content area instructors for suggestions on individuals whom students might write about. Organize a class visit to the school library or bring to class some resources for research. Read through the instructions with the class, and call on students to paraphrase the steps. Provide students with a list of historic and contemporary individuals such as: Benjamin Franklin, Thomas Jefferson, George Washington Carver, Neil Armstrong, Eleanor Roosevelt, Maya Angelou. After the class presentations are done, have the class create an historic timeline, situating each individual that has been presented.

Viewing Activity

View and interpret illustrations Bring in illustrations from different artists of one holiday (for example, July 4th or Thanksgiving). Have students compare and contrast how artists have depicted the holiday. Discuss the colors and images used, and how they convey a feeling of emotion.

Chapter 10 Feelings

Materials

Student Book: pp. 178–191
Activity Book: pp. 105–112; Mini-Reader, pp. 150–153
Audio: Chapter 10
Student CD-ROM: Chapter 10
    Teacher Resource Book:
    Lesson Plan, pp. 111–118
    Reading Fluency, p. 134
    Resource Masters: Venn Diagram, p. 139; Web Map, p. 138; Friendly Letter, p. 147; Games
        Instructions (p. 164)
Assessment Program: pp. 63–74
Transparencies

Themes

Feelings
Future Tense with *will*

Long and Short Vowel Review
Poem

Personal Letter

Learning Strategies

Look for patterns in language
Use prior knowledge
Monitor oral and written production and use self-corrective techniques
Use contrastive analysis to acquire new vocabulary
Use learning strategies such as synonyms and non-verbal cues
Make connections across content areas

Listening

Use active listening comprehension to follow directions
Listen to and extract meaning from audio recording
Analyze and evaluate discourse for appropriateness of purpose with a variety of audiences
Infer meaning from actions and visual context

Speaking

Identify people, places, and events
Share prior knowledge with peers to foster respect for others
Express ideas and feelings
Arrange phrases, clauses and sentences into correct and meaningful patterns
Produce phonological elements of vocabulary such as long and short vowels

Reading

Read authentic text
Participate in shared reading
Read silently with increasing ease for longer periods
Use graphic organizers as pre-reading activity
Use verbal cueing strategies and non-verbal cueing strategies such as facial expressions, and gestures
    to enhance the reading experience
Retell, role-play, or visually illustrate the order of events

Writing

Use basic capitalization and punctuation correctly in the format of a personal letter
Edit writing toward standard grammar
Demonstrate knowledge of the future tense
Demonstrate knowledge of negatives and contractions
Construct correct sentences

Viewing and Representing

Describe how illustrations convey emotions
Respond to media such as film by expressing likes and dislikes
Distinguish the purpose of various media forms
Explore and describe how color, shape, and line influence a message
Produce communication using technology and appropriate media such as e-mail emoticons
View and interpret media

Listen, Speak, Interact

How do you feel?

1 Listen and repeat. (Student Book, p. 179)

a. Listen to and extract meaning from audio Have students find the activity and read the directions. Play the audio or read the script. Give students visual cues to listen and repeat.

b. Understanding cultural differences While human emotions are universal, our expression of these emotion is bound by cultural norms. It is therefore important to provide as much contextual background for your students so that they may begin to understand the cross-cultural non-verbal cues. Explain to students that Americans tend to be very expressive of their emotions. In fact this expressiveness may seem exaggerated to individuals from other cultures. Try to provide various scenarios to help contextualize the emotions presented in this activity.

Audioscript

1. Listen and repeat.
Listen and repeat the words.
bored, bored / embarrassed, embarrassed / excited, excited / happy, happy / mad, mad / sad, sad / scared, scared / shy, shy/ surprised, surprised

2 Listen and identify. (Student Book, p. 179)

a. Have students find the activity and read the directions Then ask students to provide various visual cues for boredom, such as yawning, looking away, filing nails, etc.

b. Expand vocabulary through synonyms Explain to students that synonyms are words that mean the same thing. For example: *mad/ angry, happy/cheerful, scared/afraid.* You may also want to introduce antonyms for the adjectives of feelings such as: *happy/sad, shy/outgoing, scared/confident,* etc.

Audioscript

2. Listen and identify.
How does the person feel?
1. *Happy Birthday!*

   Wow! A party for me? When did you plan this? I didn't tell you it's my birthday today! I can't believe it!
2. *Oh no. I'm wearing two different socks! Why didn't you tell me? Everybody is probably looking at me. Is that girl laughing at me? Oh! I have to go home and change.*
3. *This movie isn't very good. The characters aren't interesting at all. I think I'm falling asleep. Wake me up when the movie is over.*
4. *Hello? Hello? Is anybody here? Did you hear something? I'm sure I heard a sound. I don't like this place. Let's leave!*

Answer Key

2. Listen and identify.
1. shy / scared / **surprised**
2. **embarrassed** / happy / mad
3. shy / **bored** / mad
4. surprised / **scared** / excited

3 Pair work. (Student Book, p. 179)

a. Interpret non-verbal cues Have students find the activity and read the directions. If possible, pair students from different cultural backgrounds. Remind Spanish-speaking students that in English adjectives are placed before nouns and that adjectives should not be made plural.

b. Use context appropriate language to express an idea or emotion Give students some social settings and ask them to discuss what they think would be appropriate emotional response to the event. What would be inappropriate? Here are some possible scenarios: *A store clerk gives you the wrong change. Someone bumps into you and you drop your things. Someone gave you a present.* Ask students to think: *How would you feel? What would you say?*

VISIONS BASIC Teacher Resource Book • Copyright © Heinle

c. **Share prior knowledge to foster respect**
Ask students to talk about appropriate and inappropriate ways of expressing one's feelings in various situations. Have them compare and contrast differences they have observed in their native country and in the United States.

Culture Note

There are significant cultural variations in how emotions are expressed. Although overgeneralizations about cultural behavior lead to stereotypes, there are some generalities that can be helpful. For example, Asian cultures typically tend to be less expressive particularly of negative emotions for fear of offending someone. Students from these cultures will be reluctant to make direct eye contact, and may prefer a greater degree of personal space. Latin students, on the other hand, may be more expressive of emotions and may make more physical contact and direct eye contact. Make students aware of these cultural differences and encourage tolerance.

④ **Group work.** (Student Book, p. 179)

Use prior knowledge Have students find the activity and read the directions. Write feelings students suggest on a large piece of paper to hang up in the classroom. Refer to this list as you go through the chapter.

Build Vocabulary
When I'm Happy, I Smile

⑤ **Listen and repeat.** (Student Book, p. 180)

a. **Derive meaning from visuals** Have students find the activity and read the directions. Play the audio or read the script.

b. **Interpret meaning in fine art** Bring in a picture of Da Vinci's *Mona Lisa*. Ask students if they are familiar with the painting. Ask students what they think of the painting. *Does the woman seem happy? Why or Why not?* Have students look into her eyes. Then have them look at her mouth. Ask: *Does her expression change?*

Audioscript 🎧

5. Listen and repeat.
Listen and repeat the words.
smile, smile / shout, shout / shake, shake / blush, blush / jump, jump / laugh, laugh / cry, cry / yawn, yawn

⑥ **Fill in the blanks.** (Student Book, p. 180)

Derive meaning from context Have students find the activity and read the directions. Ask students if the actions can express other emotions. For example: *What other time do you blush? Would you jump if you were surprised, or scared? Do you ever smile when you are nervous?*

Answer key
6. Fill in the blanks.
1. When I'm excited, I **jump.**
2. When I'm sad, I **cry.**
3. When I'm bored, I **yawn.**
4. When I'm embarrassed, I **blush.**
5. When I'm scared, I **shake.**
6. When I'm happy, I **laugh.**
7. When I'm happy, I also **smile.**
8. When I'm angry, I **shout.**

Activity Book, p. 105: How Do You Feel?

Grammar Focus
Future Tense with *will*

a. **Demonstrate knowledge of the future tense** Point to the chart and review the information about the future tense. Call on volunteers to read the sample sentences in the chart.

b. **Demonstrate knowledge of negatives and contractions** Review the negative form and its contraction *won't*. Practice the pronunciation, as this will be challenging for many students.

⑦ **Choose.** (Student Book, p. 181)

Give information about yourself Have students find the activity and read the directions. Go in a chain around the room, going through the items several times so that each student has a turn.

⑧ **Write.** (Student Book, p. 181)

Demonstrate knowledge of future tense Have students find the activity and read the directions. Then have them change the sentences to the future tense. Make sure that students only use contractions with pronouns. Also remind students that the -*s* for the third person singular is not used in the future tense. Students should not say: *Mario will calls his friend.*

Answer key
8. Write.
1. Mario will call his friend.
2. We will go to the library.
3. You will rent a movie.
4. She will be bored.
5 We will eat lunch at 12:00.
6. The cat will sleep here.

⑨ Write. (Student Book, p. 181)

a. Use the correct verb tense Have students find the activity and read the directions. Then have students work in pairs.

b. Alternative ways of expressing time You may want to introduce the structure *going to + verb* as an alternative way of expressing the future.

c. Demonstrate knowledge of negatives Remind students that the auxiliary verb *will* is used with *not* when making a sentence negative in the future tense. Be sure to mention that there is no contraction for *will not*. Have students switch papers with their partners and rewrite their partner's sentences in the negative.

d. Express time with modifiers Teach time phrases used with the future tense: *soon, later, tonight, tomorrow, the day after tomorrow, in a few days, next week, next month, next year, in a second, in a minute, in a week,* etc.

Language Transfer and Interference

Haitian Creole: The present tense is used for the future. Students may say: *I do it tomorrow.*
Spanish: The present tense can be used in place of the future tense.
Vietnamese: Recall that there is no tense inflection in Vietnamese. These students will need reminders to use the proper verb tenses. Their tendency will be to include expressions of time instead.

Activity Book, p. 106: What Will You Do?
Activity Book, p. 107: More about the Future Tense

Word Study
Long and short vowel review

⑩ Choose. (Student Book, p. 182)

a. Recognize and distinguish phonological elements Have students find the activity and read the directions. Then have them identify the correct vowel sound.

b. Produce phonological elements You may also want to play a game of Pronunciation Bingo with the class using contrasting pronunciation pairs. See the Games Instructions Resource Master (p. 164).

Answer key
10. Choose.
1. pen   **long e** / **short e**
2. dime **long i** /short i
3. hat   long a /**short a**
4. nose **long o** /short o
5. cup   long u / **short u**
6. fish long i / **short i**
7. ear   **long e** / short e
8. cake **long a** / short a

Language Transfer and Interference

Haitian Creole: The short vowel sounds *e* and *u* do not occur in Haitian Creole.
Spanish: Spanish has none of the short vowel sounds except the short *e*. While Spanish does have all the long vowel sounds, they do not necessarily correspond to the same vowel letters as English.
Vietnamese: Vietnamese has approximations for the short vowel sounds *a, e, o,* and does not have the short *i*. Vietnamese has only approximate sounds for the long *a* and *o*. Also, vowel sounds are often represented by different letters than in English.

⑪ Listen. (Student Book, p. 182)

Distinguish phonological elements Have students find the activity and read the directions. Remind students what *rhyme* means. Before you play the audio, see if students can determine if the words rhyme.

Audioscript 🎧
11. Listen.
Do these words rhyme?
1. *run, sun*   3. *lip, rip*   5. *leave, life*
2. *bag, big*   4. *pay, day*   6. *way, say*

Answer key
11. Listen.
1. yes   3. yes   5. no
2. no   4. yes   6. no

⑫ **Pair work.** (Student Book, p. 182)

   a. **Look for patterns in language** Have students find the activity and read the directions. Have them identify the vowel sound in the word sets.

   b. **Using prior knowledge** Ask students to think of other rhyming words they may already know in English.

Answer key
12. Pair work.
1. cat, bat, **hat**
2. dish, wish, **fish**
3. ten, then, **pen**
4. take, bake, **cake**

Activity Book, p. 108: Long and Short Vowel Review

Into the Reading
Use Prior Knowledge: Feelings About the First Day of School (Student Book, p. 183)

   a. **Use prior knowledge** Ask students to mention two opposite feelings one might have about the first day of school. *Why do we have these mixed feelings? What are some things that worry you about something new? What are some things that excite you?*

   b. **Use graphic organizer as pre-reading tool** Copy and hand out the Web Resource Master (p. 138). Have students brainstorm a list of adjectives describing how they might feel about the first day of school.

Build Background: Monsters (Student Book, p. 183)

   a. **Share prior experience to foster understanding** Be particularly sensitive to the students' personal experiences and backgrounds. Some students may have experienced very difficult and traumatic events. To them monsters can be quite real. You may want to convey that American kids also experience these anxieties. Focus on the universality of emotions.

   b. **Tell important events and ideas through graphic arts** Sometimes people are able to express through art what they cannot say in words. Allow students to do an art project to express their fears or anxieties. Have students create images of their personal monsters.

   c. **Respond to media such as film, print, and technology by explaining likes and dislikes** Ask students: *What are some famous monsters?* (Frankenstein, Dracula, Werewolf, Mummy, Godzilla) *Do you like such characters? Why or why not?*

Reading and Understanding
Text structure: Poem

Reading 🎧 (Student Book, p. 184)

   a. **Pre-teach vocabulary** You may want to pre-teach some or all of the potentially new vocabulary from the reading: *scare away, doubts, scared silly, average, outfit.*

   b. **Use active listening comprehension** Have students listen to the poem. Replay the audio and monitor your students' emotional reaction to the poem. You may also have students copy the poem and underline the future tense verbs.

   c. **Read authentic literature** Read the passage with the class as a choral reading. Then do a chain reading with the class. Stop after each line and ask students to discuss the feelings of the girl.

Beyond the Reading
Reading Comprehension. (Student Book, p. 185)

a. **Derive meaning from text** Have students answer the questions based on the poem. Have students work with partners to ask and answer more questions about the reading.

b. **Answer higher order thinking questions** For more challenge, discuss these questions with your students.

   1. How would Patti would feel if she were going to school in your country?

   2. What advice would you offer an American girl living in your country?

   3. In what ways are Patti's feelings similar to yours?

Answer key
Reading comprehension
1. Does Patti want her father's help? **yes**
2. Is Patti starting middle school or high school? **high school**
3. How does Patti feel? **afraid, worried, scared**
4. What does Patti want her father to say? **that everything will be fine**

Compare and contrast (Student Book, p. 185)

Have a volunteer read the box that explains the strategy. Hand out copies of the Venn Diagram Resource Master (p. 139) and remind students how to fill it in.

Activity Book, p. 109: Science: Stress and Your Body
Activity Book, p. 110: Reading Fluency

From Reading to Writing

A Personal Letter (Student Book, pp. 186–187)

a. Become familiarized with various forms of writing Have students review the model personal letter, and have a volunteer read the explanation. Point out the date at the top, the greeting, and closing. Remind students of proper capitalization and punctuation rules, especially with regards to proper names, the greeting and closing, as well as the date. Explain to students that the word *Dear* is used as a general greeting and it does not necessarily connote romantic feelings. Point out the closing and offer students several alternative closing expressions such as: *Your friend, Miss you, Fondly, Affectionately, Warmest regards,* etc. Then have students read the letter silently. Hand out copies of the Friendly Letter Resource Master (p. 147).

b. Use appropriate written form for various purpose and audience Present students with a sample of a business letter. Compare the form and function of a business letter with a personal letter. Also show students how to address an envelope. You may also want to introduce students to e-mail. Discuss the degree of informality in e-mail correspondences due to the medium of communication. As an alterative to the personal letter, have students write an e-mail.

c. Edit writing toward standard grammar Have students read their letter out loud to their partner. Have them check their work with the Editing Checklist. Then have students exchange their letters with a partner and read each other's work. Ask partners to use the Peer Editing Checklist.

d. Ask students to read their letters to the class Have students discuss the strengths and weaknesses of the writing and to set goals for future writing. Display student work in class.

Activity Book, p. 111: Blending Paragraphs
Activity Book, p. 112: Writing about Your Life

Review

Words (Student Book, p. 188)

Teach students how to play *Hangman* as a vocabulary and spelling activity. You may want to incorporate feelings by having students change the facial expression of their *hanging man* throughout a word puzzle.

Grammar

Future Tense with *will* (Student Book, p. 188)

Have students work in small groups to create a hope list for the future. Have students think of what they hope they will do in their personal lives, what their country will do, and what humanity will do. Have students share their hopes with the class. Explain to students what a time capsule is. Have each student suggest a small item they would like to include in a time capsule along with their hopes for the future.

Word Study

Long and Short Vowel Review (Student Book, p. 188)

Have students work in small groups to come up with a *Monster Chant* using long and short vowel rhymes to create a strong and steady rhythm that will drive away monsters of all sorts. Have groups perform their chants in front of the class.

Assess (Student Book, p. 189)

Vocabulary

1. He often feels _____ around new people.
   a. shy   c. surprised
   b. mad   d. blush

2. I got an A on my exam! I'm so
   _____.
   a. bored   **c. happy**
   b. mad   d. shy

3. The movie is really sad. I'm sure you will
   _____.
   a. shout   c. laugh
   b. cry   d. shake

Grammar

1. He _____ dinner tonight.
   a. cooked   b. cook   **c. will cook**

2. I will _____ tonight.
   a. studying   b. studied   **c. study**

3. They _____ come to class tomorrow.
   a. will not   b. not will   c. not

Word Study

1. lip   **a. hip**   b. sick   c. win
2. bag   a. sit   **b. flag**   c. bat
3. street   a. stop   **b. meet**   c. teeth

Activity Book: Ch. 9 Mini-Reader

Projects

Project 1: Keep a Diary (Student Book, p. 190)

a. Various functions of writing Explain to students that writing serves various functions. It is used to share information, to entertain, and to persuade. Perhaps the most important function of writing is the opportunity of self-reflection that it provides the writer. A diary is one of the most personal forms of expression.

b. Chronicle events in a linear progression One important aspect of a diary is that it is a way for us to record and document events in a chronological manner. This form of thinking is not necessarily intuitive for some students. Many cultures display a circular or thematic way of organizing thoughts. It is therefore very valuable for students to practice and learn thinking in a linear progression. Help students become diligent in documenting events in their days accurately. You may want to have students keep a journal throughout the school year as a form of personal narrative.

c. Make connections across content areas Explain to students that often historians have to rely on personal letters and diaries as some of the most reliable sources of historical research. Reading through these documents helps historians capture a glimpse into events from the past. Have students think of themselves as spokesmen of their generation. Encourage them to provide as much detail for an anonymous future reader. Also encourage them to think and analyze daily events in broader contexts and to become critical thinkers as they record their thoughts in their diary. Have students end each diary entry with a sentence using the future tense of what they will do later that day or what they hope to do tomorrow.

Alternatively, you can make connections to literature that students may be required to read. Have students write a diary entry from the perspective of a character in a reading. Have students write about the important incidents that may have happened in the reading or how the character may be feeling.

Project 2: Act It Out (Student Book, p. 191)

If possible, invite the drama teacher from your local high school or a community theatre group to visit your class. Have them share with the class some acting exercises. Have students practice various skits. Ask students about their favorite actors. Then have students think of how the actors are able to convey such a varied range of emotions in front of a cameras, crew and an audience. Have students give the presentation in front of the class. Then have them try again in front of a video camera. Have them discuss the difference in how they felt between the two performances.

Viewing Activity

View and interpret media Bring in a variety of magazines. Have students cut out illustrations of people with different emotions. Compare and contrast the media used (photo, illustration, etc.) and discuss how effectively the message is conveyed.

Activity Book Answer Key

VISIONS BASIC   Activity Book Answer Key

Chapter A

Left to Right Directionality (p. 1)
2. 3, 2, 4, 1   **3.** 4, 2, 3, 1   **4.** 2, 1, 3, 4

Reading (p. 8)
2. conversation with Mrs. Garcia and Tran
3. conversation with Ana and Mrs. Garcia
4. conversation with Mrs. Green and Miss Rana

Chapter B

Greetings (p. 11)
Exercise A
2. b   **3.** a   **4.** c   **5.** a

Exercise B
Answers will vary.

Conversations (p. 12)
2. A: Hi. I'm Irina. What's your name?
B: My name is Emilio. Where are you from?
A: I'm from Russia.
3. A: My name is Pablo. What's your name?
B: My name is Tran. I'm from Vietnam. Where are you from?
A: I'm from Colombia.
4. A: I'm Ana. I'm a student. What's your name?
B: My name is Lisa. I'm American. Where are you from?
A: I'm from Mexico.

Blending Sounds (p. 13)
Exercise A
2. dog   **4.** dot   **6.** pot   **8.** nap
3. fan   **5.** cat   **7.** cap

Exercise B
2. dot   **3.** fan   **4.** pen   **5.** cap
6. nap (pan is also acceptable)

Numbers (p. 14)
Exercise B
2. 3, three   **5.** 1, one   **8.** 8, eight
3. 7, seven   **6.** 9, nine   **9.** 6, six
4. 2, two   **7.** 4, four   **10.** 10, ten

Colors (p. 15)
Exercise A
Answers will vary, but follow model: *Yes, it is* or *No, it isn't. It's (color).* Students answer according to colors they use.

Exercise B
2. It's in the backpack.   **4.** It's on the chair.
3. It's under the chair.   **5.** It's under the desk.

Mathematics (p. 16)
Exercise B
2. 9, Two plus seven equals nine.
3. 7, Ten minus three equals seven.
4. 4, Nine minus five equals four.
5. 6, Two times three equals six.
6. 9, Three times three equals nine.
7. 4, Eight divided by two equals four.
8. 2, Ten divided by five equals two.

Chapter C

Classmates and Clothing (p. 17)
Exercise A
Row 1: jeans   Row 8: hat   Row 15: sneakers
Row 2: friend   Row 9: skirt
Row 5: jacket   Row 12: shoes
Row 7: shirt   Row 14: sweater

Exercise B
Answers will vary.

Consonants: h, j, l, v, x; Vowels: i, u (p. 18)
Exercise B
2. jacket   **3.** leg   **4.** six   **5.** van   **6.** hug

Classmates (p. 19)
Exercise A
2. Irina is 14 years old.
3. Emilio is 15 years old.
4. Irina is 14 years old and Linda is 15 years old.

Exercise B
Answers will vary.

Numbers (p. 20)
2. 13, thirteen   **5.** 18, eighteen   **8.** 20, twenty
3. 11, eleven   **6.** 12, twelve   **9.** 15, fifteen
4. 16, sixteen   **7.** 14, fourteen   **10.** 19, nineteen

Vowels: i, u (p. 21)
Exercise A
2. lip   **3.** in   **4.** his

Exercise B
2. under   **3.** up   **4.** cup

Exercise C
2. lip   **3.** six   **4.** cup   **5.** up

Parts of the Body (p. 22)
Exercise A
1. head   **5.** arm   **9.** knee
2. neck   **6.** hand   **10.** foot
3. stomach   **7.** fingers
4. elbow   **8.** leg

Exercise B
Answers will vary.

Friends (p. 23)
Answers will vary, but should follow this format:
This is…. Her/His hair is…. Her/His eyes are….

Chapter D

In the School (p. 27)
2. elevator, next to
3. cafeteria, across from
4. the right
5. next to
6. nurse's office, across from

Where is it? (p. 28)
Exercise A
2. order: 1, 3, 2   **3.** order: 3, 2, 1

Exercise B
Answers will vary.

Vowel: Short e (p. 29)
Exercise A
2. red   **3.** yes   **4.** left

Exercise B
2. queen   **3.** jeans   **4.** teeth

Exercise C
2. ten   **3.** wet   **4.** jet

People and Rooms (p. 30)
1. principal, office, floor, inside, entrance
2. gym, first, left, next to
3. nurse, second, across from, desk, bed

Mine and Yours (p. 31)
Exercise B
Answers will vary but should follow this format:
This is my… This…is mine.

Exercise C
Answers will vary but should follow this format:
This is your… This…is yours.

Social Studies: Reading a Map (p. 32)
Exercise B
2. Louisiana is south.
3. North Carolina is east.
4. Oregon is west/northwest.
5. Kansas is in the center.

Chapter 1

In the School Office (p. 33)
Exercise A
2. printer   3. keyboard   4. stapler   5. telephone

Exercise B
Answers will vary.

Exercise C
Answers will vary.

Exercise D
Monday (Oct. 2), Tuesday (Oct. 3), Thursday (Oct. 5), Friday (Oct. 6), Saturday (Oct. 7)

Subject Pronouns (p. 34)
Exercise A
<u>I</u> am in the school office. <u>I</u> ask the secretary, "Where is the printer?" <u>She</u> says <u>it</u> is next to the computer and the mouse. <u>They</u> are to the left of the door. <u>We</u> look at the printer. "Do <u>you</u> need to print?" the secretary asks me. "Yes, please," <u>I</u> say. "Let me help," <u>she</u> says. <u>We</u> print out my report. <u>It</u> is two pages long. "Thanks," <u>I</u> say. "<u>You</u> are welcome," <u>she</u> says to me.

Exercise B
2. He   5. They   8. They
3. She   6. They   9. She
4. It   7. It   10. It

Possessive Adjectives (p. 35)
Exercise A
<u>My</u> friends and I are in the secretary's office. <u>Her</u> desk has a computer and a printer. We want to print <u>our</u> reports. She says we can use <u>her</u> printer. First I print <u>my</u> report. Then <u>my</u> friends print <u>their</u> reports. <u>My</u> report is two pages and I need a stapler. The secretary says we can use the principal's stapler. <u>His</u> stapler is on <u>his</u> desk. <u>Our</u> reports are ready. Is <u>your</u> report ready?

Exercise B
2. This is his pen.   4. This is my notebook.
3. This is their stapler.   5. This is your backpack.

Short Vowels (p. 36)
Exercise A
2. bet, ten, leg, her   4. job, jog, cot
3. hit, sit, pin.   5. bun, hug, gum

Exercise B
2. feet   3. hi   4. foot   5. June

Exercise C
2. hat, a   3. fish, i   4. dog, o   5. egg, e

Social Studies: Holidays (p. 37)
Exercise B
2. a   3. b   4. a

Dates, Phone Numbers, and Addresses (p. 39)
Exercise A
2. a   3. d   4. e   5. b

Exercise B
2. November 1, 2001 = 11/1/01
3. April 18, 2003 = 4/18/03
4. May 5, 2000 = 5/5/00

Exercise C
2. (212) 349-4920   5. (617) 430-9343
3. (503) 249-0523   6. (314) 635-7873
4. (415) 348-0348

Exercise D
2. Chicago, IL   5. Los Angeles, CA
3. Houston, TX   6. Miami, FL
4. New York, NY

Exercise E
2. Tran Nguyen, 58 Main Street, Boston, MA
3. Mrs. Garcia, 568 Hawthorne Street, Dallas, TX
4. Miss Tan, 2 Madison Street, Chicago, IL

Chapter 2

My Family (p. 41)
Exercise A
Answers will vary.

Exercise B
Answers will vary but should follow the model.

Simple Present: be (p. 42)
Exercise A
Answers will vary.

Exercise B
Answers will vary, but should use verb forms indicated:
2. is not   3. are not   4. are not

Contractions: be (p. 43)
Exercise A
Answers will vary.

Exercise B
Answers will vary but should use the forms indicated:
2. isn't   3. aren't   4. aren't

Long vowels: a, i, o, u (p. 44)
Exercise A
2. I, white, kite   4. June, cute, rule
3. nose, phone, stove

Exercise B
1. can   2. lip   3. body   4. bus

Exercise C
2. face, a   5. nose, o   8. white, i
3. cake, a   6. cute, u   9. rule, u
4. like, i   7. phone, o   10. kite, i

Science: Genes (p. 45)
Exercise B
Answers will vary.

Capitalization and End Punctuation (p. 47)
Exercise A
1. You and I are students at Central Junior High. Our teacher is Mrs. Garcia. We have class on Monday, Tuesday, Wednesday, Thursday, and Friday. We do not have class on Saturday and Sunday or in June and July.
2. I live with my parents. Our address is 28 Main Street, Denver, CO.

Exercise B
2. My name is Irina. How old are you? Where are you from?
3. I'm fourteen years old and I'm from Vietnam. Where are you from?
4. I'm from Russia. My mother is from Russia.
5. Is that your mother? She is very beautiful!
6. Thank you!

Chapter 3

Sports and Activities (p. 49)
Exercise A
2. meet friends   6. shop
3. read   7. play the guitar
4. work   8. listen to music
5. write e-mail

Exercise B
Answers will vary.

Simple Present (p. 50)
Exercise A
2. shop   5. exercises   8. swims   11. read
3. write   6. dances   9. meets
4. paint   7. plays   10. eat

Exercise B
Answers will vary.

Simple Present Negative (p. 51)
Exercise A
2. does not   4. don't   6. doesn't
3. do not   5. don't

Exercise B
Answers for second part of each item will vary.
2. Does   3. Do   4. Does   5. Do

Long e sound: ee, ea (p. 52)
Exercise A
2. green, three, jeans

VISIONS BASIC Teacher Resource Book • Copyright © Heinle

3. sneakers, cheek, teeth
4. screen, week, year, street
5. meet, knee, ear

Exercise B

2. Green sn<u>ea</u>kers and j<u>ea</u>ns are r<u>ea</u>l cool this y<u>ea</u>r.
3. Our ch<u>ee</u>ks and t<u>ee</u>th help us <u>ea</u>t a m<u>ea</u>l.
4. F<u>ee</u>t and kn<u>ee</u>s let us dance with <u>ea</u>se.
5. <u>Ea</u>rs help us h<u>ea</u>r sp<u>ee</u>ches and gr<u>ee</u>tings.

Exercise C

2. meal	6. team	10. cheek	
3. green	7. year	11. street	
4. eat	8. teeth	12. three	
5. ear	9. teacher		

The Arts: The Statue of Liberty (p. 53)

Exercise B

2. b   3. a   4. b   5. b   6. a   7. a

Combining Sentences and Using Quotation Marks (p. 55)

Exercise A

2. Our teacher writes e-mail, but she doesn't write letters.
3. Sometimes we listen to music, but we never dance.
4. You play football, and you swim.
5. My friends play sports, but they don't play instruments.

Exercise B

2. Tran says, "I'm from Vietnam."
3. Ana says, "I'm fourteen years old."
4. "I'm from Russia," Irina says.
5. "Can I help you?" the secretary asks.
6. "This is the gym," says the gym teacher.

Chapter 4

Rooms at Home (p. 57)

Exercise A

Row 1: home   Row 2: living room
Row 4: house   Row 5: apartment
Row 8: bedroom   Row 9: bathroom
Row 11: kitchen

Exercise B

Living room: sofa
Kitchen: cabinets, oven, refrigerator
Bedroom: bed, dresser
Bathroom: bathtub, shower, toilet

Exercise C

Answers will vary.

There is / There are (p. 58)

Exercise A

2. There is   3. There are   4. There are   5. There is

Exercise B

Answers will vary.

Is there? / Are there? (p. 59)

Exercise A

Are there   Are there   kitchen
Is there   Is there

Exercise B

Answers will vary.

Compound Words (p. 60)

Exercise A

1. bed / room	6. foot / ball		
2. bath / room	7. note / book		
3. class / room	8. class / mate		
4. book / case	9. book / shelf		
5. back / pack	10. key / board		

Exercise B

2. e   3. f   4. a   5. d   6. g   7. b

Exercise C

2. birdhouse   5. headphones
3. armchair   6. bathtub
4. mailbox

Social Studies: The White House (p. 61)

Exercise B

1. 1600 Pennsylvania Avenue, Washington, D.C.
2. the President of the United States (and his family)
3. twenty-eight
4. Five chefs
5. jog, swim

Use of Commas (p. 62)

Exercise A

1. Our house is in Minneapolis, MN.
2. My birthday is April 18, 1990.
3. This house is big, but the rooms are small.
4. The kitchen has three windows, and the living room has two windows.
5. There is a sofa, a lamp, a rug, and a bookcase in the living room.
6. There are three chairs, a refrigerator, an oven, a sink, and a table in the kitchen.
7. In the bedroom there is a bed, a dresser, a closet, and a pillow.

Exercise B

I'm happy! Today we go to our new home. It is a big house. It has two bedrooms, two bathrooms, a kitchen, and a living room. There are windows in all the rooms. It is so beautiful! We bring our sofa, our beds, our tables, our desks, and our chairs to the new house. The kitchen has an oven, cabinets, and a refrigerator, and the bathroom has a shower and a shower curtain. My teacher says, "What is your new address?" I say, "It is 1349 Elm Street." I am so excited to live there!

Chapter 5

Places and Times (p. 65)

Exercise A

2. hospital   4. supermarket
3. library   5. video store

Exercise B

2. It is eight forty-five. It is a quarter to nine.
3. It is three twenty-five. It is a twenty-five past three.
4. It is ten twenty. It is twenty past ten.
5. It is six forty. It is twenty to seven.

Present Continuous (p. 66)

Exercise A

2. painting	5. playing	8. swimming	
3. shopping	6. jogging	9. writing	
4. dancing	7. exercising	10. working	

Exercise B

2. He is reading.   5. They are sitting.
3. We are talking.   6. I am writing.
4. You are listening.

More about the Present Continuous (p. 67)

Exercise A

2. Are the students writing? No, the students aren't writing. The teacher is writing.
3. Are you talking? No, I'm not talking. The teacher is talking.
4. Are we working? No, we're not working. The teacher is working.
5. Is my classmate studying? No, he/she isn't studying. I am studying.

Digraphs: ch, sh, th, wh, ng (p. 68)

Exercise A

2. where, why   4. teeth, bath, three
3. shop, bookshelf   5. finger, walking

Exercise B

2. <u>ch</u>air   3. ri<u>ng</u>   4. <u>wh</u>eel   5. mou<u>th</u>

Exercise C

2. when   3. shirt   4. math   5. month   6. chair

Social Studies: The Government and Elections (p. 69)

Exercise B

1. We have elections to choose our leaders.
2. The city council works with the mayor. They make decisions about the city and the community.
3. schools, parks, police, libraries
4. Answers will vary.

Arranging Phrases Correctly (p. 71)

Exercise A

2. The bus arrives <u>at the community center</u> <u>on Saturday, March 3,</u> <u>at 4:35 PM.</u>
3. To go <u>to the park,</u> you can take the train <u>on Wednesday, April 19,</u> <u>at 10:15 AM.</u>
4. At <u>9:15 PM,</u> there is a new movie <u>at the movie theater</u> <u>on Thursday, February 20.</u>
5. We meet our friends <u>at the restaurant</u> <u>at 6:30 PM,</u> <u>on Sunday, March 4.</u>

Exercise B

2. The bus arrives at 4:35 PM on Saturday, March 3, at the community center.
3. The train arrives at 10:15 AM on Wednesday, April 19, at the park.
4. There is a new movie at 9:15 PM on Thursday, February 20, at the movie theater.
5. We meet our friends at 6:30 PM on Sunday, March 4, at the restaurant.

Chapter 6

Breakfast, Lunch, and Dinner (p. 73)

Exercise A

breakfast: cereal, eggs, toast
lunch: hamburger, pizza, salad, sandwich, soup
dinner: beans, chicken, peas, potatoes, rice, steak (soup and salad also possible)

Exercise B

Answers will vary.

Exercise C

Answers will vary.

Count and Noncount Nouns (p. 74)

Exercise A

2. bananas, hamburgers, eggs
3. beans, pancakes
4. peas, sandwiches

Exercise B

2. soup, cereal, pasta
3. chicken, salad, rice
4. meat, spaghetti, bacon, fruit

Exercise C

2. Do you cook ~~a~~ rice?
3. Do you want a hamburger for dinner?
4. Do you like ~~a~~ chicken?
5. Does your family eat ~~a~~ cereal for breakfast?

Expressing Quantity (p. 75)

Exercise A

My brother does not like to eat. He does not like a lot of foods. For breakfast, he sometimes eats <u>a little</u> cereal. Usually, he eats <u>a little</u> toast. For lunch, he eats <u>a few</u> potatoes and <u>a little</u> soup. He sometimes eats <u>a little</u> fish. At dinner, he eats <u>a few</u> beans, <u>a few</u> peas, and <u>a little</u> salad. Sometimes he eats <u>a little</u> chicken. He is very thin because he never eats a lot of food!

Exercise B

Answers will vary.

Plural Count Nouns: Spelling and Pronunciation (p. 76)

Exercise A

2. bodies
3. lunches
4. libraries
5. days
6. pencils
7. mouths
8. gyms
9. addresses
10. paintbrushes

Exercise B

2. videos, goggles, rugs
3. bookcases, houses, dishes
4. plates, cabinets, parks

Social Studies: Where Do Foods Come From? (p. 77)

Exercise B

2. Austria
3. Italy
4. China
5. Mexico
6. China
7. U.S.
8. Mexico

Arranging Phrases (p. 79)

Exercise A

2. We have gym class at 2:00.
3. We go for a walk after we eat in a restaurant.
4. I eat breakfast before I go to school.

Exercise B

2. At 2:00, we have gym class.
3. After we eat in a restaurant, we go for a walk.
4. Before I go to school, I eat breakfast.

Chapter 7

Dollars and Cents (p. 81)

Exercise A

2. $ .30
3. $ .31
4. $24.30
5. $25.20
6. $6.27

Exercise B

2. salesperson
3. salesperson
4. customer
5. customer
6. salesperson

Comparative Adjectives (p. 82)

Exercise A

2. thinner
3. cheaper
4. cheaper
5. more expensive
6. more expensive

Exercise B

Answers may vary.

1. A sweater is more expensive than a T-shirt.
2. A cap is cheaper than shoes.
3. A tablecloth is more expensive than a napkin.
4. A jacket is more expensive than pants.

More about Comparisons (p. 83)

Exercise A

2. No! Sofas are less expensive than houses.
3. No! My father is less handsome than Tom Cruise.
4. No! Pizza is less healthy than vegetables.

Exercise B

Answers will vary.

Prefix: re- (p. 84)

Exercise A

2. g
3. h
4. f
5. a
6. c
7. b
8. e

Exercise B

Answers will vary.

Exercise C

2. rewrite
3. retell
4. refill
5. repay

Social Studies: The European Union and the Euro (p. 85)

Exercise B

b

Exercise C

a, b, c

Clauses (p. 87)

Exercise A

2. I
3. D
4. D
5. I

Exercise C

2. e
3. b
4. c
5. a

Chapter 8

Jobs and Tools (p. 89)

Exercise A

2. f
3. d
4. a
5. e
6. c

Exercise B

2. A cashier uses a cash register to take money and give change.
3. A firefighter puts out fires with a hose.
4. A hairstylist cuts hair with scissors.
5. A child-care worker takes care of children.

Object Pronouns (p. 90)

Exercise A

2. them   4. them   6. you
3. it   5. us   7. him

Exercise B

2. A mechanic uses it.
3. The cashier gives the change to them.
4. The chef cooks food for us.
5. The waiter brings dinner to her.
6. Hairstylists use them.

More Practice with Object Pronouns (p. 91)

Exercise A

2. at   3. to   4. to   5. with   6. with

Exercise B

2. You throw the ball at him.
3. I give the notebook to them.
4. Friends write e-mail to us.
5. I eat breakfast with her every day.
6. Our teacher meets with us.

Exercise C

Answers will vary.

The Suffix -er (p. 92)

Exercise A

2. drive / driver   5. paint / painter
3. write / writer   6. dance / dancer
4. play / player   7. read / reader

Exercise B

2. firefighter   4. waiter
3. child-care worker   5. carpenter

Arranging Clauses (p. 95)

Exercise A

My sister and I work in a restaurant <u>when we finish school.</u> She works with the chef, and I am a waiter. She washes vegetables <u>when the chef needs help.</u> <u>When the food is ready,</u> I serve it to the customers. <u>When the restaurant is not busy,</u> my sister and I do our homework. Sometimes we talk to the chef. We like our jobs <u>because they are very interesting!</u>

Exercise B

2. I call the doctor when I am sick. / When I am sick, I call the doctor.
3. I go to a hairstylist because my hair is too long. / Because my hair is too long, I go to a hairstylist.

How do you do it? (p. 96)

Exercise A

5, 4, 1, 3, 2

Exercise B

Answers will vary.

Chapter 9

Holidays in the U.S. (p. 97)

Exercise A

Thanksgiving: pie, stuffing, turkey
Fourth of July: fireworks, flag, parade
Valentine's Day: card, chocolates, flowers, heart

Exercise B

2. e   3. g   4. b   5. f   6. a   7. d

Exercise C

Answers will vary.

Past Tense: be and Regular Verbs (p. 98)

Exercise A

2. Tran was happy with his card.
3. You were hungry for your chocolates!
4. Ana's flowers were beautiful.

Exercise B

2. Yesterday we weren't hungry in the morning.
3. Yesterday the day wasn't beautiful.

Past Tense: Negative of Regular Verbs (p. 99)

Exercise A

2. On Tuesday, you exercised at the gym.
3. On Wednesday, I studied math.
4. On Thursday, we rented a video.
5. On Friday, the dog played in the park.

Exercise B

Answers will vary.

Consonant Clusters: s blends (p. 100)

Exercise A

2. spaghetti, sport, speak   4. stuffing, steak, station
3. skate, skin, skirt

Exercise B

2. sp, spoon   3. st, stairs   4. sk, skirt

Exercise C

2. stars   6. spoon   10. skip
3. stripes   7. stuffing   11. ski
4. sport   8. spend   12. stomach
5. skate   9. skirt

Arranging Sentences (p. 103)

Exercise A

2 simple   4. complex   6. complex
3. compound   5. compound

Exercise B

Answers may vary.

We celebrate Thanksgiving in November. We shop for food at the supermarket, and we bring it home. We cook a turkey, and we bake a pie. After we cook, the family comes to the table. Before we eat, we say thank you. I always eat a lot at Thanksgiving because the food is so good.

Chapter 10

How do you feel? (p. 105)

Exercise A

2. embarrassed   6. sad
3. mad   7. bored
4. excited   8. happy
5. scared   9. surprised

Exercise B

2. shake   4. jump   6. cry
3. shout   5. laugh

Exercise C

Answers will vary.

What will you do? (p. 106)

Exercise A

2. Ana will go to school on Monday.
3. Tran and Emilio will read in the library on Tuesday.
4. You will work at the community center on Wednesday.
5. You and I will take the bus to the mall on Thursday.
6. The dog will play in the park on Friday.
7. I will walk to the post office on Saturday.

Exercise B

Answers will vary.

More about the Future Tense (p. 107)

Exercise A

2. I'll meet new friends next year.
3. You'll work after school today.
4. They won't rent a video this weekend.
5. We'll do our homework tonight.
6. I won't play football this weekend.
7. She won't go shopping on Saturday.
8. He won't buy CDs at the mall.

Long and Short Vowel Review (p. 108)

Exercise A

2. long i   5. long a   8. long u
3. long e   6. short o   9. short e
4. short i   7. short a   10. long o

Exercise B

2. hose   3. star   4. jump   5. shake

Science: Your Body and Stress (p. 109)
Exercise B

Wording of answers may vary.

Causes stress: eating unhealthy foods, lack of sleep, being sad

Helps fight stress: exercise, eating healthy foods, sleep, being happy

Exercise C

Answers will vary.

Blending Paragraphs (p. 111)
Correct order: 2, 3, 1

Answer Key for Mini-Readers

Chapter 1: First Day of School
A. Do you understand?

1. Tuesday, September 7   3. Mrs. Mendez
2. Tom   4. Victor

B. Word Study

Short a: at, lab, math   Short o: hot, Ron, locker
Short e: second, next, ten   Short u: study, lunch, sun
Short i: in, is, print

Chapter 2: Here Is My Family
A. Do you understand?

1. teacher   2. tall   3. tall, handsome

B. Word Study

1. a. is   c. is   e. is
   b. is   d. are   f. are
2. Possible answers: brown, short, curly, average height, blue, wavy, cute, tall, thin, gray, black, average weight, good, smart, beautiful, handsome, happy

Chapter 3: Work After School
A. Do you understand?

Jolene: Friday, Saturday
Dean: Saturday, Sunday
Colleen: Monday, Wednesday, Friday
Juan: Tuesday, Thursday
Gene: Thursday, Saturday
Ana: Monday, Sunday

B. Word Study

1. Possible answers: week, needs, weekdays, Colleen, sweet, Three Green Teeth, Street, Thirteenth, see, Fourteenth, coffee, meets
2. East, team, teaches, easy, tea
3. Possible answers: helps, sees, loves, rents, needs, practices, babysits, takes, reads, teaches, shop, plays, writes, makes, meets

Chapter 4: Teenagers in the Morning
A. Do you understand?

1. 3
2. She helps her mother with housework.
3. Yes, there is.
4. He lives in an apartment near the school.

B. Word Study

1. flowerpot, windowsill, bedrooms, bedroom, bathroom, classmates, classmate, bookstore, homework, bookshelf, grandmother, bookcase, sometimes
2. Answers will vary.

Chapter 5: Saturday Afternoon
A. Do you understand?

1. 4:00 PM
2. The mall on Fifth Street (music store, pet store, sports store)
3. Rasheed
4. Sheree orders cherry ice cream. Rasheed orders chocolate ice cream.

B. Word Study

1. Possible answers: are going, is playing, are shopping, is holding, is standing, is talking, are/is looking, are getting
2. Possible answers: Charlie, watching, chocolate, cherry
3. Possible answers: Rasheed, Sheree, shopping, English, Spanish, show
4. Possible answers: they, eleventh, Fifth, the, theater, there, that's, South, thirteen, eighth, then
5. Possible answers: what, The Who, when, who's
6. Possible answers: studying, having, reading, playing, shopping, looking, holding, watching, standing, hungry, buying, talking

Chapter 6: Friends at Lunch
A. Do you understand?

1. Rafael orders two eggs, three slices of bacon, two pieces of toast, and a large glass of juice.
2. Miranda
3. Hector is a vegetarian. Vegetarians eat vegetables, beans, rice, and sometimes eggs, milk, and cheese. They do not eat meat.

B. Word Study

1. friend, restaurant, spoon, egg
2. Possible answers: juice, soup, candy, bread, meat, bacon, rice, milk, cheese, water
3. Miranda: Bowl of potato soup, large chicken sandwich
   Eva: Bowl of potato soup, a glass of milk
   Rafael: two eggs, three strips of bacon, two pieces of toast, a large glass of orange juice
   Hector: large salad, lots of bread, a glass of water

Chapter 7: Working at the Supermarket
A. Do you understand?

1. He's a cashier at the supermarket.
2. carts
3. Customers usually pay with ATM cards.

B. Word Study

cleaner, easier, more convenient, more delicious

You Do the Math

1. 10 hours   3. 2 weeks   5. $9.98   7. $3.18
2. $60   4. $7.96   6. $10.02

Chapter 8: Career Day at School
A. Do you understand?

1. He works at Children's Hospital.
2. A chef prepares food in a kitchen.
3. Karen Smith is a carpenter.
4. He paints pictures of birds and animals.

B. Word Study

1. Answers will vary.
2. firefighter, carpenter, painter

Chapter 9: Holiday Scrapbook
A. Do you understand?

1. Yes, they did.
2. They visited Skinner Forest Park. They planted trees.
3. Yes, she did.
4. Answers will vary.

B. Word Study

1. Possible answers: learned, was, were, visited, helped, planted, called, declared, watched, carried, waited, walked, started, carved, shined, dressed, showed
2. Possible answers: spring, spruce, Sperry (Park), spread, spooky
3. Possible answers: last, States, Steven, Stella, started, stuck, costumes, stuffing

Chapter 10: Joel's Senior Yearbook
A. Do you understand?

1. Yes, he will.
2. Marisa is embarrassed about her picture.
3. Sometimes they are excited. Sometimes they are bored.
4. Zhi will.

B. Word Study

excited, bored, surprised, mad, happy, shy

Name _____ Date _____

Reading Fluency Chart

How many words did you read in one minute?

Color in the graph up to the number of words that you read.

When you read silently, color in the chart with red.

When you read orally, color in the chart with blue.

Key: **Silent Reading = Red**
Oral Reading = Blue

Words Per Minute										
180										
175										
170										
165										
160										
155										
150										
145										
140										
135										
130										
125										
120										
115										
110										
105										
100										
95										
90										
85										
80										
75										
70										
65										
60										
55										
50										
45										
40										
35										
30										
25										
20										
15										
10										
Reading Exercise	1	2	3	4	5	6	7	8	9	10

Reading Fluency Teacher Notes for Activity Book, Chapter 1

Name _____ Date _____

Use with student text pages 57–59.

Build Reading Fluency
Rapid Word Recognition

➤ **Rapidly recognizing words helps increase your reading rate.**

A. ➤ **Listen and repeat.**

address	week	machine	date	machine	address
screen	date	week	machine	date	machine
date	year	screen	address	year	screen
machine	date	machine	screen	address	year
year	screen	address	year	week	date

B. ➤ **Practice.**

With a partner, read the words aloud three times.

C. ➤ **Read.**

Your partner will time you for one minute.

Total words in one minute	
– Minus words missed	
= Words read correctly in one minute	

38

Purpose: Rapid word recognition is an excellent activity for all students who struggle to memorize words with irregular orthographic patterns.

Directions: Have students listen as you pronounce each word. Read the words in the direction of the arrow. Then have students repeat each word. Remind them of the arrow to show the direction they will be reading.

You or a partner should time students for one minute as they read the words in the chart aloud. Have them record their results on the Reading Fluency Chart on page 125 of this Teacher Resource Book.

Reading Fluency Teacher Notes for Activity Book, Chapter 2

Name _____ Date _____

Use with student text pages 71–73.

Build Reading Fluency
Echo Read Aloud

➤ Echo reading helps you read with expression. Pay attention to the question marks (?) and exclamation points (!) as you read.

A. ➤ Listen and repeat.

Who is a Family
by John Mundahl

Who is a family?

There's mother, mom, mama.
There's father, dad, papa.
There's brother, sister, daughter, son.
And that's not everyone!

There's grandma, grandpa, uncle, aunt,
And remember baby!
There's cousin,
And a dog and cat,
Remember that!

B. ➤ Read.

1. Do echo read aloud with a partner.
2. Read the poem three times.
3. Read with expression.

C. ➤ Present.

Read your three best sentences to the class.

46

Purpose: Echo read aloud helps students understand how to read with expression. Have students point to the question marks and exclamation points. Model how your voice goes up for a question and down for an exclamation.

Directions: Model reading aloud with expression. Read one line at a time. Ask the class to read (echo) the same line you just read before going on to the next line.

Ask students to share their favorite stanza with the class. Remind students that as they present, they should read with expression.

Reading Fluency Teacher Notes for Activity Book, Chapter 3

Name _____ Date _____

Use with student text pages 85–87.

Build Reading Fluency
Rapid Word Recognition and Decoding Long *e* Words

➤ **Rapidly recognizing words and decoding /ee/ and /ea/ words will increase your reading rate.**

A. ➤ **Listen and repeat.**

feet	meal	teach	greet	teach	feet
read	greet	meal	teach	greet	teach
greet	meet	read	feet	meet	read
teach	greet	real	read	feet	meet
meet	read	feet	meet	meal	greet

B. ➤ **Practice.**

With a partner, read the words aloud three times.

C. ➤ **Read.**

Your partner will time you for one minute.

Total words in one minute	
– Minus words missed	
= Words read correctly in one minute	

54

Purpose: Students need practice reading long *e* words. In English, two vowel sounds (for example, *ee* and *ea*) make one long *e* sound, as opposed to Spanish where usually one vowel sound has one spelling. For your Spanish-speaking students, you will need to point this out.

Directions: Have students listen as you pronounce each word. Read the words in the direction of the arrow. Then have students repeat each word. Remind them of the arrow to show the direction they will be reading.

You or a partner should time students for one minute as they read the words in the chart aloud. Have them record their results on the Reading Fluency Chart on page 125 of this Teacher Resource Book.

Reading Fluency Teacher Notes for Activity Book, Chapter 4

Name _____ Date _____

Use with student text pages 99–101.

Build Reading Fluency
Reading Key Phrases

➤ **Reading key phrases helps you
stop reading word by word.**

A. ➤ **Practice reading silently.**

We use numbers in school. Our teacher teaches us mathematics.

B. ➤ **Read aloud.**

1. With a partner, read three times.
2. Did you read in phrases?

A House of My Own
by Sandra Cisneros

Not a flat. Not an apartment in back. Not a man's
house.
 Not a daddy's. A house all my own. With my porch and
my pillows,
 my pretty purple petunias. My books and my stories.
My two shoes waiting beside the bed. Nobody to shake a
stick at Nobody's garbage
to pick up after.
 Only a house quiet as snow, a space for myself to
go, clean as paper before the poem.

62

Purpose: Reading key phrases helps students move beyond reading word by word. It also helps students learn to read with expression.

Directions: Demonstrate and explain to the class that reading key phrases of underlined words helps improve their reading fluency. Ask students to listen as you model reading phrases before they practice silently.

After students feel comfortable, have them read aloud with a partner. Check to make sure they read three times each.

Reading Fluency Teacher Notes for Activity Book, Chapter 5

VISIONS BASIC **Chapter 5** The Community

Name _____ Date _____

Use with student text pages 113–115.

Build Reading Fluency
Rapid Word Recognition of High Frequency Words

➤ **High frequency words are words you read a lot in stories. Some words begin with the /th/ sound.**

A. ➤ **Listen and repeat.**

the	your	are	they	are	the
you	they	your	are	they	are
they	there	you	the	there	you
are	they	are	you	the	there
there	you	the	there	your	they

B. ➤ **Practice reading silently and aloud.**

1. Read the words silently one time.
2. With a partner, read the words aloud three times.

C. ➤ **Read.**

Your partner will time you for one minute.

Total words in one minute	
– Minus words missed	
= Words read correctly in one minute	

70

VISIONS BASIC Activity Book • Copyright © Heinle

VISIONS BASIC Teacher Resource Book • Copyright © Heinle

Purpose: Struggling readers often have difficulty reading high frequency words. Practicing reading these words will allow students to focus on the meaning of the words they encounter while reading.

Directions: Have students listen as you pronounce each word. Read the words in the direction of the arrow. Then have students repeat each word. Remind them of the arrow to show the direction they will be reading.

You or a partner should time students for one minute as they read the words in the chart aloud. Have them record their results on the Reading Fluency Chart on page 125 of this Teacher Resource Book.

Reading Fluency Teacher Notes for Activity Book, Chapter 6

Name _____ Date _____

Use with student text pages 128–129.

Build Reading Fluency
Chunking

➤ **Reading chunks of words helps you read faster.**

A. ➤ **Listen and repeat.**

or fork	or core	or pit	or stem	or pit
or core	or fork	or core	or pit	or stem
or stem	or skin	or stem	or fork	or fork
or pit	or stem	or pit	or skin	or fork
or skin	or pit	or fork	or fork	or core

B. ➤ **Practice reading silently and aloud.**

1. Read the chunks of words silently one time.
2. With a partner, read aloud three times.

C. ➤ **Read.**

Your partner will time you for one minute.

Total words in one minute	
– Minus words missed	
= Words read correctly in one minute	

VISIONS BASIC **Chapter 6** Food

VISIONS BASIC Activity Book • Copyright © Heinle

78

VISIONS BASIC Teacher Resource Book • Copyright © Heinle

Purpose: To help students get over the habit of reading word by word.

Directions: Demonstrate and explain to the class that reading chunks of words helps improve their reading fluency. Ask students to listen as you model reading chunks before they practice silently with a partner. Then monitor the class to make sure they read aloud three times each. Have them record their results on the Reading Fluency Chart on 125 of this Teacher Resource Book.

Reading Fluency Teacher Notes for Activity Book, Chapter 7

Name _____ Date _____

Use with student text pages 141–143.

Build Reading Fluency

Scanning

Scanning is reading fast. Look for key words when you scan.

$13.89 watch	$3.95 soccer ball	$99.99 skateboard

A. ➤ Read silently and answer.

We use numbers in school. Our teacher teaches us mathematics.

Items on Sale

1. What is the most expensive item?

_____

2. What is the least expensive item?

_____

3. How much are the watch and soccer ball together?

_____

4. How much more is the watch than the soccer ball?

_____

5. What is the total price of the skateboard and watch?

_____

6. What is the title?

_____

B. ➤ Check.

Check your answer with a partner.

1. Which problem was difficult?

2. Why?

86

Purpose: To help students adjust their reading rate when reading math word problems. Scanning is the fastest type of reading.

Directions: Model a think-aloud on how to scan. Show how you focus on key words. Remind them that they have had several of these words in their student book. If necessary, go over the meaning of *most, least, how much, together, more than,* and *total.* Tie the key words to either addition or subtraction operations.

Next have students read silently and answer the questions. Monitor as students check their answers with a partner. Discuss as a class what is easy and what was difficult and why.

Name _____   Date _____

Reading Fluency Teacher Notes for Activity Book, Chapter 8

Name _____   Date _____

Use with student text pages 155–157.

Build Reading Fluency
Key Phrases and Echo Read Aloud

➤ **Key phrases and echo reading help you read with expression.**
  Pay attention to the question marks (?) as you read.

A. ➤ **Practice reading silently.**

We use numbers in school. Our teacher teaches us mathematics.

Who is Working Today?
by John Mundahl

Who is working today?
  A lawyer is busy in court.
  A teacher is busy in a class.
  A cashier is busy in a store.
  A chef is busy in a restaurant.

Who is working today?
  A doctor is helping people.
  A hairstylist is cutting hair.
  A student is reading a book.
  An actress is making a movie.

Who is working today?
  A pilot is flying a plane.
  A police officer is directing traffic.
  A mechanic is fixing cars.
  A dentist is directing teeth.

Who is working today?
  Me too!

B. ➤ **Read.**

1. With a partner, read the poem three times.
2. Read with expression.

C. ➤ **Read.**

Read your five best sentences to the class.

94

Purpose: Reading key phrases helps students move beyond reading word by word. It also helps students learn to read with expression.

Directions: Remind students that they have already learned to read "Key Phrases" in Chapter 4. Demonstrate and explain the benefits of reading key phrases of underlined words. It helps improve their reading fluency. Ask students to listen as you model reading phrases before they practice silently.

Next have students read aloud with a partner. Check to make sure they read three times each. Encourage them to share their favorite stanza. Remind them to read with expression.

Reading Fluency Teacher Notes for Activity Book, Chapter 9

Name _____ Date _____

Use with student text pages 169–171.

**Build Reading Fluency
Shared Reading**

➤ **Shared reading helps you read with expression.
Pay attention to the exclamation points (!) as you read.**

A. ➤ Listen.

Celebrating American Holidays
by Jamelle Nnakwe

The Fourth of July is spectacular.
There are great parades, barbecues
And colorful fireworks in the sky.
Sparks of red, white, blue, green
And gold.
What a sight in the night!

Thanksgiving is when families gather
Together for a big feast.
Taste the turkey with stuffing and
Delicious hot apple, pumpkin or
Sweet potato pie.
What a wonderful treat!

Christmas is a joyous time for
Bright lights outside of homes
And on the pine smelling trees.
Dear friends and family give and
Receive gifts.
Kiddies, don't forget!
Santa Claus is on his way!
Riding on his sleigh!

Valentine's Day is a sweet, fun
Loving time.
You give from your heart by
Exchanging cards, giving flowers,
Kisses and boxes of chocolates.
What a way to celebrate a holiday!

B. ➤ Read and present.

1. With a partner, take turns reading the different stanzas.
2. Share your favorite stanza with the class. Did you read with expression?

102

Purpose: Shared reading helps students practice reading fluency by taking turns reading the different stanzas of the poem.

Directions: Model reading the poem aloud with great expression as students listen. Emphasize the words that rhyme. After reading the poem, ask students which words rhyme. If they have difficulty, say the word pairs: *sight/night, feast/treat, way/sleigh,* and *way/holiday.* Have students point to or underline the words that rhyme.

Have students take turns reading the stanzas of the poem. Let them practice three times reading the poem. Ask each student to share their favorite stanza and present it to the class. Check for good expression.

Ask students what holidays they like from their culture. This poem is about a few holidays they studied in their student book. You might encourage students to write their own poem about holidays they enjoy.

Name _____   Date _____

Reading Fluency Teacher Notes for Activity Book, Chapter 10

Name _____   Date _____

Use with student text pages 183–185.

Build Reading Fluency
Comprehension

➤ **Comprehension means understanding what you read.**
Comprehension is very important in reading fluency.

A. ➤ **Read silently.**

A Very Rich Man

Ben Garza grew up poor and unhappy. He wanted to be rich. He became a millionaire. But he still was not happy. He was very sad. He decided to make more money. He worked day after day and every weekend. He was still sad. He was embarrassed and mad. Being a millionaire did not make him happy.

B. ➤ **Answer.**

What is the lesson from this story?

a. Poor people are always happy.

c. Money doesn't buy happiness.

b. It's better to be rich than poor.

d. Millionaires are embarrassed.

C. ➤ **Read silently.**

Maria's Day

Maria was feeling excited. She sang in the chorus. She played in the band. She did not know why she was so happy. She worked hard playing the trumpet. She practiced many long hours. Before she started singing she felt sad and bored. She was scared she didn't have any friends. Now every day she feels happy.

D. ➤ **Answer.**

What is the lesson from this story?

a. Maria didn't have friends.

c. Maria played the trumpet.

b. Maria feels wonderful.

d. Maria was sad and bored.

110

VISIONS BASIC Chapter 10 Feelings

VISIONS BASIC Activity Book • Copyright © Heinle

Purposes: To prepare students for the type of comprehension questions they will encounter in more difficult academic material. Students will practice reading silently and answering questions about:

a. the "theme" or lesson of a story

b. the "main idea" of a story

Directions: Before students read silently, explain that stories often have a lesson to learn. This is the **theme** of the story. Authors do not write the exact words of a lesson or theme in their story. The reader must work this part out. Give students an example of a "lesson to be learned," such as "Never give up" or "Practice makes perfect." Encourage them to share any lesson from their culture.

The **main idea** is the most important point of the story. Note that in "Maria's Day," the choices may include supporting details, but only one is the main idea of this particular story.

Personal Dictionary

Use a Personal Dictionary to build your vocabulary.

Use this page two different ways:

1. Use one page for each chapter of your student book. Write a chapter number and title at the top of each page. Write new words you learn in each chapter.

2. Use one page for each letter of the alphabet. Write the alphabet letter at the top of the page. Write new words you learn on the correct page of your Personal Dictionary.

Letter of the Alphabet *or* **Chapter Title:** _____

Student Information Form

```
        STUDENT INFORMATION FORM

DATE: [        ]            GRADE: [        ]


LAST                FIRST              MIDDLE
NAME: [        ]    NAME: [        ]   NAME: [        ]


ADDRESS

STREET: [                                      ]


CITY: [              ]      STATE: [         ]

ZIP CODE: [         ]       PHONE: [         ]

                           DATE OF BIRTH: [         ]


PARENT OR GUARDIAN: _____

ADDRESS: _____

DAYTIME PHONE: _____
```

Editing Checklist

☐ All dates have a month, a day, and a year.

☐ All phone numbers have an area code.

☐ The address has a number, street, city, state, and zip code.

Web

➤ A Web is useful for building vocabulary or for main idea and details.

1. Write the main vocabulary word or main idea in the large oval in the middle.
2. Write related vocabulary words or details in the smaller ovals.
3. Add or delete ovals as needed.

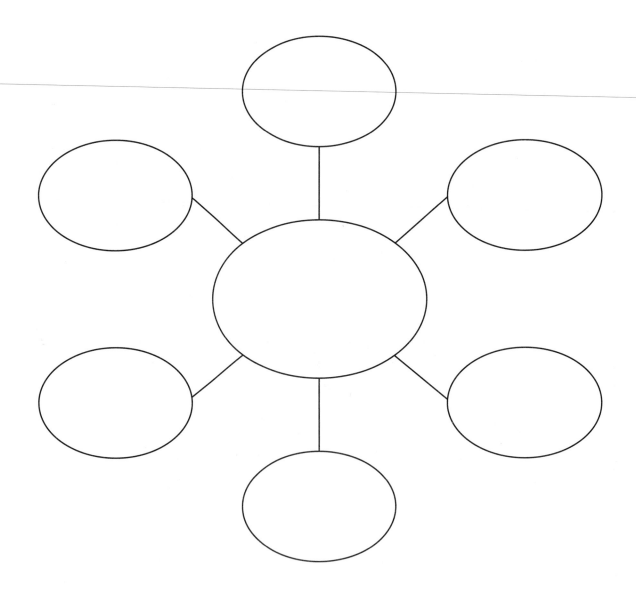

VISIONS BASIC Teacher Resource Book • Copyright © Heinle

Name _____ Date _____

Venn Diagram

Compare and Contrast

➤ Use a Venn Diagram for listening and speaking, writing, and viewing activities.

1. Write the two things you are comparing on the lines in the two circles.
2. List ways the two things are different under the lines.
3. List ways the two things are alike in the space where the circles overlap.

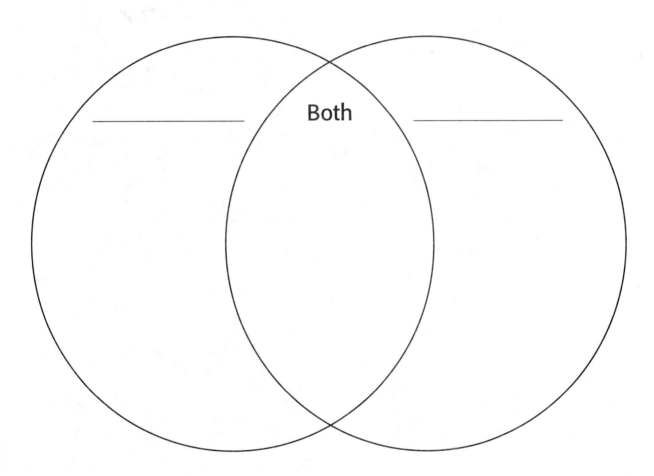

Cluster Map

Compare and Contrast

➤ Use a Cluster Map to help you organize your ideas.

1. Write the topic in the largest circle.
2. Write the main ideas about the topic in the medium circles.
3. Write details about the main ideas in the smallest circles.

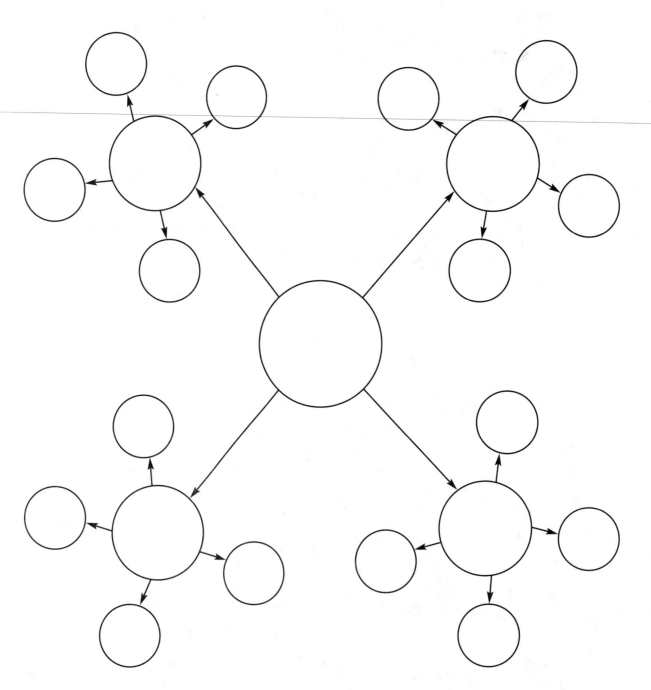

Name _____ Date _____

Sunshine Organizer

Reporting

➤ Use a Sunshine Organizer to help you answer questions about a story or to write a report.

1. Write the topic in the circle in the middle.
2. Write answers to the *wh-* questions next to the triangles.

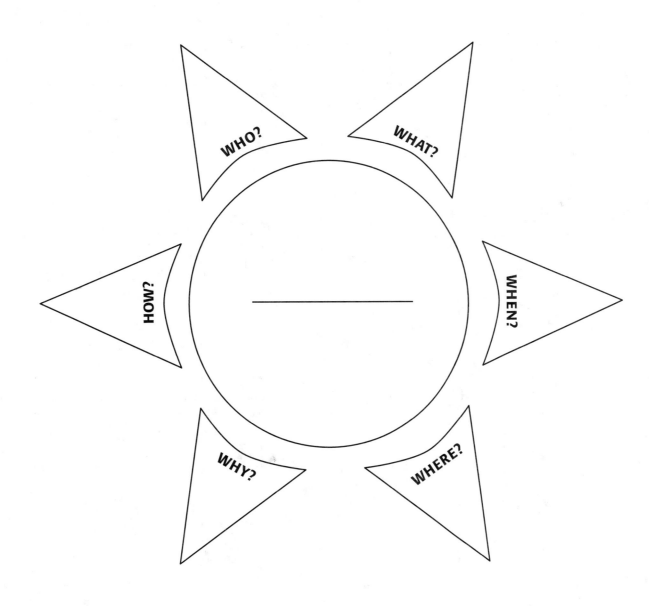

Timelines

➤ Select one of the timelines to show order of events.

1. Write the events in the order they took place.
2. On the left, write the first event and the date.
3. On the right, put the latest event and the date.

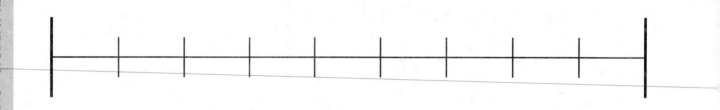

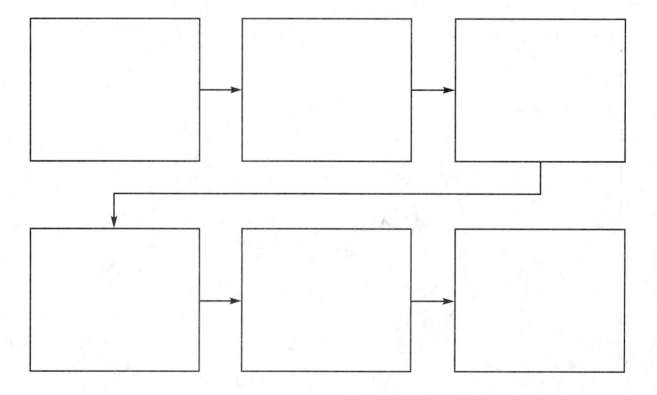

Name _____ Date _____

Sense Chart

Description

1. Write the name of the object or thing in the first column.
2. Write down what you see, hear, smell, and touch.

Title:

Name of Thing	See	Hear	Smell	Touch

Paragraph

1. Indent the first line of your paragraph.
2. Check for correct capitalization and punctuation.
3. Use a dictionary to check spelling and to find words.

Title

Indent

Name _____ Date _____

Interview

1. Write a list of questions.
2. Record the interviewee's answers.

Interview questions for _____

(Name of interviewee)

1. **Question:** _____**?**

   Answer:

2. **Question:** _____**?**

   Answer:

3. **Question:** _____**?**

   Answer:

4. **Question:** _____**?**

   Answer:

5. **Question:** _____**?**

   Answer:

Step-by-Step Instructions

Procedural

➤ Use this graphic organizer to explain how to do something.

Fill in the chart with information. Then use the chart to plan for a paragraph or an oral presentation.

INTRODUCTION
What are you going to explain?

_____

_____

STEPS
What are the steps?

1. First, _____

_____

2. Then, _____

_____

3. Next, _____

_____

4. After, _____

_____

5. Finally, _____

_____

CONCLUSION

_____

_____

Friendly Letter

➤ This format is used for writing a letter to a friend.

1. Write on an 8 1/2 by 11 inch piece of paper or on personal stationery.
2. Write using good penmanship.
3. Proofread your spelling and punctuation.

_____
(Date)

Dear _____ **,**

Indent

Indent

Indent

Yours truly,

(Your name)

Writing Lines

Name _____   Date _____

Print Alphabet (A–I)

Write the capital and lowercase letters.

A a A a

B b B b

C c C c

D d D d

E e E e

F f F f

G g G g

H h H h

I i I i

Print Alphabet (J–R)

Write the capital and lowercase letters.

Jj

Kk

Ll

Mm

Nn

Oo

Pp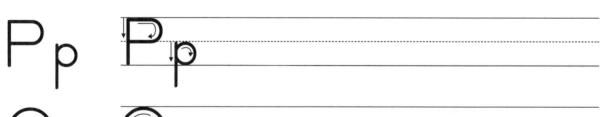

Qq

Rr

Print Alphabet (S–Z)

Write the capital and lowercase letters.

S s

T t

U u

V v

W w

X x

Y y

Z z

Cursive Alphabet (A–I)

Write the capital and lowercase letters.

Aa   Aa _____

Bb   Bb _____

Cc   Cc _____

Dd   Dd _____

Ee   Ee _____

Ff   Ff _____

Gg   Gg _____

Hh   Hh _____

Ii   Ii _____

Cursive Alphabet (J–R)

Cursive Alphabet (S–Z)

Ss   Ss

Tt   Tt

Uu   Uu

Vv   Vv

Ww   Ww

Xx   Xx

Yy   Yy

Zz   Zz

Letter Tiles: Capital Letters A–M

A	B	C	D	E
F	G	H	I	J
K	L	M		

Letter Tiles: Capital Letters N–Z

N	O	P	Q	R
S	T	U	V	W
X	Y	Z		

Letter Tiles: Lowercase Letters a–m

a	b	c	d	e
f	g	h	i	j
k	l	m		

Letter Tiles: Lowercase Letters n–z

n	o	p	q	r
s	t	u	v	w
x	y	z		

VISIONS BASIC Teacher Resource Book • Copyright © Heinle

Name _____ Date _____

Word Tiles: Short and Long Vowels

cap	pen
lips	dog
bus	cake
ear	dime
nose	computer

Word Tiles: Digraphs and Blends

<u>ch</u>air

<u>sh</u>irt

mou<u>th</u>

<u>wh</u>eel

ri<u>ng</u>

<u>sp</u>oon

<u>st</u>ar

<u>sk</u>irt

VISIONS BASIC Teacher Resource Book • Copyright © Heinle

Name _____ Date _____

Numerals 1–10

1 1

2 2

3 3

4 4

5 5

6 6

7 7

8 8

9 9

10 10

Numerals 11–20

11

12

13

14

15

16

17

18

19

20 20

Name _____ Date _____

Calendar

month _____

Sunday	Monday	Tuesday	Wednesday	Thursday	Friday	Saturday

Games Instructions

Game	Instructions
Simon Says	One player is Simon, the person who gives commands. The other players must stand up and follow "Simon's" commands. Each command begins with "Simon says." For example: Simon says touch your arm. Other players must follow the command, and if they fail to do so, they must sit down. If the command given does not begin with "Simon says," then students must not obey the command. Those who follow such a command must sit down. The last person left standing is the winner.
I Spy	One player observes an item in clear view and calls out "I spy something that begins with the letter . . ." The rest of the players must call out the names of objects they see beginning with the letter until they guess the item.
Scavenger Hunt	Players are given a set of clues to try to locate various items. The winner is the person (or team) who first finds all the items.
Twenty Questions	One player thinks of a word. Other players need to guess what the word is by asking no more than 20 yes/no questions.
Bingo	Make Bingo cards with five rows and five columns. In each square write a letter, sound, or vocabulary word that students have been studying. Hand out the Bingo cards. Call out letters, sounds, or vocabulary words one at a time. Have students cross off each letter, word, or sound if they have it on their card. The winner is the first player to cross off five squares in a row, either horizontally, vertically, or diagonally.
Charades	One player is given a word, and must act it out so that the others can guess the word. The player may also give clues. For example, he or she may show with his or her fingers how many syllables are in the word.
Picture Dictionary	Make cards with vocabulary words. One player takes a card, and must draw pictures to help the other players on the team guess the word. Points are given for each word the team guesses correctly. Set a time limit for each turn. At the end of the time, the opposing team may try to guess the correct word to win points.
Word Building	Using the Letter Tiles Resource Master (pp. 157–158), assemble a large pile of letters. Divide the letters between two teams. Each team makes as many words as they can with the letters they have. Give each team one point for each three-letter word, two points for every four-letter word, etc. The team with the most points wins the game.
Hangman	This is a good game to review vocabulary at the end of a chapter. Think of a word. Draw a "hanging stand" with one blank for each letter of the word you are thinking of. Students call out letters, one at a time. If the letter is in the word, write it in the correct blank. If not, draw one part of the hangman, starting with the head. The game is over when students either guess the word, or when enough incorrect letter guesses have been made to complete the hangman.
Go Fish	Create a set of cards that has pairs of matching words. Shuffle the cards, and hand out five cards to each student. The object is to ask for and complete pairs of cards. For example, a student who has only one card with the word "book" might ask the other student, Do you have "book"? The other student says Go fish, or gives the card. To "go fish" a student draws a new card from the center pile of cards. When students get a pair, they put the pair down on the table.